CALL ME HERMAN

An Autobiography

By Robert B. French, Jr., BS,LLB,JD

Also by Robert B. French, Jr.

AN ADVENTURE WITH JOHN

THE LAWyer

Beaten, Battered and Damned -The Drano Murder Trial

My life is dedicated to the magical women who influenced me: My mother, Nina Lois French, my wife, Celeste French, my daughters, Michelle French and Tammy Prewitt, my granddaughters, Kaitlin Prewitt and Victoria French, and Karen Holcomb my companion in my twilight years.

TABLE OF CONTENTS

FORWARD

By our very nature, trial lawyers are storytellers. To persuade you to accept our version of the facts, we must paint a word picture in a story that allows you to see the action. Being as old as I am, I have thousands of stories to tell, and it seems I tell one or more of them every day to illustrate a point.

Based upon my storytelling, several people have asked me to write my memoirs. I have thought long and hard about it. Some of the things that have happened to me during my 85+ years may be worth repeating. Certainly, my children, perhaps my nieces and nephews, and my friends might be interested. It has been a captivating life. Sort of a long trip on a rocky road.

I have always claimed to be the luckiest man alive. I have enjoyed being in the right place, at the right time, doing the right things. That has been the basis of my so-called good luck.

Actually, I have always believed that the Lord loves me in particular because few human beings have been blessed as I have.

Several people have said that I am the Renaissance Man.

Maybe. I have been fortunate to rise out of poverty, to become well educated, and to excel in a number of areas.

I have been blessed to succeed at almost everything I attempted. Throughout it all, I have constantly searched for the new, different, exquisite, and even spiritual adventures.

I learned very early in life never to be bothered with what others thought of me. I have always thought that my ideas about me were the only ones that counted.

My philosophy, at an early age, was – as you believe things are, so they are. Perception, perception, everything is perception. I have lived by the rule: That which you can realistically conceive, truly believe, accurately visualize, relentlessly pursue, anxiously anticipate, and claim as your own, must inevitably come to pass.

I have carried this motto in my wallet for more years than I can remember.

I have always believed that life is basically a point of view--how you see yourself, and how you see others. Remember, **NOW** is all you have, and it is passing at the speed of light.

How one uses the **NOW** depends upon choices. I always knew I had the choice of walking away, sometimes running, from whatever was happening. I always had a choice, and sometimes that was all I had.

Those admissions describe my life. I didn't design it, the Good Lord did. Plus, I have been blessed by having wonderful, beautiful, intelligent women take an interest in me, helping me along. They kept me on the path toward accomplishment of whatever I was undertaking.

So, I have decided to tell you my story-my history-part fact, part fiction. It may not be accurate because I am going to tell you how I remember the events in my existence.

My memory may be clouded by later years. I don't know. I'm just going to put it down in a stream of consciousness the way I remember it. Hopefully, it will be fairly accurate. However, the thick fog of time can fool the best of us.

However, I've never been one to let the true facts interfere with a good story. My tale may turn out to be exaggerations, imagination and out right lies, but I am going to write it in the first person so it may read like a letter to you. Having outlived almost all my childhood friends, and most of the people mentioned in this book, there are few who can contest the facts as I remember them.

It's not bragging. It's a torrid tale told by an old man. Fasten your seat belt and grab on to something safe; there will be turbulence ahead.

CHAPTER ONE
IN THE BEGINNING

Nothing much was happening on Friday, September 15, 1933. The country was in the 4th year of the terrible economic depression. Other than the Civil War, it was the worst time in American history. The country was in a vicious downward spiral from which it could not extricate itself. People could not buy because they did not have any money. People didn't have money because they could not find jobs. Jobs did not exist because manufacturers and retailers could not sell their products. They couldn't sell anything because people did not have any money. And so it went, a vicious cycle creating a desperate time.

Times were especially hard in the South. Contrary to common knowledge, the South was still recovering from the Civil War. In addition, the carpetbaggers had visited their own kind of hell in the area. Although the rest of the country was suffering, the South was near desolate. Alabama did not survive the Civil War until after WWII.

The 15th was a clear day. The crisp fall air poured in through the driver's window of the gray 1932 Chevrolet. There were two brothers in the front seat, and a tall beautiful sister in the back.

They were traveling North on two-lane Pulaski Pike, out of depression - smitten Huntsville, Alabama. They were bound for Winchester, Tennessee.

The sister, Nina Lois Sibley French, had been married to Robert B. French for almost 6 years. Now, after years of trying, she was finally 9 months pregnant and wanted to see her husband.

Robert had left the Tennessee Valley Bank as Vice President when it closed on Black Friday. Now in hard times, he was working as a lineman hanging telephone wires across Southern Tennessee. It didn't utilize his college education in Finance, but it was good-paying work, and that was hard to come by in North Alabama.

Nina had asked her brothers, Arnold, the driver, and Ira, Jr., to borrow their father's car and take the day off from the dairy to drive her up to see her husband.

Motels had not been considered, and there were no hotels nearby. For overnight travelers in the country, people took in roomers or borders. There were boarding houses and rooming houses in every small town. Robert had been boarding with the Mapes family in the small community of Howell, Tennessee. Nina had not seen him in more than 6 weeks. Hanging the lines went on 7 days a week – often daylight to dark.

When the trio arrived at the Mapes farm, it was a little past mid-day. Robert would not be free until dark. They had found him, ridden by, honked, and waved to let him know they were there. He was wearing huge tan leather gloves, pulling wire off a large wooden spool on the back of a truck. Nina hoped he might get off a little early. Although the car had good lights, they didn't want to travel at night.

While the brothers smoked, leaning back against the car, Mrs. Mapes, who was very kind to Nina, took her to see the horses down at the barn. Nina was a horsewoman and was very interested to see the saddle horses that the Mapes raised and trained.

SADDLE UP

At the large unpainted barn, smelling of hay and animals, Mr. Mapes was grooming a chestnut mare named Susan. She was a beautiful tall horse and spirited. When Nina admired the mare, Mapes said she rode like a rocking chair. He was going to saddle her up and ride her around the whitewashed three-board training ring a few times for exercise.

As he cinched the saddle girth strap, Nina, who had been quietly rubbing Susan's muzzle, while feeding her from her other hand, said, "Let me ride her."

Mrs. Mapes, standing nearby, said, "You shouldn't do that, Mrs. French; you are in a family way."

3

"It won't hurt. Mr. Mapes said, "She rides like a rocker."

After tucking her dress between her legs, Nina struggled to get her pregnant belly up behind the saddle horn as her brothers arrived.

"Nina!" Ira Jr. exclaimed, "What are you doing?"

"I'm just going to take her around the ring," she responded, as she made a clicking sound with her tongue, and urged Susan forward out of the barn with her heels.

When the horse recognized the ring, she broke into a gallop. Nina loved it! She did ride like a rocking chair. She urged the mare on lightly with the excess bridle. Susan responded, and away the horse and rider went, full gallop around the white-fence enclosed training ring. Her long brown hair was flowing out behind her as she and the mare joined that rider/animal relationship where they are almost one.

After four rounds, Susan broke a sweat, and Mr. Mapes walked to the edge of the training ring. As horse and rider came by, he told Nina that was enough.

She guided the horse back into the barn, and with the help of all in attendance, she dismounted.

"Thank you so much, Mr. Mapes. Susan is a beautiful animal."

In the semi-light of the barn, Nina sat on a feed sack and watched as Mapes exercised two more horses. As he finished, Robert arrived early from work.

"The foreman let me and my 'ride' off early, knowing my wife and brothers-in-law were here."

ARRIVAL

Approaching dark, Mrs. Mapes invited the guests to stay for dinner. Robert ate at their table as part of his room and board. A short time later, it was dark, and Mrs. Mapes had dinner on the table. While eating, Nina bent double with pain.

"My word!" Mrs. Mapes exclaimed, "You are going into labor!"

4

Robert and the brothers became all excited. "Call Dr. McCown!"

Mrs. Mapes responded, "We have plenty of time. This is her first child and it will not come quickly. I suggest we let the good doctor have dinner and call him around nine or ten."

And, so they waited. Nina prided herself on being strong. She did not whine nor cry with the labor pains. She simply gripped Robert's hand as they came stronger and stronger. When the pains began to occur every five minutes, as timed by Mrs. Mapes, she called the doctor on her new 4-party-line telephone. She asked him to come over. At his request, she gave him a full report. He said that he would be over before midnight.

The doctor arrived at a little past eleven thirty. He checked Nina's vitals, timed the pains, and announced that the baby would be coming soon.

At exactly 12:05 a.m., September 16, 1933, I appeared on earth. "8 pounds, 6 ounces." "A Boy, $25.00," the doctor's receipt reported.

Mother and child were fine, except for the fact I was born in Tennessee. Eight generations of my relatives, four of whom mustered out of George Washington's Army, settled in Madison County, Alabama. But I had to be born in Tennessee, a curse that would follow me all my life. It has been particularly upsetting during football season.

CHAPTER TWO
BABY YEARS

My first clear memory is when I had started walking. I was in diapers, wearing a pink and yellow sun suit that featured blue flowers. It was a beautiful sun-filled spring day, too pretty to stay indoors. My mother carried me in her arms down the gray wooden stairs that led to where we lived - a three room, upstairs apartment in Huntsville. It may have been on Randolph Street. I remember my mother mentioning that address. On the ground, she deposited me with some other children to play in the mouth of an empty automobile garage.

I thought the children were very big and knew everything. Probably, the oldest was five years old, and most of them were eighteen months to three years. There were several young mothers around.

One girl allowed me to hold and inspect a small blue metal globe of the earth. She didn't let me keep it long, but I had it long enough to make it out, and remember, that it was a globe of the earth. A boy let me hold a silver jack. It was one of those small, six-sided metal jacks that kids played with by bouncing a small rubber ball. He took it back shortly, and after a bit, my mother took me back upstairs.

I was a pretty baby with golden blonde hair. My parents decided it was time for my dad to take me to have my hair cut. He was working locally in the telephone central office. Down the stairs we went and walked to a barbershop. He carried me most of the way. I can remember that he was very strong and had large, comfortable arms.

When it came my turn, the barber sat me on a wooden board laid across the arms of the "Token" barber chair. He dressed me in the barber's gown and began to cut. Naturally, being a baby, it scared me, and I began to cry. My father told me I had nothing to fear, as the barber was not going to hurt me, and I would feel better after my hair was cut. I stopped crying and began to watch myself in the mirror. When the barber brushed me off and let me down, I was fine. Ten cents. So much for a haircut.

My father was a short man; 5'6" tall, all bone and muscle. He was very strong, and sometimes called, "Mr. 5 by 5." He had been a college football player and a minor league baseball catcher. Although his original nickname through high school and college had been "Short Dog," he didn't mind being called "Shorty." He acquired that name when he went to work on the railroad. All railroad men had a nickname and his stuck. He had married Nina Sibley who was 5'9", and people said they looked like Mutt and Jeff, a popular comic strip of the day involving a short man and a tall man, his opposite.

THE DAIRY

When I was perhaps two years old – certainly not more than two and one-half -- mother and daddy moved us to my grandfather's dairy on Pulaski Pike, just North of Huntsville. I later learned it was called Bean's Dairy, and that my Grandfather, Ira T. Sibley, rented the farm and cattle from Mr. Bean. My grandfather was not a sharecropper. He always had a contract, and a real estate lease. He paid Mr. Bean rent, and made a tidy profit for both families.

Times were ugly; deep in the depression. President Roosevelt was trying everything he knew to bring recovery to the nation. Nothing would work until WWII.

My father left the telephone company and had gone to work on the Southern Railroad Bridge Gang. We had moved into one of the four-room tenant houses on the dairy. My grandfather and grandmother lived in the two-story "big house" with my Aunt Mildred, Uncle Ira, Jr., and Uncle Arnold.

My mother, her oldest brother Edgar, and older sister Pauline Baker, Moved their families into the other four-room houses scattered around the dairy property. Other than my dad and Uncle Ed Baker, the men worked the dairy managed by my grandfather.

We had 32 cows that had to be milked twice a day, seven days a week. Granddaddy had a big, solid black, cantankerous bull named Tommy Toole. He kept the cows

7

happy and constantly produced a spring calf crop. He was said to be descended from Lily Flagg, the most famous cow in American history. She had produced more butter than any cow ever recorded at a world's fair sometime in the distant past.

Later, Tommy Toole was bred to one of Lily Flagg's descendants, owned by the Jones family from Jones Valley. According to what I was later told, a calf of the Jones cow won an award at the World's Fair in New York in 1939. The Huntsville-Madison County International Airport is named after Mr. Carl T. Jones. Later in life, I did business with his sons, and Son-in-law Peter Lowe, engineers who dabbled in the mineral business.

One bright summer day, when I was approaching three years old, my mother, hanging out clothes on the clothesline, failed to watch me closely. I walked down the hill from our small white clapboard house to the little brown pump house. The smokehouse, another small brown structure, loaded with meat, was located nearby. While childishly exploring the trickle of water runoff from the pump house, a large tom turkey knocked me down, put his foot on my chest, and began to closely inspect me. I can still remember his eyes, beak, ugly face, and red wattles.

Fortunately, my mother came   running in her gingham dress and shooed the bird away. That night, at dinner in the big house, she told the story to the family. My grandmother said that I was very lucky the turkey didn't peck my eyes out. I was pretty happy about that too. The sight of that   blue and red-faced bird standing over me has stayed with me all my life. 83 years later, I can still see him in my mind's eye.

It was about this time that I came down with colitis. The childhood strain of this sickness resulted in a right inguinal hernia. That affected my life until I had surgery when I was 16 years old. I was consoled by the fact my grandfather had a dual hernia and had to wear a truss every day to prevent strangulation. I also survived diphtheria about this time. The doctor said that I got it from drinking contaminated water. I was told I nearly died from the high fever associated with the illness.

We were a large family trying to survive the Depression, so we lived close together. My grandfather must have had a good deal with Mr. Bean because he traded for a new car every two years. I would sit on the running board and look at the stagecoach metal decal, "Body by Fisher." My grandmother had a maid, and a cook in the big house. Both ladies lived down the road. Their husbands worked on the dairy. Uncle Arnold was able to attend some sort of veterinarian school in Huntsville.

Although times were horrible, Granddaddy saw to it that the 15 of us lacked for nothing. We had a hen house full of eggs and chickens, a pigsty producing pork and bacon, beef in the field, potatoes rolled under the floor, and a huge garden every year. Plus, there were apple and peach trees on the place, as well as a vineyard. Except for being a little short on money, we did well.

The dairy had tractors, plows, harrows, small trucks, large trucks, two silos and all the equipment necessary to produce enough milk to fill a truck bound for the creamery on Clinton Avenue West in Huntsville.

When electric milking machines became in vogue, my grandfather and Mr. Bean bought enough of them to milk the cows. This greatly increased production and speeded operations significantly. However, the men spent more time cleaning the machines and barn than they did anything else. The rubber boots and rubber hoses functioned for at least 6 hours every day.

It was as though milking and processing was secondary to keeping the barn and machines clean. Granddaddy was constantly inspecting, finding fault, and making corrections in cleanliness.

Mother would let me go down to the barn when the cows were milked by hand. Sitting on a short metal milking stool, my Uncle Edgar would catch me looking at him, pulling on the teats, spraying the milk into the milk bucket. I went up close to hear the squirt-squirt sound of the milk hitting the bottom of the bucket. He let me come closer to see him milking, and then he turned the teat up, and sprayed me in the face. He then laughed uproariously. I didn't cry. I dried my eyes with my sleeve and never went that close to him again. Electric milking machines ended that trick anyway.

Approaching sundown, the cows would gather at the pasture gate and bellow until they were let in. They wanted to be milked, they wanted to eat, and they let you know it.

The barn had 16 stalls to the side. Each cow would walk up, the metal halter would clamp around her neck, her udder would be scrubbed, and she would start eating from the feed trough as she was being milked. The following morning the same procedure endured. The cows knew the drill and would walk directly to their assigned stalls. They didn't hesitate to butt another cow if she tried to go into the wrong stall.

Granddaddy said that contented cows gave more milk. My Uncle Arnold bought a small brown Majestic Radio, and put it on a shelf in the barn. It was played loudly when the cows were in the stalls. Before he passed away, he gave the radio to me, and I still have it on the roll-top desk in my office. It takes a while for the tubes to warm up, but it plays and is still tuned to WSM, Nashville, Tennessee.

When "a cloud" would come up – our name for a serious thunderstorm – the entire family would gather in the barn, sometimes with the cows. Being concrete, it was the strongest building on the dairy.

I can remember my cousins Marie, Earl, Ira George Baker, and me sleeping on the large rolling feed cart that rolled down the feed trough area between the stalls. The feed was removed from the big buggy into the trough feeding the cows as they were being milked. Mother would bring a blanket, put it down on the feed, and lay me on it with another blanket on top. Later, when my sister Doris was born, she was laid on the blanket with me. My cousins were sleeping on the other end of the feed buggy. Earl, the oldest, would eventually become Police Chief of Huntsville.

Sister Hester, named after my grandmother, was born in June 1938, and she was laid on the feed buggy with us as an infant. That barn was the family storm shelter. Plus, it was a lot of fun when the family was all-together.

ELECTRICITY

It was a milestone day when TVA ran electricity through the small houses on the property. The big house, barn, pump house, and other necessary places had electricity, but the small houses that had been vacant, or used by field hands, did not have service.

There were three TVA electricians who came to our house. They took green and yellow cloth-covered wire, drilled a hole in the side of the house, and ran the wire through. They came inside and stapled the wire up the wooden walls, across the ceilings, and left enough for a drop cord and light bulb. A socket was wired on. They screwed in a bulb, and put a large brown switch near the door where the wire ran up the wall. They did this in all four rooms. Now you might think this was unsightly, but to us, those wires were beautiful.

The men then went outside and put a meter where they had drilled the hole in the wall. One of the men went back into the house, turned a knob on the switch, and we had light. We had electricity! It was a happy day in the French household. We no longer went to bed at sundown and got up with the chickens. It was a totally new freedom. Electricity was great!

Before the electricity, our greatest entertainment had been sitting on the small porch at night looking at the flashing light on the hotel in Huntsville.

The hotel had been built sometime during the 1920's and was pretty close to 12 stories high. It may have been the tallest building in Huntsville. "Russel Erskine," it would flash in red, then "Hotel," with a red arrow pointing down. My mother told me what the sign said as it flashed red for all to see. I would say, "Russel Erskine - Hotel," in cadence with the light, over and over again until I would tire of it, and then do it again the next warm summer night.

Now, we had lights! Soon we would have an electric stove, an electric iron, and even a radio. With electricity, times were definitely improving.

DORIS NEAL FRENCH

I was approaching three years old in September 1936. My sister had been born in June. One day she was not there and the next day we had a premature baby to take care of with all kinds of problems. She weighed less than 6 pounds when she was born. The entire family was worried that she would not live. She was seriously premature, small, frail, with little chance for survival.

My father put a pull-socket on the light bulb in his and Mother's room. He then tied a string from the chain on the pull-socket to the headboard of their bed. During the night, he simply pulled the string, and he, or Mother, could see how to get up to take care of my sister Doris, whom we now called Dot.

Dot could not keep anything on her stomach and was slowly dying. The doctor told Mother to give Dot light coffee in her milk. This worked, and when I got some, it started my love for coffee that continues until this day. My mother, and other relatives, worked hard to bring Dot around to a healthy child after about nine weeks.

Mother had a color picture made of me kissing Dot when I was five years old and she was almost three. It was Sunday, and I was sitting on a small child's chair in a hay field, wearing short pants and a dress shirt. She had on a small dress and was looking up to kiss me. That picture stayed in the French household until I lost track of it when I went into the service. I recently found an old black and white of it. Ah, precious memories.

PRANKS

My Uncles, Arnold and Ira Jr. were teenagers who constantly teased their nephews. One hot summer day they were sealing a boat that they had built for fishing. They had taken the flat bottom boat, put it up on saw horses, and filled it with water to swell the planks together.

Cousins Earl, Ira George, and I were playing around the dairy. We walked the plank across the manure ditch that

12

flowed into a holding pond, converting cow manure into fertilizer for the coming planting season. We began inspecting the boat filled with water. Arnold and Ira, Jr. sneaked up behind us and put all three of us in the boat filled with water. I went home determined to tell on them, but by the time I got home, I was dry, and my mother laughed about it. She said, "At least, they cooled you off."

Sometimes they would claim to hear things that we couldn't hear. They would put their hands up to their ears and agree that they could hear a train, airplane, or a truck. We would listen as closely as we could, and we couldn't hear it. After a while, they would laugh at us for falling for the trick.

Of course, they always threatened to put us in the manure ditch if we didn't do exactly what they instructed. They were just country boys having fun with their nephews.

LITTLE EVA

There was a Sunday that is indelible in my mind. A child was born to my grandmother when I was a little past four years old. The child lived about three months and died. The girl baby had been named Eva, after her mother, my Great-grandmother, Eva Chandler, who had married John Preston Maples. When the child died, my grandmother grieved terribly. This was her 10th child, yet she was inconsolable.

On Sundays, the entire clan ate dinner (lunch) in the big house. The table would seat the fifteen of us. Sometimes my Uncle Eugene and Aunt Nita would drive out from Huntsville and eat with us. When that happened, the kids ate at a side table in the kitchen.

Wherever I was seated, I would always say the blessing that usually consisted of, "Christ, save us. Amen." This earned me the nickname of "Preacher." Nicknames were a big thing back then. My Uncle Ira was called Peck's Bad Boy, after a movie character, earning him the nickname of Uncle "Peck."

My Uncle Arnold would squint an eye and wink, earning him the nickname of Uncle "Popeye," after the cartoon character. I was unable to say grandmother so I tried to call her mother. It came out "Wauva," and that nickname stuck. My Aunt Mildred was a tomboy, so we called her "Bill." My Aunt Pauline Baker was Aunt "Poppy."

On this particular Sunday, the entire family had gathered after dinner, and were sitting around in the front yard under a very large oak tree.

My grandmother was saying, "Oh, if I only knew that she was all right. If the Lord would just give me a sign, I could stop hurting so badly. I know she is in heaven, but I need a sign that she is happy."

Right then, she stopped, and looking into the summer sky said, "Oh, there she is, I can see her in the sky! She's smiling, she's happy! Oh, thank you Lord! Thank you! Thank you! Now I can quit worrying."

Everybody was looking up in the sky trying to see Little Eva. I saw her! I saw the baby face in the sky! She was beautiful and smiling. All the family was trying to see what Wauva saw. I didn't say anything. Some of the family was shouting, praising the Lord, and then we had prayer, a prayer of thanksgiving by my grandfather.

When we got home, I told my mother, "Mother, I saw Little Eva and she was laughing. I just saw her head and curly hair."

My mother said, "Son, that was just your imagination."

"No, Mother, I really saw her. I really did."

"If you really saw her, then you should remember it the rest of your life because you are a mystic. And I don't doubt you because mysticism runs in the family." ·

I still see the child in my mind's eye. This experience put me on notice to look for the strange, mystical events which have taken place in my life. When I became a serious Biblical student and lecturer, I realized that I had been given the gifts of the spirit discussed in the New Testament. I have found them to be a great adventure as I have traveled the road of life. I'll probably talk about some of these mystical experiences as I write this book.

My mother told me that my sign that I was a mystic was that I have a perfect triangle of the lines in my right hand, and a double crown on my head. I don't know whether there is anything to that or not. I did go to a palm reader once, at the Ringling Brothers Barnum and Bailey Circus. when I was a boy. She looked in my hand and refused to tell my fortune, "You tell mine," she said.

I had paid a quarter, and I insisted. She said that two women would figure prominently in my life; I might marry them both. I would make a great success in the newspaper or writing business. I must say she was right on. Writing for the Goodrich Industrial Newspaper did change my life and two women have figured prominently in my existence. I married only one of them.

I have had a lot of fun with mysticism on the path. I've enjoyed teaching people to witch for water. They are always amazed when they feel the invisible energy. When I was so inclined, I enjoyed telling fortunes. I'd just look in the person's palm and say the first thing that came into my mind. I couldn't read palms nor anything else – just whatever came to me. I did not do it often. Unbelievably, the fortunes came true! Oh, if I could tell what was going to happen to others, why could I not predict my future? I could, and did. The hard thing about it is, whatever is going to happen - good or bad - I can't do anything about it. It's going to happen and does.

My fortune telling dreams always include water. Mother said that water was my sign. I guess it is. If the water is dirty, the future is bad. If it is clear, things are going to be great. After the dream, I just look for the future. After thousands of dreams, it never fails.

I'll share one in a little more detail. After my darling wife Celeste, died, I wanted the diamond gold encrusted cross that I had given her. I was going to wear it in her memory. Unfortunately, it was nowhere to be found.

Neither of the children had seen it since their mother had passed away. No one knew where it was. I took the house apart looking for it.

Then, I had a dream. A man standing by a clear water stream said, "You are looking for Celeste's cross. The wolf got it."

As usual, I immediately woke up wondering, what in the heck did that mean? "The wolf got it." This is one time my mysticism has failed. I discarded the dream believing that the dream had failed because I was growing old.

Several weeks later, a Saturday, I was cleaning house. I noticed some *National Geographic* magazines laying in a stack of magazines on a small stand in our bedroom. As part of my cleaning ritual, I was going to take the magazines and put them in the collection going back to 1957.

I noticed that the top magazine had the picture of a wolf making up the entire cover. There was an article about wolves in that issue. I picked it up to see the article and there lay the cross!

Not only thankful, I was amazed. I was so happy I had not lost the gift. Plus, I had the cross and still wear it. "The Wolf got it." Okay. I got it back.

SCRAP IRON AND THE JAPS

In 1938, or the early part of 1939, when I was five years old, my uncles, Arnold and Ira Jr., heard that there were some little yellow men down on the square in Huntsville who were buying scrap iron and paying a good price for it.

They took the largest old truck we had on the dairy, put me on a pillow under the steering wheel, put a brick on the gas pedal, reached in the window to put it in gear, and told me to drive. One of them would reach in and put the floor shift out of gear to stop the vehicle. They, along with their best friend, Edward Hunkapiller, hung out on the back wooden flatbed, looking around the doors telling me where to steer the vehicle. The dairy was large, and machinery had been left where it had broken down years ago.

I did as I was told, and we slowly accumulated near a truckload of scrap plows, hay balers, mowers, and you-name-it. Then they had me drive back to the barn. My mother was there and practically went into cardiac arrest seeing her precious baby boy driving that big truck.

She dressed her brothers down for being silly. They thought it was funny. Uncle Peck said that I wanted to drive the truck all the way to his girlfriend's house.

Hearing all the commotion, my grandfather came out of the barn. He learned what his sons and Edward Hunkapiller had done, and he told them, "Boys, Nina is right. That was a terrible mistake. Preacher could have missed the bridge and ran that truck into the manure ditch. Then where would we be? Don't do that again."

My uncles knew they had not heard the last of it as my grandfather had the reputation of being a raver, i.e., a person who, once started on a subject, didn't seem to know when to stop. Family rumor was that my great-grandfather, Mills Jenkins Sibley, was a raver, and his son, Ira Taylor, came by it honestly. So, Granddaddy did discuss their actions for several more days at supper after a day's work. Certainly, they would never do that again. You just didn't want to get him started.

However, in compensation for my good work, they let me go through the scrap iron on the bed of the truck and pick out my part to sell to the little yellow men. I picked out what I thought was a plenty, and away we went down to the square in Huntsville. Edward Hunkapiller was riding on the back with the scrap iron.

It was a festive occasion on the north side of the courthouse square. I think it was on the corner of Jefferson Street and Spring Avenue. The little yellow men had set up at that northwest intersection, weighing, buying scrap iron, and loading it onto trucks to haul to the railroad depot about ten blocks away.

My uncles and Edward Hunkapiller took in folding money. I got fifteen cents for my part. It was the first money I ever made! One of the little yellow fellows gave me a dark blue top that ran up and down a string. I had never seen such a thing in my life. He carved some palm trees and a boat on it with his pocketknife. He called it a yo-yo. That little toy became my proudest possession.

Edward Hunkapiller needed to go to T.T. Terry's Drug Store across the square. It was very dark in the store.

17

Everything was dark wood. Uncle Arnold lifted me up on a stool at the counter and told me to order a chocolate milkshake. When the soda jerk came around, I made my order. It cost a nickel and was the most fantastic thing I had ever tasted. It was in a big glass, and I drank it all.

After we had finished our shakes, we went back into the pharmacy, in the dark of the store. Edward Hunkapiller wore an asphidity bag around his neck. It was a small bag, about the size of a quarter, with yellow drawstrings that tied to a rawhide string around his neck. I had seen it every time I had ever seen him. It was so filthy; it was almost black, even the strings were black. He wore the horribly smelling thing to keep away colds, flu, and evil spirits.

He told Mr. Terry that he needed a new nickel bag of asphidity. I watched as Mr. Terry brought out an ugly smelly brown chunk of something, cut off a little piece of it, put it in a new white cloth bag, and handed it to Edward.

"That'll be five cents."

"My family has an account here. I would like to charge it."

"What's the name on the account?"

"Hunkapiller," replied Edward.

"Just keep it," Mr. Terry said, holding the small charge book in his left hand with his pencil in his right. "I wouldn't write asphidity and Hunkapiller for a nickel."

Edward smiled, said thanks, and we were on our way out and back to the dairy. I yo-yoed as we walked by the huge courthouse, back across the square. My uncles interrupted me every now and then to yo-yo themselves.

The end of the story: Years later, my Uncle Peck was sent home after being shot up on the beach of Iwo Jima. Both he and my Uncle Popeye were in the Navy, and both were recipients of the Purple Heart.

During WWII, very few people in Huntsville had gas for an automobile, nor could anyone get tires. As a result of shortages, wounded soldiers and sailors were shipped to their hometowns on Red Cross hospital troop trains. The families would meet the train and carry their wounded home on their gurney walking across Huntsville.

18

With all the white sheeted gurneys going in every direction from Union Depot, it looked like rays of light spreading across the town. As far as you could see, in every direction, there were families carrying their wounded home. War truly is hell.

When the boys went off to war, Granddaddy could not run the dairy shorthanded. He bought a house at 331 Clinton Avenue West, two blocks from the Russel Erskine Hotel, at 123 Clinton Avenue West - downtown Huntsville. Von Braun Civic Center eventually took the property. Year's later, practicing law, I got the heirs a good price for it before the Von Braun was built.

With Granddaddy gone, Mr. Bean sold the dairy to Meadow Gold, the company that owned the creamery. All the families moved away. My father moved us to Atlanta Avenue in Sheffield. He was now a flagman on the main line and soon became the Baggage Master on the Joe Wheeler, the first diesel locomotive owned by the Southern Railway System.

We got word Uncle Peck was coming home, and we took the train to Huntsville where the family had gathered at granddaddy's. We walked to the railroad station, which was about 10 or 12 blocks away. When the train arrived with the large red cross flags draped on the sides of the cars, Daddy asked the conductor where Ira Taylor Sibley, Jr. might be found. In his round black conductor's cap and conductor's uniform, he searched his manifest. He located the car that my uncle was in. Daddy and Uncle Edgar went on the train, and brought Uncle Peck down the steep steel steps.

He was all ensconced in white sheets on the gurney. Like the other families, we had our wounded. Daddy and Uncle Edgar began carrying him through the streets of Huntsville. Although all of us were thrilled he was home, he would be bedfast from his wounds for more than a year from the day we were at the station.

As my daddy and Uncle Edgar lifted Uncle Peck down the curb stone at Holmes Avenue, right by the federal post office, he looked up at me.

"Preacher, do you remember that scrap iron we sold to the Japs?"

"Yes, sir," remembering driving the truck, earning fifteen cents, drinking the milkshake, and having the yo-yo.

"Well, I went and got some of it, and brought it back home." Then he tried to laugh, but the pain was too much. Everyone else thought it was funny.

It wouldn't be long before we went through the same process again with Uncle Arnold.

Grandmother and Granddaddy had their hands full taking care of two wounded veterans while Granddaddy guarded German prisoners that had been brought to Redstone Arsenal. It was there that granddaddy became friends with Wernher von Braun. They became such buddies that the scientist taught Granddaddy some German. He enjoyed speaking German to the grandchildren. All I can remember was he called a nail a "nagel." We had no idea that the man my grandfather was guarding was the world famous German scientist.

SELECTING A CHURCH

After the halcyon times on the dairy, and we had moved to Sheffield, I started to school in Mrs. Nathan's first grade class. I wanted to go to church, and Mother let me pick out which church I wanted to attend. I picked the First Baptist as it was the closest in walking distance from the house. I thus became the first Baptist in my family. My Great-grandfather, John Preston Maples, had been the Methodist minister at New Hope, Alabama. My Grandfather, Neal Robert French, had been the Presbyterian minister at Gurley, Alabama.

Having introduced the family into the Baptist tradition, I would one day lay claim to being the first Republican in the family.

We were union people and devout democrats. On my grandfather's seventieth birthday, my Uncle Eugene Sibley bought him a new suit. He wanted to take him for a ride in his new Buick around Huntsville. I went with them.

Uncle Gene drove around the square, and Granddaddy remembered his many terms of jury service there. Then he drove us up Monte Sano Mountain. He stopped at the

Highway 231 overlook, a scenic view of Jones Valley. He said, "Dad, just look at how Huntsville has grown."

"Yeah, Son, I see them. In every one of those little cracker box houses there's either a Nigger, Yankee, or Republican, and any way you cut it, it spells nothing but trouble."

As I grew up, I worked with and became close friends with many black people, I married a New Yorker from Midtown Manhattan, and I became a founder of the modern Republican Party in the South. Granddaddy must have rolled over several times.

Although my grandfather may have been a victim of his time, and held prejudicial views, we were always a deeply religious family. We were taught that all people were God's Children, and that we were no better than anyone else. Northern Soldiers had killed Granddaddy's grandfather for no reason, and he firmly believed President Hoover had caused the Depression. He called all gravy, "Hoover Gravy."

Still, prejudice and all, we always gave thanks before meals; always said prayers before going to bed; and had Scripture reading after supper. Neither myself nor any of my four sisters were allowed to believe in Santa Claus because Christmas was Christ's birthday. As older children, we tried to persuade our younger siblings to believe in Santa, but it didn't work.

We were urged to memorize Bible verses and recite them from a very young age. Mother would quiz us to repeat the verses we had memorized that day. I can still repeat almost all those verses, including the entire 12th Chapter of Romans, and the 13th Chapter of First Corinthians. Of course, the Christmas Stories were the first verses we learned.

Later I would teach Sunday School -- or Chapel in the service -- for more than fifty years. I taught the Baraca Class thirty-six years. Plus, I have written six books on the Gospels. My family was very influential so far as my service to my beliefs was concerned.

CHAPTER THREE
<u>A YOUNG MAN</u>

I have no idea why we moved around as often as we did. I remember Christmas on Atlanta Avenue. Our neighbor built a mechanical Santa that he placed in his window facing the street. It waved its arms and legs up and down.

We then moved into a beautiful antebellum house on Main Street in Tuscumbia, across from Deshler High School. It was not far from Ivy Green, the home of Helen Keller. The rooms were high and large. There were huge oak trees in the expansive yard. I got my first bicycle while we lived there.

After a short time, we moved again. I believe the big house was too expensive to heat. Every basement had a coal bin, and with central heat, coal was the only way to heat. With 9-foot high ceilings, it was expensive. This time we took residence at 501 East 4th Street. We were living there when the war broke out. I was in the third grade, Miss Shaw's room.

During the winter, between the second and third grades, I came down with whooping cough, measles, mumps and pneumonia all at the same time. My lips were so swollen that the little string everyone has at the top of the front gum broke and remains so today. Someone said it was called a procheilion.

While lying on the couch in the living room, I spiked a temperature of 106. My mother called Dr. Whitman. He came with his black doctor's bag and examined me.

He told the family, "I'm sorry, this boy is gone."

My mother began to cry uncontrollably. My father picked me up in his arms and paced the living room floor with my draped limp body. I knew everything that was happening, but I couldn't respond. The doctor was trying to console the family. He suggested that my father put me down and call the funeral home.

Daddy put me back on the couch, and somehow, I moved. The doctor raced back to me and yelled, "He's alive! Unbelievable, this boy is still alive! I hope his brain is all right. He's been dead a little more than five minutes!"

They put ice packs and cold rags all over me to get the fever down, and slowly I recovered. Unfortunately, the mumps "dropped" on me, resulting in my being practically sterile. When I was past 60 years old a urologist told me that I had been sterile, or practically sterile, all my life. I never knew it. I should have realized something was wrong when Celeste and I had to go to the fertility clinic at UAB in Birmingham in order for her to get pregnant with Michelle.

A few days later, Sunday, December 7, 1941, the Japanese bombed Pearl Harbor. I didn't understand what was happening. The Sunday before, my Uncle Ira, Aunt Mildred, and Ira's future wife, had visited us, and my picture was taken sitting on the steps of the house. Now, in the late afternoon, my father was pacing the floor snapping his fingers saying, "This is terrible! We are at war on two fronts. Thousands are going to be killed. This is a world war! Quick, turn the radio on!"

Mother tuned the radio to the Mutual Broadcasting station. Gabriel Heater was announcing to the world that the Japs had pulled a sneak attack on us, and many boys had been killed. "We are a nation in a world war!"

We listened to President Roosevelt say that December 7, 1941, was a day that will live in infamy.

On Monday morning Miss Shaw asked if we knew what had happened on Sunday. We said that we didn't understand. She then spent the rest of the morning explaining war and wars throughout history. She told us the implications of war, and the hardships we could expect. Three weeks later, she was gone. She had joined the Women's Army Corps. Everyone was participating in the war effort.

RAILROAD ACCIDENT

A month or so later, my father, who was now a conductor on a freight train, was working with a problem in the railway yard in Huntsville. He had his left hand down between the rail car couplings called buffer plates. The steam engine jumped and crushed his hand. Doctors at Huntsville Hospital said all they could do was amputate the hand. This was doubly hard as he was left-handed.

Daddy said he would do anything to save his hand. The doctors told him that there was a doctor at Campbell's Clinic in Chattanooga who might be able to save it. He was placed in an ambulance and taken to Campbell's Clinic.

The Chattanooga doctor thought he might be able to do him some good. The hand would never be normal, but he could knit some of the bones back together. Daddy asked him to do it. The doctor said that he needed him awake at the time he was working to move what was left of his fingers. They had a brand new anesthetic called a spinal injection that would kill the pain, yet allow daddy to remain conscious during the procedure.

Although it would be the first use of this new spinal anesthetic in the South, daddy agreed, and they proceeded to administer the painkiller. The doctor worked on the hand for 6 hours, and then said that he had done all he could do. He stitched Daddy up and sent him to recovery.

The repair was wonderful. The hand was not normal, but it was better than losing the hand. My father could never close his hand, but he could use it.

Unfortunately, the spinal didn't go as well as the doctors imagined. Somehow the fluid injected into my father's spine traveled up the spinal cord to his brain causing great damage. A man who had been brilliant with figures and letters, an athlete, a husband and father, became like a small child. The French family began to experience hard times.

If my father was going anywhere I had to go with him, as he would forget how to return home.

We shopped at the Railroad Supply Store in Sheffield. It was called "The Grab" because it grabbed your check, and deducted what you owed, before you received your money. Although Daddy was drawing some kind of small Railroad Act disability check for being injured, we would have to walk to The Grab and get what was on Mother's list. Sometimes, we would take my red Western Flyer wagon to haul the groceries back.

We did not have nursing homes nor assisted living facilities at that time. When a person became old and could not care for themselves, a member of the family had to care for them, or they were moved in with some family that would take them in as a roomer. They would have constant care, be treated well, bathed, fed, and generally attended to.

In order to make ends meet, our family had to take in a roomer. We took in Mrs. Martin, the mother of some railroad men, and she lived with us until she died several months later. I believe her sons paid Mother $40 a month. With Daddy unable to work, this was survival money for us in 1942.

After a period of time, I don't know how much-the railroad quit paying injury benefits. My sister Daina had been born in June, 1940. Mother now had four children, and a sick husband. She couldn't work, and we were getting into dire straits. The union made up a fund for Daddy and gave it to us, saving us for a while.

Mother believed that Daddy could perform some kind of work. He was improving, no longer getting lost, and generally beginning to recover. People urged Mother to sue the railroad under the special laws that applied only to railroads. She refused but made a decision.

TIME TO MEASURE UP

It was summer of 1943. I was in the 4th grade and had passed to the 5th.

Mother called me in, "Young man, your father is able to return to work. They don't pay any attention to me because I am a woman. So, I want you to take his pass, and this union book, go to the yard in Sheffield, see Mr. Cooper, the Division Superintendent. Tell him that your daddy is ready to go back to work. Do not take no for an answer.

"If he refuses, go to the station, use this pass to go to Cleveland to the B of RT (Brotherhood of Railroad Trainmen), and ask for Mr. Green. He's the president of the union. Tell him your daddy's story, and ask the Union to file a grievance. We need to get your daddy put back to work. Then take the pass and come home. Here's $4 to eat on. You'll just have to sleep in your clothes on the train."

I had absolutely no idea what I was doing. I was approaching 10 years old. However, my mother told me what to do, and I set out to do it.

It was a sun shining summer day as I walked across Tuscumbia, into Sheffield, and on to the Southern Railroad Yard. The management building was an imposing two-story brick building at the end of the tracks. It was the only brick building on the yard, so I headed there. I went in the imposing front door, and I could see offices lined up two walls.

Otherwise, everything was vacant, except for a wide, imposing set of stairs, leading from the front door to the second level. Nothing seemed to be going on downstairs. I could hear typing noises upstairs so I went up.

There was an isinglass window in the door flanked by isinglass windows on either side of the entrance. Isinglass is a glass that is smooth on one side, and slightly beveled all over the other, resulting in a glass you can't see through, but light can penetrate it. I opened the door.

As I entered a large bare room with maybe eight chairs around the front wall, I noticed a light wooden desk in the middle of the room. It appeared to be made of maple. A woman was seated behind the desk with an upright typewriter, on a small table to her right. I could see a Dictaphone and an upright black telephone, among the papers scattered around the top of the desk. She was listening to the Dictaphone and typing. She looked up at me.

"What do you want, boy?" she said, genuinely wondering how I got into the place.

"If this is Mr. Cooper's office, I want to see Mr. Cooper."

"This is Mr. Cooper's office, but I doubt you have an appointment, and he is very busy. You can't see Mr. Cooper."

"I'll wait," I replied, and sat down on one of the hard-wooden chairs near the front of the room under the isinglass. I noticed that Mr. Cooper's office was also wood on the bottom and isinglass on the top, as was his door. So I sat.

The lady kept looking at me now and then with a mean look. I just smiled back. "Always return good for evil," my mother had said.

After an hour or so, a be speckled man with green bands around his forearms, holding his white shirt, came out of his office and approached the woman.

He saw me. "What's going on here?" he asked.

Exasperated, the lady said, "Mr. Cooper, this boy is waiting to see you. I have told him that you do not have time for him today, but he has been here almost two hours."

He looked me over again. "All right. I'll see him. Come in, young man. Let's see what's on your mind."

He didn't invite me to sit, so I stood. He stood on the other side of his desk with his hands on his hips.

"What is it?"

"Mr. Cooper, I'm Robert French, Shorty French's boy. You know, my daddy was hurt in Huntsville and has been out of work for more than a year. He is now ready to come back to work, and we need him to work. I have come to ask you for his job back."

"I know Shorty French. Everyone knows Shorty, but I have no work for him. Sorry. That's just the way things are. Every job we have here is filled."

I held up my pass and $4. "Well, I was hoping you would help us, but I'm not through. I'm taking this pass and money to Cleveland, and I'm going to see Mr. Green and ask the B of RT to file a grievance. I'm leaving on the next train out."

Mr. Cooper grinned, "You are a determined young man. I wish my son had your gumption. I don't have a job here, but I may be able to find something for Shorty in Chattanooga. Send your daddy to work Monday morning. I'll find something for him to do

28

around here. He may have to sweep the floors until I can transfer him to Chattanooga."

I thanked him profusely. He came around the desk and patted me on the shoulder. "You are a good young man."

As I was leaving, I heard him tell the lady at the desk, "That boy will amount to something."

Walking home I was so happy that I didn't have to go to Cleveland. Plus, the family needed the $4. I thanked the Lord over and over because I had prayed hard coming to Sheffield that Daddy would go back to work.

Mother was so happy, she cried, and daddy was glad to go back to work on Monday. In less than a month, we packed up everything we had and all rode in the cab of the moving truck. We moved to Red Bank on Dayton Boulevard just outside Chattanooga.

We rented a bungalow with a creek in the back. Out front was the biggest street I had ever seen. Across the street was the estate of Mr. Christensen who owned a hardware store in town. We watched him cut his grass with a gasoline lawn mower. We had never seen such a machine in our lives.

The summer, before school started, on occasion Dot, Hester, and I would take Daddy's lunch to him at the Union Station in Chattanooga. We would walk down Dayton Boulevard and have a big time when we walked through the tunnel yelling at the top of our lungs to hear the echo. Other-wise, we enjoyed throwing rocks at snakes in the creek behind the house.

I started the 5th grade at Red Bank Elementary School. I was given a spanking for refusing to eat vegetable soup. Mother went to the school and told the teacher off for hitting her son who suffered from a hernia.

That Halloween, we didn't have any way to dress up and scare the neighbors, so we took some of Daddy's railroad carbon paper and smeared it on our faces. Bad mistake. We like to have never removed that blue stuff. Trick or treat had not spread to the South at that time. We simply knocked on the neighbor's back door, and when they came, we said, "boo."

About half the way through the school year, Daddy was transferred to the Decatur, Alabama, yard. Here, I will include an excerpt from my book, *Beaten, Battered and Damned, The Drano Murder Trial.*

April 10, 1944, I was eleven years old, and I stood quietly frightened before the huge double brown oak doors of the gothic red brick building emblazoned, "Joe Wheeler Grammar School." It was located on 9th Avenue, West, Decatur, Alabama. I was a fresh boy transferring in from the 5th grade at Red Bank Grammar School in the suburbs of Chattanooga, Tennessee.

My father had been transferred to the Decatur, Alabama, Southern Railroad Yard. This meant that my three younger sisters and I had to enter the school year interrupted. I was nervous. Classes had started, and I had to enter that strange "new boy" territory accompanied by the principal. She had gathered all the information about the French children from my mother who had walked with us from our newly rented "defense" home on 6th Avenue to the school. Defense homes were small, two bedrooms, four- room houses built 25 feet from each other during the war. Ours was the only thing my father could find on short notice.

Mrs. Harvey welcomed me to her 4th and 5th grade classes of about 40 children.

"Boys and girls, this is Robert French. He is new to Joe Wheeler, as he has just moved to Decatur from Chattanooga, Tennessee. Robert is a fine person, with a good school record, so please make him welcome."

All the boys and girls looked up from their work expressionless as Mrs. Harvey guided me to one of the old-fashioned desks in front of Barbara Hurst.

Mrs. Harvey instructed the 5th graders to turn to their workbooks and complete an assignment in Chapter 7. Meanwhile, she taught the 4th graders arithmetic. I went to work in my 8 X 12 pulp-paged book.

During recess, I got to know some of my classmates. There was one girl who impressed me immediately because she was the only person in school with red hair - Bobbie Mae Mooney. She was tall, pretty, and in the 4th grade. Little could either of us have known then what fate awaited us 55 years later.

While I was in the 5th grade, Daddy came over to watch me catch in a baseball game. He had been professional catcher, and had taught me the tools of the trade. I was catching this country boy and Daddy yelled, "Get up under his butt, son!"

I did, and rather than placing the bat on his shoulder, the boy swung the bat back, and hit me squarely in the forehead. I have carried the knot of that day throughout my life.

When I reached the 9th grade, I was tired of school. I asked my mother to let me quit. She would have none of that. We were going through some hard times. We were dirt poor, due to my father having been injured in another on-the-job accident. We lived out in the country, without running water or many other conveniences of the time. However, my mother was firm.

She said, "Young man, you will not quit school. Education is all we have. I went to college, your father went to college, and we read. Remember that. We are not trash because we read books. Now get back to your schoolwork."

Although I remembered the incident all my life, I was determined to quit school. I'd show my mother. I promptly failed the 9th grade. I was put back with the class one year younger. Bobbie Mae Mooney was now a classmate of mine. We graduated together from Decatur High School in 1952. I went off to the University of North Alabama and, after two semesters, into the Korean Conflict. She went off to Auburn, and I lost track of the redheaded girl.

Our paths would cross again more than 50 years down the road. The renewal will impress Alabama forever and give the folks something to talk about for generations.

CHAPTER FOUR
HARDTIMES

The war raged on and was difficult for the French family. Uncle Peck and Uncle Popeye had gone off to war.

Daddy had fallen from an ice-covered rail car, injured himself, and was out of work again. Plus, it seemed the jarring of the fall had caused the old spinal trouble to come back with a fury. He was home all the time, and I was taking care of him again.

In addition, I had a morning paper route delivering the *Birmingham Post Herald* to 265 homes; then I worked in a grocery store as a delivery boy using one of those delivery boy Schwinn bikes with the big wheel in the back, a little wheel in the front, and a big basket for groceries.

Groceries had to be delivered because people did not have gas for cars nor rubber for tires. So baskets filled up during the day to be delivered when I got there. And all the time I was attending the 5th grade.

My day consisted of getting up at 4:00 a.m. riding my bike to the newspaper pick-up, rolling papers and putting them in my bag, riding down Johnson Street, Grant Street, and prospect drive, throwing papers. Then I had to ride home as fast as I could, eat breakfast, wash up, and go to school. Immediately after school, ride to the grocery store, and deliver groceries until I had delivered them all. After supper, homework and a bath, get into bed about 8:00 p.m., and start the same thing again the next day. After I collected from my paper customers on Saturday, I had to work at the store the rest of the day. I threw the Sunday papers, and then finally got some rest, usually after church. I was bringing home $16 to $18 a week, and the family needed it.

Looking back on it, I wonder how an 11-year-old boy could do that. Back then, it was just normal, and things were going to get worse.

The National Safety Council held a contest for kids, under 12, to suggest safety ideas that would help the war effort. I saw the ad in a magazine and decided to enter.

My suggestion was that, since it was war time, kids did not have many toys. As a result, they dug holes, and made play roads into the hole in the ground, or dug down, and went sideways, and made a cave.

My suggestion was that since defense workers went to work at night, and walked across places where kids played, children should fill up their holes as a worker might step in it and break his leg. This would hurt the war effort. I won a beautiful medal. It was another memento that I kept until I went into the Air Force and lost track of it.

The unpaved roads in Decatur were covered with railroad cinders. The city hauled them away from the yard. The railroad was glad to get rid of them as they piled up with every train that came through. They were small, about the size of a dime, jagged, and sharp as glass.

I was overloaded with groceries, got into the shoulder of unpaved 7th Avenue West, and fell into the cinders on the bike. I still carry the scar, slightly below my right knee, where I was injured. It became infected and I couldn't ride. I became unemployed in the early summer before I started the 6th grade.

THE TROLLEY

Ronnie Newsome, who would later become a high ranking Naval Officer; Harold Howell, who would later become Chief Pilot United Air Lines; and I, were walking down the railroad tracks going somewhere boys go on a beautiful warm summer day. We stumbled upon about 65 feet of steel cable laying between the tracks. We decided to drag it to Ronnie's house where there was a vacant lot. As we tugged and strained, pulling that heavy cable a little over a mile through the streets of Decatur, we decided what we would do with it.

Getting into Ronnie's daddy's toolbox with a hammer, nails, a saw and other tools, we captured some three-foot boards that we nailed as a ladder to the trunk of the highest tree. About 30 feet up, we found the limbs we were looking for and built a platform out of an old wooden pallet.

We then nailed one end of the cable to the tree. We got a two foot piece of pipe and threaded the cable through it. We then nailed the loose end of the cable to another tree, about five feet above the ground some 66 feet away. We called our construction a trolley.

"Who's going to ride it first?" Harold asked.

I volunteered, climbed the hand holds we had nailed to the tree, took to the platform, grabbed the pipe, and away I went. Great ride! The hand pipe got a little hot going down, so we oiled the cable with most of the motor oil we could find in Ronnie's garage and taped the pipe. Heat problem solved.

After a couple of days, everyone began riding it. We would have a line of kids at the bottom of the tree waiting their turn.

It was great fun. The rider arriving on the ground had to sling the pipe back up the cable for someone to catch on the platform.

A few days later, Bobby Glenn Redding, or Paul Marion, I can't remember which, slid the pipe back up to me. Regardless, I missed grabbing it, lost my footing, and fell out of the tree. If my mother didn't have enough problems, her son now had a broken right arm.

One of the neighbors drove me across town to the Nungester Clinic. Dr. Nungester set the arm and wrapped it with a splint, rather than setting it in Plaster of Paris.

After a few weeks wearing my splint, I returned to work at the grocery store. I was not able to deliver papers, but I could ride and deliver groceries.

My sister Dot slipped off down to Ronnie Newsome's house and rode the trolley. It was now the most popular thing in West Decatur. After a few rides, she fell out of the tree and broke her arm. I took her to Nungester Clinic sitting in the basket of my delivery boy's bicycle.

Dr. Nungester said, "That's it! I've had four kids come in here with broken arms. Somebody is going to get killed on that trolley. It's a wonder a kid hasn't already broken his neck."

He called the police. They came, took down our trolley, and hauled away the steel cable. So much for that fun.

ROLAND OLIVER

My 6th grade class would be in Gordon Elementary School. There were three schools on the property on Prospect Drive in Decatur – Gordon Elementary, Bibb Elementary, with Decatur Junior High School sprawling across the background. I was assigned to the class of Miss Bernice Sermons.

After my arm and leg healed, I took a job delivering the same *Post Herald* route I had earlier and took a *Decatur Daily* route in the afternoon. I was throwing over 400 papers a day on a bicycle that had cost five dollars. that I had painted myself. (It wasn't a good paint job.)

While rolling papers, under the watchful eye of Mr. Layman in the newsboy room, I met a fellow who was a little younger than me, one grade back, who would influence my life until he died some 66 years later – Roland Oliver. He went to Fairview School and lived in the country. However, we became best friends and rolled our papers together.

When the war ended, during that school year, all newsboys were let out of school to go sell extra papers announcing the end of World War II in Europe. It was a joyous time. Finally, we would be out of the ration system, we could devote our entire effort to defeating Japan, and the boys would be coming home soon.

I left school at about 11:00 a.m., went to the newsboy room, and got my extras. I knew where I was going to sell the historic papers--the corner of Second Avenue and Johnson Street by V.J. Elmore's 5 & 10 Cent Store. When I got to my spot, I started yelling, "Extra! Extra! Read all about it! Germany has surrendered! Get your Decatur Daily, 25 Cents!"

I was selling papers as fast as I could make change.

I looked across the street, and there, in front of Haggerty's Drug Store, was Roland Oliver trying to outyell me and outsell me. That began a competition that lasted until he passed away. We competed at everything - golf, ping pong, root the peg, baseball, softball, football, auto racing, motorcycle racing, skiing, everything – mostly golf.

This account of my history would not be accurate without a generous telling of Robert and Roland stories. Believe me, there will be many.

Funny how life works out. Roland always wanted to be a lawyer and I always wanted to be a businessman. Changes and circumstances reversed our lives.

All the newsboys did a repeat when the Japanese surrendered, and a new world began. The economy was booming; the boys were coming home; the housing was out of sight; and babies were being conceived.

Unfortunately, for the French family, things began to become worse.

WORST TIMES ON THE HORIZON

After having recovered enough to return to work, my father began to drift mentally again. He became like a child once more. We wondered when the stuff they had injected into his spine would wear off. He began to work off and on. We could not survive that way. My mother had to go to work.

Mother went all over Decatur trying to find a job in an office. She could not find a job that would pay her enough money to support the family with four children. Although she had a college degree from Madison Business College, she had to take a job where she could meet production in a factory. She went to work on the midnight shift at Goodyear Mills that made cord for tires.

It was so terrible for us. Mother had to catch the last bus out of West Town to go across town to the mill. In the morning, she would catch the bus back. It was 10 cents each way. I was running the household, as Daddy was like a child again. He even got into a broom fight with Billy Joe Clark, a 10-year-old, from across the street. That was a mess. I straightened it out with Billy Joe's father.

Sometimes, Mother would have to walk to work through the dark part of West Town, near midnight. She carried Daddy's straight razor with her for protection. For safety, she would walk in the middle of the street.

One dark night, a black man stepped out from behind a large oak, "Where you going, Missy?"

Cool as could be, Mother never stopped walking. She said "I'm taking this straight razor to work. It's razor sharp, but I need it strapped."

The man said, "I shore hope you get it strapped. I'd hate to get cut by a dull razor."

"You go about your business, and you have nothing to worry about."

He stopped, and Mother walked on. That was the only time she ever came close to having any problem walking to work at night. So sad.

Even the memory of the sacrifice of my mother still hurts me. She lived her life for her family. I did all I could, but I wonder if I could have done more. I excuse myself, as I was only a boy. She worked at night so she could take care of the family during the day. It was very hard on my mother. I still do not know how she did it. I certainly love her for her sacrifice.

CLARENCE CAMPBELL

One Saturday I had collected off my paper route and was on my way home with fellow paper boy, Clarence Campbell. I had $13.75 in my pocket to take to my mother. Clarence suggested we go Into the Mayflower Café on Moulton Street and buy a chocolate milkshake.

It was still wartime winding down, and I had not had anything sweet in what seemed like forever. Unable to buy sugar, we sweetened our coffee with Karo Syrup. I felt all the change in my pocket.

"How much do you think one would cost?" I asked, remembering the one I had before the war.

"Not much, 25 cents."

We went in and took our places at the soda counter. I was drinking my chocolate milkshake when my mother appeared in the door. She had her hands on her hips. She looked at me and turned and walked away going home.

I'll never know how she found me. I was broken-hearted. I had intended to take the quarter out of my collection and say that was all I had earned. Now she knew differently. I was getting something that the three girls did not get.

When I got home, I told my mother, "Here's the money from my paper route."

"Just keep it. You'll need it to buy milkshakes that no one else gets."

I laid the money on the kitchen table and went for a walk. I was so broken- hearted with myself. I was a cheater - a selfish cheater. I had taken family money and spent it on myself. I had a hard time on that walk. When I got back home, all my collection on the table was gone, and all was forgiven. I would never put myself before the family again.

Clarence Campbell got me into more trouble that summer. His father had rented a mule for the day to plow his garden. He was through, and he had tied the mule to a tree awaiting the owner to come get it.

"Let's ride that mule," Clarence suggested.

I thought it was a great idea. I untied the mule and climbed on. Mr. Campbell had put the halter and bridle back on the mule. So, away I went.

When I got to Moulton Street, a truck loaded with horses went by. One or more of them neighed. That mule bolted after the truck. I fell off and hit my head on the street. I lay in the busy street until someone came by and picked me up. Clarence told them where I lived, and they took me home. I remained unconscious for almost three days. That would come back to haunt me when I tried to become a jet pilot during the Korean War.

TOUGH TIMES GET WORSE

For some reason, we could not live as we were living. Daddy was not working at all so we moved to Austinville, two miles out of Decatur.

He finally went to work in a chicken plant that was stinky, filthy work, but he hung in there until he could get a job at American Oak Leather as a day laborer. It wasn't much, but between the three of us, we were making ends meet.

I had passed the 7th grade at Decatur Junior High a year after the war ended. It was there I would acquire the nickname that accompanied me the rest of my life-- Herman.

Everyone had a nickname, and a boy in my class, who combed his hair regularly, was named McCoy. I began calling him Pretty Boy McCoy, and it stuck. He hated it, and wanted to get back at me. He had read a book, and had given a report, *Henry French Indian Fighter*. He began calling me Henry.

It wasn't long before someone else took it up, but now it was not Henry French, it was Herman the German.

For the rest of my life I became known as Herman French in Decatur, Alabama. Throughout my life, many people have thought that was my real name. Worse yet, all my younger sisters, other than Rebecca, who came along much later in life, were called "Little Herman."

Now I would enter the 8th grade at Austinville, where I knew absolutely no one. We lived near the school, but it was out in the country. We did not have indoor plumbing, just an outhouse out back.   I used to take those long, leaping steps across our garden to the outhouse on cold mornings, and say as I went "I will never do this again. I will do better than this."

And then… things got worse.

Mother was having a hard time getting to work with "rides," or worse yet, walking at least four miles each way.

We had a small two-eye laundry heater to heat the entire house, and we cooked on it when we could. Mother bought a two-eye hot plate, and we cooked on that.

Saturdays were our regular bath night. Fortunately, being the only boy, I got to take the first bath. Mother had bought this little heater that you dropped into a #3 washtub of water, and it would heat the water. Until it wore out, I got a warm bath, then we might heat a pan of water on the stove to knock the chill off the water and climb in. Often that was too much trouble, so I just climbed in, freezing water and all.

We had a well, and it took quite a bit of running back and forth to fill a #3 wash tub. About that time, our hot plate broke. I had repaired it as many times as I could. Now, we were without a stove. We put a Dutch oven on the stovepipe of the laundry heater but it would not get hot enough to cook in. The sides of the little heater would get red hot, but the top wouldn't. So, there was nothing to do but go into the back yard, dig a hole, and cook out there until we could swing another hot plate. I made good use of the time. I earned my cooking merit badge with the Boy Scouts. Plus, I learned how to cook when you have very little to work with.

RIDING BARE BACK

It was Halloween, 1945, and daddy was taking work wherever he could get it. He worked almost a year for a farmer named Raymond Matthews, $25 a week. During the summer, he had persuaded Mr. Matthews to hire me on at 35 cents an hour. I pulled dog fennel that made the milk taste bad. I plowed old Het, his mule, and anything else necessary around the farm.

One day Mr. Matthews told me to take the mule to Decatur and have her shod. I rode the mule bareback through Cedar Lake, the Black community, right down 2nd Avenue, to the blacksmith shop below the Princess Theatre.

The Farrier nailed new shoes on Old Het and said he would charge the $3 to Raymond Matthews. I got back up on the mule, straw hat, overalls, brogans and all.

Everything was fine until the mule hit the pavement with the new shoes. She bucked me off and started running up 2nd Avenue, the main street of "New" Decatur. The harder she ran, the louder the noise from the new shoes, and the farther away she got from me. She was running straight up 2nd Avenue, on a Saturday, being chased by a boy holding his straw hat, and running as fast as he could.

Fortunately, when Het hit the intersection of 2nd Avenue and Johnson Street, where I had sold papers a little while back, some farmers stepped out in the street, and caught Het. They boosted me back up on her, and that mule and me became one until I got her back to Raymond Matthews' barn.

HALLOWEEN

Shortly after the episode with Old Het, it was Halloween. Matthews had a very large stump in the cotton patch adjoining our house. Our house was a four-room white cinder block affair whose yard joined the cotton patch. The farmer was tired of plowing and otherwise working around the stump. It was big. He wanted it removed, and would pay to have it done. He hired daddy to dig it out.

I went out with daddy. We dug around the stump about two feet deep. He then hooked Old Het to the stump, and told her to get up. The mule pulled, hunkered down, and pulled, and pulled again. Daddy started unhooking the singletree.

I said, "Daddy, beat that mule. Make her pull up that stump."

Daddy replied with a lesson that has remained with me until this day. He said, "Son, when a mule has done all it can do, that's all it can do. We have to do more digging."

I have reflected on that experience all my life. When a person has done all he or she can do, that's all that can be done. In other words, try something else.

So we dug, and we dug, and we dug. Finally, we had loosened the stump to where Old Het could pull it out of the ground. I noticed as the stump came out it left a huge hole about eight feet by six feet, and 6 feet deep. After we sawed up the stump, it filled almost two truckloads of debris. It left a big hole.

"We'll have to fill that hole in tomorrow," daddy said at the end of the day.

That night, Halloween, Ki Roper, who lived across the freshly plowed cotton field from us, came toward our house to borrow a cup of sugar.

Ki was a welder at Decatur Iron and Steel. He lived in a little brown, pine clapboard, two-room house. He worked hard all week, but come Friday night, Ki Roper got drunk. He got drunk and stayed drunk the entire weekend. He wasn't much trouble. We could hear him across the cotton field cursing at imaginary demons or singing at the top of his lungs. All that was his business.

Ki, like everybody else, walked everywhere he went. So he never knew about mine and Daddy's work on the stump. Instead, in his drunken stupor, on a dark moonless night, he headed across the cotton patch to borrow a cup of sugar.

Ki Roper fell headlong into the hole. He tried to climb out, he tried to jump out, and he tried everything he knew to get out, including yelling, "Get me outta here!" at the top of his lungs. Finally, he gave up and said, "To hell with it."

He squatted down in one corner of the hole, fished a pint out of his overall's bib pocket, and made the most of a bad situation.

At about 1:30 a.m., Waymon Hamilton was coming home from Ingalls Shipyard. Instead of walking down Spring Street to the field road that went to his house one-half mile away, he decided to cut across the cotton patch. Bad decision.

Remember, it is pitch black, and Waymon did not have any light. As fate would have it, he stumbled into the hole. He immediately began to jump up and down, trying to get out. He tried to dig his feet into the wall and get out. He tried everything.

While he was huffing and puffing, Ki Roper though he might help him get them both out of the hole. In his most sober voice, he said, "You can't get out of here."

He did, and ran all the way home.

A little after daylight, I heard Ki yelling for help. I knew he was in the stump hole. I went out and gave him a hand, and he climbed out. We found Waymon's old crushed lunch bucket. Apparently, he stood on it to get out of the hole.

Ki had to go to the house and tell everyone what had happened. He thought it was the funniest thing that

45

he ever knew. He told it far and wide, and Waymon never denied it.

DIVING OFF THE KELLER MEMORIAL

It was the following summer. I was 15 years old, and had already thrown my morning papers. I peddled over to the river to see what was going on.

It was a beautiful Saturday on the river. One of the guys, David Roe, had a motor boat, water skis, and a disc. To heck with the skis! They were too tame. We each took turns riding the disc. Swimming trunks? Heck no. We didn't have them. We pulled off our pants, and participated in our briefs - white underwear.

Either Paul Marion, David Roe, Jack Scott, or Frank Blackwell, came up with the brilliant idea of diving off the Hellen Keller Memorial in the middle of the bridge over the Tennessee River at Decatur. I remembered that war ships used to pass through that draw bridge during the war.

Somebody had said, "Let's dive off the Keller Memorial."

"I donno," another boy said. "That's pretty high up there. More'n 60 feet, I would say. Plus, they say that 20 feet down in the channel there is an undertow that will carry you down river. You can't fight it strong enough to get back to the surface. They'll find your body somewhere below the railroad bridge a half mile down river."

That brought on conversation about seeing a drowned body – all fat, white and ugly. We had all seen one. We didn't want to be one, but that bridge held a calling for teenage boys. So, we decided we would walk up there and look around.

Cars were going by, we were in our skivvies, but we didn't care. They couldn't see anything. We climbed up on the memorial railing that protruded out from the bridge about 10 feet. From that perch, we looked down at the water.

"That's further down than I thought," Frank Blackwell said.

"Maybe we ought to go back down to the river bank," Paul Marion opined.

Just about then, David Roe pulled the boat out below us in the river. He had picked up another boy to help him pull us into the boat after we dove off.

"What are you, a bunch of chickens?" Roe yelled up from the surface far below. He would later become a dentist in New Orleans.

"That's it! I'm over the edge," Jack Scott said, and let go of the Washington Monument shaped Memorial to Alabama's Helen Keller. He stepped a couple of paces out on the wide concrete railing and dove off. He hit the water, surfaced and was helped into the boat. His shorts were down around his ankles. He pulled them up, looked up at us and waited.

"Who's next?" David Roe yelled up to us.

"I guess I might as well go," Frank Blackwell said in a resigned voice as he stepped away from the Memorial and dove into the river. He came up and was helped into the boat. His briefs stayed up.

Paul Marion looked at me. "Well, what do you say, Herman, you or me?"

"Go on. I'm just not ready yet."

Paul stepped away from the Memorial and dove as far out from the bridge as he could. He surfaced and was helped into the boat.

Before I could even think about it, Jack Scott was hollering, "Herman! Dive off the bridge!"

"I'm worried about the undertow," I yelled back.

"Then come up soon. We're here to pull you out."

47

with that, I stepped away from the Memorial, said a prayer, and dove off. I hit the water and surfaced as quickly as I could. I was afraid of the undertow.

The boys pulled me into the boat, briefs in place, and one said, "That's the quickest I have ever seen anyone come up from a dive. It didn't look like you went 5 feet into the water and then you were up."

"I was afraid of the undertow," I replied.

When I got home, Mother said, "The *Decatur Daily* called. They said you dove off the Helen Keller Memorial into the river. Were you so silly as to do that dangerous thing?"

"Yes, Mam."

"Well the reporter wants to know if you will come back tomorrow at 2:00 o'clock and dive off again so he can get a picture. I told him that you would not do that. And, you will not."

"Yes, Mam."

Who dove off the next day for the paper? Roland Oliver.

HOPPING A FREIGHT CAN BE DANGEROUS

That same summer, after our paper routes, Roland and I decided to go down to the railroad station and look around. We stood with our bikes north of the depot building, and watched the freights pass under the highway, and go across the river on the railroad bridge. The bridge was a turnstile bridge in that rotated the center of the bridge up and down the river when a large boat needed access to the channel.

As boys will, we became a little bored, watching and listening to freights and enjoying that old railroad smell.

"What would you think about hopping a freight across the river?" I asked Roland.

"That would be a lot of fun, but how would we get back. We sure can't walk that bridge back because its barely wide enough for a railroad car."

"We could wait on the other side and hop a freight coming back. You know they all have to slow down to cross the river. I think the maximum they can go is 7 miles per hour."

"That might work. Let's park our bikes over there near those rocks and jump this one that's passing through right now."

We parked the bikes and jumped the box car ladders. The lower part of the box car ladder may have been called the grab. I can't remember. Anyway, Roland was on the rear of the car in front of me while I was on the rear of the next car.

When we got to the river, the train was slowed to a crawl. I got off and held on to the ladder and Roland did too. We walked in the gravel on the ties with the train up to the point where the ground became the river bank and the railroad bridge began.

At that point, like hoboes, we swung back up on the ladder. That is, Roland swung back up on his ladder. I lost my grip and fell. I was fortunate to grasp on to the lower step of the ladder, the one that hangs down from a box car. I'm swinging on that thing, holding my feet and legs up off the bridge as we went across the river.

Safely on the other side, both of us got off the train as it began to pick up speed. "Herman, I thought I had lost you for a minute when you fell," Roland commiserated.

"Yeah, I thought I had a bad day. I could just see losing my legs in a freak accident. It was hard to hold that sitting position on that ladder all the way across the bridge. But, win some, lose some, and some are rained out."

We stood around, kicked clods, threw rocks, explored and waited for a train going back toward Decatur. In about 4 hours, a slow-moving freight provided us transportation back to our bikes at the depot.

That night, when I said my prayers, I thanked the Lord for saving my life. Even though Roland and I made light of it, I could have easily been killed or lost both legs.

That was the last time I ever hopped a freight.

COTTON PICKING TIME IN DIXIE

I guess neighbors somehow heard how hard we were having life. Certainly, we didn't tell anybody. We were too proud. The fact that we couldn't afford a radio didn't matter. We read everything we could find. We made up stories and told them to each other. We used old magazines for toilet paper. Once in the outhouse, I said, "Thank God for *Collier's Magazine.*"

Regardless, the welfare woman came around one Saturday.

"Mrs. French, if you will just sign some papers, I can get you $18.00 a week from the State."

Mother said, "Lady, we are not trash. We are educated people having a hard time. We read. We do not want your money."

I thought that if it had been me, I would have taken it. Maybe we could move out of the hellhole we were living in. But it was a good lesson for me – always keep your values, and never be ashamed of your circumstances as long as you are trying to change them.

When school started that year, I was the new boy in the 8th grade. I had to wear hand-me-downs from my cousins Bill and Tom Hasty, and from my Uncle Arnold's navy clothes. Kids would laugh at me because "Sibley" was stenciled across the right back pocket of my overall pants. Jeans had not been invented at the time.

"Your name is not Sibley, why do you have it on your pants?"

"They're my uncle's Navy pants, and I'm proud to wear them."

There were a lot of embarrassing moments during the 8th grade at Austinville. I had holes in my shoes, and I was wearing my uncle's socks tucked down in my shoes. We couldn't afford to have my shoes resoled. It rained one day and the toe of the sock came out the hole in my left shoe. Everyone laughed. I didn't care. My opinion was the only one that counted, and I was proud to have something to wear.

We got out of school for three weeks in the fall to pick cotton. I borrowed a cotton sack from Mr. Calvert, and off to the field I went. I learned how to pick cotton - and pick a lot. They were paying $3.50 per 100 pounds picked. I could pick almost 100 pounds a day.

An older gentleman, Castor Lott, picked 200 pounds a day. I watched him and caught on as to how to pick cotton in a hurry. I earned enough that first year to buy shoes and socks for myself, Dot, Hester and Daina. Mother was proud of me.

In the 9th grade, I had traded for my own sack, and Mother sewed another old discarded sack to it. This resulted in my being able to pick without going to the weigh wagon so often. I was picking above 100 pounds a day. Again, I bought the school clothes for all of us that year. That was the year I intentionally failed the 9th grade.

When school started the next year, after I had been put back, who do you think showed up? The Oliver family had moved to Austinville, and Roland and I were joined at the hip again. We lived about a quarter of a mile from each other.

Back right after the war he and I had left our paper routes and had begun caddying at Decatur Country Club. We could make $3 a day if we were lucky. Although I had not seen him often, when I could get a Saturday or Sunday off, and get a ride, I would go to the country club and caddy, even if it meant walking the seven miles back home.

It was also early on that golf became our passion. Roland and I had caddied at the Decatur Country Club as often as we could. We always found golf balls. I wanted to play so badly, but I could not afford the game. So I made myself a golf club.

I looked around the trees and bushes for a couple of days before I found exactly what I needed. I cut the "club" out of the bush and nailed a tin can lid on its face. I would spend hours in the unplanted cotton field hitting balls, chasing them down in the prepared rows, and hitting them back. Roland laughed at me for being a club manufacturer. However, I could hit my homemade club as far as he could hit a three wood he had bought from the pro, Mr. Lowery, for $5.

In the 9th grade at Austinville, I played on the basketball team and lettered. My mother sewed the big black "A" on a white sweater so I could wear it proudly at school. It wasn't long before my sister Dot got it, and she wore it until it was threadbare.

During cotton picking time, while I was in the 9th grade, I was down on Pepper's Creek, about half a mile, across two 40's, from the weigh wagon.

I was pulling that double sack in long staple Egyptian cotton. This cotton had just been introduced into the South. It was small stalks, no more than a foot and a half high, with 3 or 4 bolls that had long staple cotton coming out of them. The ends of the bolls were sharp stickers, and any picker who tried to pick a lot had bloody fingertips.

The cotton was too low to bend over and pick it. I had tried that and wore myself out. I decided to put my basketball knee pads on under my overall pants, straddle one row on my knees, pick it, and pick the one on the right and the one on the left as I went up the field.

It had worked really well coming out from the wagon shortly after daylight and during early morning when it was cool. Now it was hot - unbearably hot - and I was dragging my heavy, half-filled sack, down on my knees in the red clay of North Alabama.

I was straining to pick three rows of cotton at once. I was tired, hungry, and just out of sorts. I noticed that my tears were splattering on the red clay leaving star-like red designs.

I stopped picking and said to myself, "There has to be a better way. I refuse to do this."

I started praying, "Lord, if you will just give me the strength to drag this sack back to the weigh wagon, I will not come into a cotton patch to pick cotton as long as I live."

With that, I gathered all my strength and began dragging that 19-foot sack packed with cotton to the weigh wagon. It took me about 30 minutes to get there.

"What are you doing, Robert?" Mr. Isley, the farmer, asked.

"I'm through. I've picked my last cotton, rode my last load of cotton to the gin, and I am never coming back into a cotton patch."

"Well, that's a big mouthful, Robert. I hope you can make it stick. Now, let's see what you've got in that sack."

He weighted me out – 137 pounds picked since dawn. He paid me, and I started to leave.

"Robert," he yelled after me, "you forgot your sack."

"I didn't forget it, Mr. Isley. I will never need it again. Give it to some other poor soul."

The next day, still being out of school, I walked into Decatur looking for a job. I was hired at 35 cents an hour to attend the stoker at V.J. Elmore's 5 and 10 Cents Store. Compared to picking cotton, it was a desk job. By the time school started back, I was a stock boy. I worked after school until summer. At that time, I took time off to devote full-time to caddying at the golf course.

9th GRADE AGAIN

Roland and I were now together in the 9th grade. The teachers would not allow us to sit next to each other. We bought a card that taught sign language. We were in Mrs. Teague's biology class. I signed to him, "That woman has the biggest feet I have ever seen."

He signed back, "And ugly too."

"I saw that!" yelled Mrs. Teague. "I knew you two were up to something so I learned sign language myself. Robert French, you go and sit in the hallway. Roland Oliver, you go sit at the door because you are going into the hallway next."

There was a rule at school that if a student was found in the hallway during class, he would immediately get a spanking of six licks with the principal's paddle. Back then, a school day paddling meant licks that would lift you up on your tiptoes. I thought that my butt was going to be burning. I was peeping through the keyhole. Roland was inside looking back.

"Roland Oliver!" asserted Mrs. Teague, "what are you looking at through that keyhole?"

"Ma'am, all I see is another eye."

"Get out! Get out! You bad boy! I hope both of you get a beating."

Roland came out red-faced. "What are we going to do now, Herman?"

"I'm getting out of here. Let's go to the outhouse. We stay here and Principal Dollar catches us, he will beat our tails off. We can't be in more trouble than we are in. Let's go."

Away we went to the men's outhouse. The school did not have indoor restrooms. We had started smoking earlier that summer, lied about it to our parents, yet we kept a pack of 23-cent Camels somewhere between us all the time. We got up to the outhouse, and fired up. I didn't need to know anything about that stinking cell anyway.

Later, Mrs. Teague told me that I was failing biology. I couldn't afford to do that because I had just failed the 9th Grade. She assigned the class the drawing of a cell for one-third of the grade for the year. She didn't know I was an artist, and I put a cell on her like she had never seen before. It was just exactly like the one in the book. I used a box of Crayola Crayons to color my work and I did it on white butcher paper. It was far and away the best cell in the class. She gave me an A resulting in my having a C for the course.

I heard that she demonstrated my cell to every class thereafter to prove what a student can do, if he or she will do it.

If you pay attention to life close enough, you will find that events repeat themselves over and over. Years later, Michelle had to draw a cell in biology class at Fort

Payne High School. I didn't paint it for her, but I did help her in drawing the cell. She got an "A" for her effort.

The Lord works in mysterious ways.

REBECCA GENE FRENCH

We moved back to Decatur – 6th Avenue West across the street from where we had lived earlier. Daddy was not working, and we were having trouble again.

Before we left Austinville, Mother noticed something about me that I had not noticed. I was growing up. I was 14 years old and had not kissed my first girl. That was going to change. It came about like this. A girl in my class at Austinville- Carolyn Robertson-was having a party. I told my mother that I had been invited.

"You're going, of course."

"No, Ma'am, I'm not interested in all that hugging and a chalking." That was the title of a popular song at the time.

"Oh, yes you are, young man. I'm concerned about you. Here you have grown up in a house full of girls, and you are almost like one. I appreciate you helping with the washing, ironing, cooking, sewing, and housekeeping, but that may not be too healthy."

"I'm going to town and get you some dress clothes, and then you are going to that party. When they play post office or go walking, I want you to kiss every girl you can. I'm afraid you may be getting funny."

My mother walked from Austinville into Decatur to Goforth's Clothing Store. There, she bought me a tan sharkskin suit on credit. She dressed me in it, put some of Daddy's shaving lotion on my face, and sent me off to the party.

I kissed three girls, and that was it. No more feminine traits for me. I had almost been an Eagle Scout, lacking three merit badges. Although I was a Senior Patrol Leader, I quit the Boy Scouts and became a girl scout.

Now we had to move again. In all, by the time I left home, we had moved 12 times. Often it was to be near Daddy's work. Other times, I guess the rent was cheaper.

We were back on 6th Avenue West and my mother delivered her last child, my baby sister, Rebecca. There was a little more to it than that.

Mother was working full-time at Goodyear Mills. She was walking back and forth to work when she could not catch a bus or a ride. I don't know how she did it.

I was running the house, and Daddy was working wherever he could. It was such hard times. Daddy chose that time to pledge to give Central Baptist Church $25. We like to have never raised that money.

Mother cried because this was a pledge that we could ill afford. We had a hard time raising the 10-cent bus fare for mother to get to work. Into this situation came Rebecca Gene French.

She was born in Hamil Clinic in Old Decatur on Bank Street. When she began labor, Mother walked some two miles to the clinic, checked in, and had the baby. They would not allow her to leave until they were paid $40. They were charging by the day. We had to get Mother out of there, bring the baby home, and get about our business. But we couldn't. We didn't have $40.

For the first time in my life, my mother had to call upon her family to help. We couldn't afford to pay for the baby. It was a terribly joyous day. To the family in Huntsville, and Daddy's family in Scottsboro, we were always doing well, and didn't need anything. Now we were desperate. I think they were charging $15.00 a day, and we didn't have it.

Mother called Uncle Popeye (Arnold) and asked for $40. He drove directly over from Huntsville, paid the $40, and brought Mother home. He complained bitterly that we had allowed ourselves to get into such a mess without telling the family. Unfortunately, we got into more messes, but we had never called upon the family for help. So far as the outside world knew, we were doing okay.

After Mother settled the baby in, she began cleaning house, and mopped the kitchen floor. Looking back on it, the woman was unbelievable. I have no idea where she got her energy and drive, but I do know that I inherited most of it.

I did my duty with the baby. I fed her, bathed her, and changed her diapers. I didn't like to change the dirty diapers. Dot refused to do it, and Hester would usually do it. Sometimes I could persuade Daina to change Becky.

When Becky was 18 months old, I was cooking bacon for breakfast. I was moving a cast iron skillet to the table. Dot wanted me to fry her an egg. I refused because we didn't have enough eggs for everyone to have one.

As I was moving the skillet, Dot grabbed the handle and said, "I'll cook it myself!"

With that, the skillet tipped, and we spilled hot bacon grease on the baby's head. Horrors, we didn't know what to do. Becky was screaming in pain, and Mother had not come home from work. Daddy was still in bed and didn't know what was going on.

I put ice on the baby until Mother got home about 30 minutes later. She was so upset that we had burned the baby. She called a cab and rushed her to the hospital.

I doctored her until she got well, and it never became infected.

Unfortunately, Becky has dealt with that scar her entire life. When she became older, she could cover it up with her hair. It has been one of my painful regrets, but what's done is done. It didn't hold Becky back. She excelled at everything she attempted.

SAVING DOT'S LIFE

I was very active in the Boy Scouts. I worked myself up to a Life Scout, one rank below an Eagle. I may have mentioned that Paul Marion and I slept outside 50 nights to get the camping merit badge. In all, I was a Senior Patrol Leader and I believe I had 21 merit badges.

One of my merit badges was in first aid. It had been a difficult one to master. However, none of them were easy. Regardless, I felt like I was pretty good at first aid. It turned out I had to be.

Dot was approaching her teenage years. She was in the shower using a glass bottle of Prell Shampoo. Naturally, she had her eyes closed. The bottle slipped out of her hand and hit the floor of the shower shattering into many different pieces.

When Dot moved to get soap out away from her eyes, she stepped on a large piece broken glass. It cut her deeply in the center of her foot. She screamed for mother.

Mother washed Dot off, all the while examining the cut. It was bad. Blood was everywhere. Mother could not get the blood stopped. She wrapped Dot in a towel and called me.

"Son, call an ambulance, your sister is bleeding to death!"

I called the ambulance and returned to the shower where everything was covered with blood. Mother had used two towels to try to stop the bleeding and they were soaked in blood.

"I don't think she is going to make it. She'll bleed to death before the ambulance gets here and transports her to Decatur General."

I ran to the bedroom and got daddy's oldest neck tie, one that was frazzled, and retrieved a wooden spoon from the kitchen. I then went into the bathroom and applied to a tourniquet to my sister's ankle.

Using the techniques I had learned in scouting, I relieved the pressure every 15 minutes.

The ambulance finally arrived. The driver and his assistant examined Dot and said, "Leave her just as she is. The tourni quet she has on will work until we get her to the emergency room."

He then turned to us, "Who put this on, it has just saved her life?"

I told him that I had learned the technique in scouting.

They took Dot away and mother rode in the ambulance with them to the hospital. Dot was stitched up and she and mother returned in a taxi cab a little later.

Scouting was a great influence on my life. I had two scoutmasters, Mr. Sims and Ed. Brazelton. Both taught me many valuable life's lessons. Scouting was particularly an advantage when I went into the Air Force.

CHAPTER FIVE
FAMOUS JAMES

We moved again. This time to 14th Street SW. I turned 15 there, and my father had been able to return to work. Between him and Mother, the French family was making a comeback. Somehow, I had saved up right at $150. I wanted to buy a motorcycle. Fortunately, my mother and daddy wanted me to have one.

Daddy bought a Famous James in Memphis where he was working with the railroad. It cost $318.00 and I loved it. Of course, he tried to ride it when he took delivery on it and promptly wrecked the front fender.

He told me that he was sorry, but it just got away from him. It hurt that he had scarred my bike, but he had paid more than half the price for it. So, I might as well be happy with it. Furthermore, I was used to Daddy messing things up. He did things like that often, and Mother would always say, "It's not his fault. He is not the man I married, but I love him just the same. He's your father; forget it."

With the Famous James, I didn't wait for morning. When daylight came, I went to Austinville to get Roland. We rode that little motorcycle until we had sore posteriors. Within a week, Mr. Oliver had bought Roland a Service Cycle, another brand of 125cc motorcycle. Now Roland and I were mobile, agile, and hostile.

Once we had wheels, we kept the road hot to the Country Club. We played golf on caddy's day. We worked for Mr. Lowrey, the professional, through the week, 45 cents an hour, and caddied on Saturdays and Sundays. We were doing well.

In order to make my James louder, we took the muffler off. It was loud! It was Monday, caddie's day to play golf, and we wanted to start early. We arrived at

Decatur County Club a little after five. Naturally, John B. Stevens, our assistant pro who ran the golf shop, was not there and neither was the pro, Melvin Lowrey.

Mr. Lowrey had been very kind to Roland and me. He said that he had lost his two boys in an ugly divorce. They lived with their mother, and her new husband, in Huntsville. She would not allow him to see them often. We reminded him of his boys, and he treated us pretty well like sons. We got the best bags on the weekends, i.e., the golfers who tipped the best, and he worked us on the golf course through the summers. On rainy days, he would take Roland and me down into the clubhouse basement and teach us the golf swing.

He and his new wife lived in a white clapboard house in the middle of the nine-hole golf course.

Quite naturally, Roland came up with a very bright idea. "Look Herman, we know Mr. Lowery is not going to open up until eight. That's more than two hours from now. Let's go ride around his house and wake him up."

That sounded like a splendid idea to me. I kick-started the James and we headed for the pro's house. On our third round of his house, Mr. Lowrey came out on the front porch dressed in his nightshirt, nightcap, and carrying a shotgun.

Over the noise of the sans-muffler James, I heard him shout, "I'll kill you sons-o-bitches if you don't leave right now."

Out of an abundance of caution, I suggested we leave. We came back at 9:30 to see if we could play.

"No, you can't play!" he screamed. "You are not only fired as greens keepers, you are run off. You may not come on these grounds again."

We rode home very sad. Mother said I had learned a valuable lesson. "Don't bother people who don't want to be bothered. You and Roland made a terrible mistake, and you are going to pay for it."

Fortunately, Mrs. Oliver called Mr. Lowery and begged him to take us back. It was after lunch, and the pro had cooled down. He laughed about it and let us come back to work on Tuesday. He did warn us about our conduct. He talked about it for days. I thought he sounded a bit like my grandfather.

Roland got a new portable radio for his birthday. Portables had just come out, and they were about the size of a washing powder box because they had large batteries. Roland called it his battry radio. That's not a misspelling. He called it battry.

"Herman, we can now ride and have music."

Sounded like a good idea to me, and we enjoyed many happy miles with the radio playing.

He had the radio about three days when we were let off early one day and headed home. I was going a little fast when we turned left off Highway 31 onto 14th Street. I lost the bike, and we were sliding in the railroad cinders with the bike on top of us.

I slid out from under the motorcycle, cut it off, and righted it. I noticed that the left leg of my thick overall pants was ripped to shreds.

Roland got up holding his radio up above his head. He pulled it down to his ear, "Speak to me WMSL, speak to me!" He was listening intently to be sure his radio worked. It worked.

He was the best dressed boy around. In fact, he was named the best dressed in the senior class when we graduated. This day he had on thin summer tan slacks. I looked at his leg, and the entire left thigh of his pants was gone. He had raw bloody skin for about a foot of his thigh. It was ugly. I pointed to it.

"You might ought to forget the radio. Look at your leg."

He looked down at his bloody limb, and let out a wail. I took him home as fast as I could. The rest of our lives he would claim that I tried to kill him on my motorcycle.

ELEPHANTS

While we were healing from our scrapes, cuts, and bruises from the motorcycle wreck, the Ringling Brothers, Barnum and Bailey Circus came to town. It set up on our American Legion baseball field. Our problem--how to go to the circus without spending money? A little after daylight, we rode my James to the site where they were putting up the Big Top. Smaller tents were already in place. They had elephants pulling the ropes that would hold the three-ring Big Top in place.

We approached a guy who was obviously the foreman. I asked him for a job.

"I can use you boys, if you'll work hard. I'll give you two passes for the circus as long as it is here. I'll pay you five dollars a day – daylight to dark."

"We'll do it. When do we start?"

"Our cooks are feeding the people in the kitchen tent right now. You boys go over there to the kitchen tent and eat breakfast; come back to the holding tent; get a #3 washtub; walk down to that creek I saw coming in here; fill the tub with water; bring it back here; and give it to the elephants in the holding tent." He talked very fast and had a Yankee accent.

We enjoyed eating with the circus people. They were all relaxing and having a good time. In addition, the food was great. After we finished, we found the holding tent, and got a #3 washtub that had seen better days.

We set off for the creek a quarter of a mile away. We didn't realize how heavy a #3 washtub filled with water was. It felt like it weighed 200 pounds. Plus, it splashed about. We could barely carry it and had to stop often to rest.

When we got to the tent, the foreman was putting the elephants back in where the hay was. "Good. You boys are back. Give that tub to Jumbo over there."

We tugged the tub over to the largest elephant in the tent. That beast stuck his trunk down in the tub, sucked the water out of the tub, and sprayed it in his mouth.

The foreman said, "Go get another tub. And when you get back, scoop up this elephant shit, and put it in those cardboard boxes by the flap."

We went to the creek, filled the tub, and hauled it back to the holding tent. This time another elephant stuck her trunk into the tub, sucked out the water, and sprayed it in her mouth.

Roland and I got a couple of coal scoops and began to scoop up elephant manure.

"I didn't know these things could crap this big," Roland mused. "My scoop won't hold half of what this elephant is doing."

"Don't stand too close, it'll splatter on you," I warned.

We continued to shovel until the foreman came around and said. "That's enough for one day, boys. You did good work, and I'm letting you off a little early so you can see the freaks and still catch the big show." He handed each of us a ticket and $5.

We headed over to where a barker was enticing people to come in and see the freaks. He had on a straw hat, red striped jacket, red bow tie and a cane.

"Step right up, folks. Come see wonders that will amaze you! See Jo Jo, the dog-faced boy! He walks, he talks, and he crawls on his belly like other man-eating reptiles! Right this way fifty cents and see it all – the giant, the bearded lady, the fattest man alive, the sword swallower, and fortune-tellers galore!"

We each gave the barker fifty cents and went into a promenade made of tents facing each other. We saw the giant drop a silver dollar through his ring. We were amazed with the sword swallower when he swallowed a green neon light that lit up his throat. I went to the fortune-teller, and she was the one who asked me to tell her fortune.

As we were leaving, a guy with three English Walnut half shells said, "Hey, boy, come here. I got a little game for you."

We went over to his counter, and he said, "See this red marble? That's called a pea. These are shells. I put this pea under this shell and move them around. Can you guess which shell it's under?"

I pointed out the shell. Sure enough, the pea was under the shell. He did it several more times and finally concluded that I had the sharpest eyesight and memory he had ever seen.

"Now, just to make the cheese more binding, I'll bet you a quarter you can't do it again."

I put a quarter up because I had guessed right every time.

He put the pea under the shell and moved the shells around, and I knew exactly which shell the pea was under. I pointed it out. Wrong. He took my quarter and wanted to play again. I said no. That quarter had been too hard to earn. Roland and I went into the Big Top to see the show.

Years later, I would tell almost every criminal jury that story and say that, sometime later, I learned why I could not guess which shell the pea was under. He had palmed the pea, and it was not under any of the shells.

"And that, Ladies and Gentlemen of the Jury, is exactly what the State is trying to do in this case." Then,

I would go into all the facts the State omitted trying to create a reasonable doubt as to the guilt of my client.

Roland got off the James at his house. "That foreman didn't get our names nor any information about us, did he?"

"No, he never asked anything about us."

"Good, cause I'm not going back. Carrying that water was hard, but shoveling up elephant shit is more than I bargained for. I think every elephant in that circus has diarrhea."

"Yeah, it was pretty loose. Some of it was like water in my scoop. I'm not going back either. I've seen all that circus I ever wanted to see.

CHAPTER SIX
BAD TIMES KEEP ON COMING

The railroad assigned Daddy to a great job in Memphis. All he had to do was go out of the flagman's shack and wave a stop sign to the trucks and cars when a train was coming.

A flagman was required because the highway ran through the switchyard, and trains were up and down the track all day. Daddy would work all week, and on Friday night he would catch a train to Decatur. I believe it was Number 45. And on Sunday, he would catch another train back; it may have been 46.

When he first got to Memphis, things were wonderful. After a year or so, he stopped bringing money home. He would come in with $12. Mother would be beside herself. We were having a rough time, and he was blowing $80 to $120 a week. He did that week in and week out. He seemed not to hear Mother's crying and complaining about our desperate needs.

Finally, when we were almost totally down and out, Mother contacted some railroad men who worked in Memphis. She asked them to find out what Shorty was doing with his paycheck. She was told that he loaned money to other men who would not pay him back. In addition, he was gambling on midget race cars. He didn't drink nor smoke, but he was betting his money away.

That was it for me! I had raised my own father. I had given up my childhood to care for him; I had never played cowboy and Indians; and when he was able, he wouldn't contribute to the family. Now, I had had it! Enough! I began to hate the man.

Mother had some of the men talk with Daddy, and they straightened him out temporarily. He began to bring his money home. By the time I was a senior in high school, Daddy appeared to be as well as he would become. Mother said that he was close to being the man she had married. I thought he would become a good father for my youngest sister, Becky. He didn't.

I felt that I was fortunate enough to have known my father when he was young, strong, and full of fun. He would play games with Dot, Hester, and me saying he was the "spellingest speller that ever spelled a spell." Then we would come up with words we didn't think he could spell, such as hippopotamus. His weakness was crossword puzzles. He worked every one of them he could find. He also liked to unravel twine that was twisted and balled up to the point it couldn't be used. He would sit for hours unraveling it and putting it in place on a spool.

Unfortunately, as a child I had the misfortune of seeing him deteriorate into an individual who didn't know right from wrong, nor have any sense of direction, time, or space. He had been the guy who came home from work, grabbed me up and raised me in the air. Then he would do Dot and later, Hester.

At 501 East 4th Street, he and I would sneak down into the basement and play with my Christmas toys before Christmas. We particularly had fun with a steam shovel that I was going to get. We always hid our play from Mother. I believe Hester was three years old when he had his accident. Then, he was never the same man. He might have days of lucidity but then lapse back into being a child.

Later, when I was trying to help raise Dot, Hester, and Daina, he compounded every problem I had. Then Becky came along. It was not an easy life for the oldest brother, but I lived through it, and it made me a better man.

After the gambling incidents, I harbored feelings that I had been cheated. For years I tried to get rid of my hard feelings toward my father, but I could not. I prayed hard about it and discussed it with my mother many times. She would beg me to forgive him because it was not his fault. Furthermore, I had lost very little by taking responsibility at an early age.

Finally, when I was 32 years of age, I forgave my dad. It was a wonderful feeling that it was over. He lived his twilight years somewhat happily sane.

When he retired mother got his retirement checks and social security. For the first time in a long time, they had money.

THOMAS BARKER

There was a cavernous hole adjoining #4 green at Decatur Country Club. It was at least 300 feet in circumference, and more than 80 feet deep. It was full of huge rocks and small trees. Due to a wet weather spring at its deepest spot, the bottom stayed wet in the winter and most of the summer.

Number 4 was a par three, and dozens of balls were lost each month in the hole. When a player sliced, or pushed the shot, the ball was gone. No one would go down there to find it. On off days, brave caddies, with big sticks, spent hours looking for balls in the depths of the hole. Mr. Lowery wanted rid of it. It was the home of snakes. It was ugly, dangerous, and gave the club a bad name. Locally, it was called "Matthews' hole."

The pro contacted the City, and it was agreed that the City would fill the hole if the wet weather spring at the bottom of the hole was stopped up. Dirt would not do it. There had to be small rocks filling in the mouth of the spring. Mr. Lowrey could not find a man who would go down into the hole and dynamite some rocks to fill the mouth of the spring.

It was a beautiful summer day when Roland and I arrived at the country club hoping Mr. Lowrey would have work for us. He did. He handed each of us a 12-pound sledge hammer and directed us to go to the bottom of the hole and break up rocks with the sledges. We were to put the rocks in the mouth of the wet weather spring.

He thought he was funny when he said, "Make small rocks out of big ones."

At 45 cents an hour, we were happy. We went down into the hole. It was cool and damp like a cave. We began to pound away. After about two hours, Roland put down his hammer, pulled a Tootsie Roll out of his pocket, sat on a rock, and began to nibble on his Tootsie.

"Herman, I'm really jealous of you. There you are out there swinging that sledge, developing all those muscles, and here I sit getting fat and flabby."

"You just sit there, big boy. I'm going to rest in a few minutes then your flabby butt will be up here making little ones out of big ones."

We pounded away until almost noon. We climbed out of the hole and went to the pro shop to get something to eat. Roland bought a Pay Day bar and a Coke. I bought a Royal Crown Cola and a MoonPie.

We went to the old abandoned Black cemetery, east of #1 Fairway, near the caddy shack. I sat on the ground with my back to a utility pole while Roland was sitting on a tomb stone that had been turned over. Thomas Barker, whose nickname was Baby Brother, one of the more popular caddies, came out of the shack.

I never could understand why he was called Baby Brother when his real baby brother was named Bobby Leon Barker. Regardless, Baby Brother came out of the shack.

"Hey, Robert French, I got 35 cents, a set of dice, and I'll fade you a nickel. Let's shoot some."

"Not me, Baby Brother. My money comes too hard. I can't take a chance."

"What about you, Roland? You're a sport. I'll give you the dice and fade you a nickel."

Roland got up off the tombstone. "Give me those dominoes and lay your money down."

The dice were hot, and Roland had won Baby Brother's money down to his last nickel. He came out with a five.

"Hit 'em seven!" Baby Brother was yelling.

"Fever in the funk house!" Roland was yelling back.

He rolled the dice, and one ended up in an engraving of the buried person's name. One of the dice was flat and the other was in the engraving. The flat dice was showing a three. The dice in the engraving was showing a two. However, it was cocked due to the slight depth of the engraving. Dice had been lodged in the engravings earlier and neither gambler had said anything.

They agreed upon the number and went on. Now, they were down to Baby Brother's last nickel.

"That's a five!" Roland screamed. He reached to pick up the two nickels.

Baby Brother put his big hand on Roland's, "That ain't no five. That's cocked dice. You gotta roll again."

The two began an argument whether it was the point or there must be a new roll. Baby Brother said, "Robert French, come here and call the point."

"I'm not getting into that," I responded eating my MoonPie.

Roland said, "Come on, Herman. Call the point. This is the end of the game."

"I'm not calling the point. I don't know what your dice looks like, but whatever I say, one of you is going to be mad at me. I'm out of it."

"Please, please, please," cajoled Baby Brother. "We won't get mad."

They continued to beg me to look at the dice for several minutes. Finally, I cut weak and went and looked at the dice. It was clear to me that it was a two, resulting

72

in a five, and Roland had won. He giggled and grabbed up the two nickels. I went back to finish my lunch.

Baby Brother pulled some Johnson grass and hit me across the face with it. "You cheated me, Robert French."

The blades of the grass stung a little, but I thought discretion was the better part of valor. "I didn't cheat you. You know it was a deuce. I didn't want involved. You begged me. Now, don't hit me again."

The Johnson grass slap wasn't worth a fight. Plus, it was almost time to go back to work in the hole.

I was eating the last of my MoonPie and drinking the end of my RC Cola. As I sat against the post, I noticed that an out-of-bounds stake had been knocked out of its hole and was laying on the ground. The stake was around four feet long, painted white, and sharpened on the end that was driven into the ground. I planned to put it back up when we went back to work.

In the meantime, I was trying to avoid trouble with Baby Brother. He was big and strong and would probably beat me up, regardless. So I ignored his mutterings about how I had cheated him. I couldn't understand his thought processes.

Roland had won all his money. I did not get a penny. I had tried to avoid making the call on the dice. Further, I made the correct call. He knew it, Roland knew it, and I knew it.

He continued to walk around saying Robert French had cheated him. I finished eating and was ready to go back to work. As I was getting up, he walked over, picked up my empty RC bottle, and in one swift move hit me in the face with it.

The blow broke my nose in several places. Blood and mucus flooded my face. I couldn't see anything. Baby Brother was wearing the bottle out on my head, neck, shoulders, and arms. I knew this man was going to kill me, and I could not see. I was helpless.

As Baby Brother was beating me to death, I spotted the out-of-bounds marker. I rolled away as he caught me again on the head. I fought for consciousness and grabbed the two-by- four marker. When Baby Brother saw me getting up with the marker in my hand he started running. He ran down the middle of # 1 Fairway. Barely being able to see, I was determined to catch him.

He made it almost to the 150-yard marker before I hit him with the 2X4 marker as hard as I could. I put all my 165 pounds into the lick. He folded up like a shot deer and lay there. I turned around and walked back to the pro shop.

Roland was waiting. He said, "Man, you are a mess."

"Yeah, I need to wash up and go home."

I went into the men's room and looked in the mirror. I was blood and mucus from my shirt to the top of my head. My nose was flattened and crooked--all over my face. I checked my teeth and they were all there. It was primarily a nose, cheek, and chin injury.

Assistant Pro John B. Stevens came into the restroom and said, "Robert French, you have killed Baby Brother. He hasn't moved since you hit him."

"John B., I tried to kill him. Look at me."

Roland and I left. Once more, Mother almost went into cardiac arrest. She sent me to a doctor who said there was nothing he could do for me. My nose was badly broken. He packed it with gauze and treated my scrapes and cuts with antibiotics.

It took about Six weeks for me to heal. I was never able to go back into the hole to finish the job. My work on the golf course was over, other than caddying on the weekends after church. Baby Brother Barker never came back to the country club.

Roland, as usual, had a smart comment, "Herman, you now have a Roman nose – roaming all over your face." Then he would laugh.

Years later, I was home on furlough. I went to the cleaners to get my uniform. Thomas Barker had just picked up his uniform and we met at the door. We were glad to see each other.

I stepped back out into the sunlight and we visited. I was in the Air Force. He was in the Army. We caught up with each other. Neither of us had married, and so on.

As the visit came to an end, Thomas said, "Robert French, you remember that day you hit me in the head with that out-of-bounds marker?"

"Yeah, I remember," rubbing my nose.

"Well, I still have headaches from that hit you put on me." He rubbed the back of his head.

"I'm sorry about that," Baby Brother. But I can't breathe through my nose, and I'm told I am going to have to have surgery for a deviated nasal septum."

"I guess I messed us up when I started it. I'm sorry," he mused.

"I'm sorry, too. Oh well, we gotta do what we gotta do. Good to see you."

"Good to see you, Robert French. God bless you."

Years later, while I was attending the University, I could not breathe through my nose at all. My darling wife Celeste arranged for me to have a sub mucus resection at Druid City Hospital.

At the end of the surgery, when the anesthesiologist yanked the airway out of my mouth, she broke off my two front teeth. The hospital paid a dentist to implant steel pins in the healthy roots of the teeth and covered them with caps.

Calling that point may have been one of the worst decisions of my life. However, there were more to come.

FALLING IN LOVE

Her name was Nancy Carolyn Long. She was tall, beautiful, and 15 years old. She lived about three blocks up the street from me. I can't remember where I first saw her or met her. It may have been at Austinville Baptist Church where I taught the primary boys in Sunday School. Wherever it was, when I met her I was smitten.

I was pretty close to turning 16 years old. I was working wherever I could, usually at the country club, and finishing the 10th grade at Austinville High School. Nancy was in the 9th grade, and I truly believed she was the most beautiful girl in the entire school.

The first time I kissed her I saw stars and all kinds of fireworks. She was an unbelievable kisser. I had kissed one or two girls before I kissed her, but now it was pure love on my part. In the summer between the 10th and 11th grade, we were inseparable when time permitted. At about that time, she began to care for me.

I was broken-hearted that I was going to Decatur High School for the 11th grade, and would lose Carolyn. Both she and Roland would be students at Austinville High School when school started in September.

Then, miracles of miracles, Nancy Carolyn Long announced she was going to Decatur High. Her father would have to drive her to school. Someone else would have to take her home. Wow! I would have a steady during my junior and senior year. Plus, I truly loved her. Truth be known, I practically worshiped her. We took long walks, played games, rode my Famous James, went to church, and hung out together as much as we could.

A HOLE IN THE CEILING

After much begging and pleading, Roland's parents arranged for him to attend Decatur High School.

He and I were going to enter our junior year, the first year the new high school building was opened. Once we knew we were going into the brand-new building, we decided to explore it.

It was the largest building we had ever been in. It was open with no one in sight. We walked from end to end exploring classrooms, the lunchroom, and on and on.

Upstairs, somehow only Robert and Roland could find their way into the dark overhead of the huge auditorium 60 feet below. We were walking, in the dark, on steel Joists that held the roof of the building above the auditorium. Don't ask me why we were doing it. We were exploring. That's what boys do.

I slipped, and my right foot went through the ceiling tile. Fortunately, I held on to the cross member of the joist and saved myself from certain death. We heard the tiles hit the auditorium floor.

"Let's get outta here before we get caught," I said, reversing my steps along the joists.

Once safely outside the building, Roland said, "Let's go back in and see what damage you did to the ceiling."

"I'll go back in, so long as we pretend we have just arrived and we are looking at the building."

Still, no one was in the building. We went in the front door, into the auditorium, turned on the lights, and there it was – a three-tile-hole in the ceiling.

I whispered, "You're as much to blame for that as I am. It was your idea to explore the building. You led the way among the rafters in the dark. You tell it, and I'll blame you."

"I'm not telling," Roland replied, and we exited the building.

Every assembly, every presentation, every chapel, every play, every time anything was happening in that auditorium for the next two years, each of us looked up at the ceiling that clearly indicated three ceiling tiles had been replaced. Seventeen years later, Roland would tell it in public; however, that is a story for another time.

A 1940 PLYMOUTH

We moved again. This time, back to Austinville, in a house that had all the amenities. It was there I turned 16 and asked my mother to let me buy a car. The family had never had a car, neither Mother nor Daddy ever had a license, and I was now a licensed driver. I had been forced to get a driver's license in order to ride the Famous James motorcycle. Daddy was back at work as a crossing watchman in Memphis. He came home on the train every weekend. He was almost back to normal. We appreciated the fact the Southern Railroad had provided a job for him that he could do.

Mother said that because I had always worked and had taken care of things growing up, she would help me buy a car. I had $100 and she put up $250. We went down to Lott Motor Company, owned by Ed Lott, the son of Mr. Castor Lott, who could pick 200 pounds of cotton a day. Ed sold me a black 1940 Plymouth. I drove Mother home in it.

I immediately went over to Roland's house to show it to him. We went riding for several hours. The car was eight years old and completely worn out, but it served its purpose for me. After dropping Roland, I went to Carolyn Long's house, and took her for a ride in my "new" car.

I learned a lot of mechanics working on that car. The first job was replacing the head gasket.

A BAD DECISION

Within two weeks, Mr. Oliver bought Roland a 1939 Chevrolet. I was following him to the country club to caddy. Naturally, we began racing. We were on 14th Street, near the house from which I had just moved. I lost control of the Plymouth, and by an absolute miracle, went between two utility poles that barely had enough room for a car between them. I was stopped by the chain link, what we called "cyclone fencing," around an electric substation. Not good.

Some men stopped and helped Roland and me push the Plymouth out from between the poles. The only damage done was that the cyclone fencing of the electric substation was dented. Roland suggested that we go and talk with his mother about it.

Mrs. Oliver said that since the police were not called and no one had seen me hit the fence, other than the men who helped me get the car out, I should just ignore it.

I didn't like that advice because I knew that Bobby and Roy Freeman's father was the superintendent of the electric company. Bobby was a classmate. Roy was one year ahead. Both were athletes. I had played baseball with both of them.

At that time, I was working as a stock boy at V.J. Elmore's. I was sweeping the walk in front of the store.

A policeman came up. "Are you Robert French?"

"Yes, sir."

"Come with me."

I was petrified. Was I under arrest? We began walking to the electric company a block away. The policeman marched me into Mr. Freeman's office. He didn't wait for any preliminary pleasantries.

"You ran into my substation on 14th Street and didn't have the courage to come and tell me about it. What have you got to say for yourself?"

"I did, and I am sorry."

"Get out. Come back in a week, and I am going to decide what to do with you."

Later, I realized that I had made a gross error presenting myself. I was dressed in pegged black pants, a black shirt, a ducktail haircut, and a pack of cigarettes in my shirt pocket. I resolved to do better.

In one week, I went back to Mr. Freeman's office. This time I was dressed in overall pants, a wine-colored corduroy shirt, no cigarettes, a flat-top haircut, and saddle oxfords. My pants were rolled up the appropriate two rolls of the day.

When I went in, Mr. Freeman said, "Who are you?"

"I'm Robert French, a friend of Bobby and Roy's. We play ball together. I'm the boy who ran into your substation, and didn't report it.".

"You don't look like the boy who was in here last week. You say you play ball with my boys?"

"Yes, sir. I'm a catcher, and I have caught both Bobby and Roy in American Legion ball. They're the best pitchers in Decatur."

"Hum, okay, I'm busy. What lesson have you learned here?"

"When you do something wrong, don't run away from it and try to cover it up. Do the best you can do to make it right."

I was thinking that I would have done that if Mrs. Oliver had not told me to hide it.

"Very good. I'm going to let you go. You did $315 damages to my substation; but working at Elmore's, you can't pay it.

"You seem to have learned a lesson. From now on be a good boy, and if you catch for either of my sons again, don't miss the ball on a strike out."

"I won't," as I thanked him profusely and made my exit. I had learned a horrible lesson.

MAN KILLED WITH MOTORCYCLE

A classmate, Duane Smith, persuaded his widowed mother to buy a used Famous James for him. He rode it about a week when he discovered it needed piston rings. He knew that I still had a Famous James and probably knew how to do a ring job. It was winter when he called and asked if I would help.

I told him to go to Athens, Magnison Motorcycle Shop, and buy three Famous James piston rings. That was the only place I knew that carried Famous James parts.

"I thought it only took two piston rings."

"It does, but we don't have a ring tool, and we'll probably break one. You'd be surprised how delicate they are."

A couple of days later he called and said he had the rings. He wanted to know if I could help him that day.

I drove over to his house. He and his mother lived in a huge, rambling old two-story white clapboard house. He met me at the back door.

"We're going to work on it upstairs. It's vacant up there, and that way we won't be cold outside."

With that, we went into his garage, and I helped him push the Famous James through the kitchen and up the stairs to the vacant second floor.

As we went up, I noticed a bed made up near the stairs. It appeared someone was in bed. When we got upstairs, we spread newspapers out on the floor where we were going to work. After we had parked the James, on its kickstand--on the papers--I asked, "Who was that person in the bed near the stairs?"

"That's Grandpa. He is very sick. I don't know what's wrong with him, but it's pretty bad because he has been in that bed more than a month. Here are the tools; let's get started."

We went to work as only two boys can work when they are determined to do something. After about four hours, we had the parts off, the head pulled, and the piston exposed. I worked the rings into the cylinder very carefully. It was difficult without a ring tool. Of course, I broke one ring. Fortunately, I was able to seat the rings in place and slide the head back down. The Famous James was ringed! Now, we had to put it back together. After a couple of hours, we had it back together, other than the tailpipe and mufflers.

Duane said, "You think we ought to try it before we get it all back together? I'd like to know the ring job is good."

"It wouldn't hurt. I'll kick it over."

I put my right foot on the kick starter, kicked down, and it started. In that cavernous upstairs the noise was intolerable. It was beyond loud. It was unbearable!

As Duane turned it off, I heard his grandfather's voice from down stairs. "Daughter, I have just heard the angels coming for me. Goodbye sweet girl, I am joining the Heavenly band."

"Daddy, don't die! Please don't go! That was not angels; that was Duane and his motor bike."

I wished Duane luck putting the tailpipe and mufflers back on the motorcycle. I was getting out of there.

While his mother was holding his dead grandfather in abject grief, I made my exit and drove very fast going home.

I didn't see Duane for a while. A little over a month later, I ran into him at a ball game. I asked him how he was doing.

"I'm doing well, but my mother has not recovered from you killing my grandfather."

This shocked me. "I didn't kill your grandfather, and you know it."

"You don't really think I would say that I agreed to start that engine, do you? You started it with me begging you not to do it because it might hurt my grandfather."

"Duane Smith, you are a terrible person and a liar."

"Maybe. But I am also the hero who tried valiantly to save my grandfather from that idiot, Robert French."

CHAPTER SEVEN
D.O. AND D.E.

Decatur High School had Diversified Occupations and Diversified Education programs. Roland and I entered the D.O. Program, which was a managerial curriculum where the student took core subjects from 8:00 a.m. until noon. The student then went to work at some local business until the end of the day. The employer graded the student, as did the teachers in the morning. Roland got a job as Assistant Manager of the Capitol Theatre, and I kept my job at V. J. Elmore's next door.

From time to time, Roland would hire me at night to run the popcorn machine and usher. The Capitol had a bad name. The students called it the "rat house." They said that you had to carry two sticks into the theater with you-- one to prop up the seat, and the other to beat off the rats.

After a few months, the manager quit. Roland was promoted to manager while still a junior in high school. It wasn't long before the WAGS were saying that Roland was the Great Capitol Rat Chaser, and I was simply Rat Man Herman.

Roland had one great adventure at the theater. A classmate, Bobby Dockery, hid in the basement of the theater. When Roland went down to check everything before closing for the night, Dockery jumped out from behind the furnace with a knife. He and Roland had not had any trouble. Although Dockery was slightly off mentally, he was passing in school. It seems he just wanted to kill someone, and Roland was to be his victim. Somehow Roland talked his way out of the dangerous situation. A few years later, Dockery could not talk his way out of prison.

When we became seniors, Roland was transferred to Decatur's primary theatre, the Princes Theatre, as assistant manager. Soon, the manager transferred, and Roland was promoted again. Classmates began to call him "Deal Beal the Big Wheel from Austinville." They shortened it to "Deal."

I learned a managerial lesson from Mr. Manker, our store manager. I would eat a sandwich in the car on the way to work. Usually, a carload of the DO and DE students would ride together. When I got to the store, my first job was to check the stoker and fill it. Then I would usually go to the bathroom. I did this almost every day. Mr. Manker called me aside one day and told me to go to the bathroom on my own time. He wasn't paying me to take a crap. I learned a lot of managerial lessons from that.

Hubert Brooks, our D.O. teacher, was one of the most humorous people I have ever met. He had a dry saying for anything going on. I believe we had to go to D.O. class once a week. It was always a lot of fun.

We went to the D.O. Convention in Tuscaloosa. Roland entered the public speaking competition. He did well discussing ancient law and how American law tracked back to Hammurabi, the first man to put the law in writing. I didn't compete, but I did do a comedy skit. The following day's *Tuscaloosa News* said "Decatur High Schooler Robert French is the most entertaining and the funniest student attending the convention at Northington Campus."

On our way home, we were traveling through Black Warrior National Forest south of Jasper, Alabama. I was in the front passenger seat. Mr. Brooks was driving. Roland had a carload of students in front of us. We spotted a huge tornado bearing down on us from across a large valley. Mr. Brooks stopped the car, "If that thing looks like it is going to hit us, get out of the car and lay down flat in the ditch. You see how it's snapping trees? You don't want to be hit by any of that debris."

We watched the tornado carve a road across the valley. It passed about 100 yards in front of us. I thought sure it got Roland's car. Fortunately, when we caught up with him, he said that it had passed behind him.

For many years later, I would always see the storm's path across the hills and valley when I traveled Highway 69 from Decatur to Tuscaloosa. I saw it on the trip that involved Celeste's toilet paper incident much later.

RESTROOM TRICK

When we weren't working, Roland and I would double date. His steady was Bess Cowan, and mine was Nancy Carolyn Long. Roland noticed that Nancy Carolyn never went to the restroom, no matter what we were doing,

"That girl has iron kidneys and a bladder the size of a basketball," Roland opined. "Let's see if we can make her go Saturday night."

I agreed. It was harmless fun.

I picked her up a little after 4:00 p.m. We then got Bess. Away we went to the Rainbow Drive-in. There we had hamburgers, fries, and a coke. I bought an extra coke for each of us as we were going to the drive-in to see a movie. Before the movie started, Roland went to the restroom, and brought back four more cokes. By the time I finished the third coke in the middle of the movie, I had to go to the restroom. Bess Cowan joined me. We went to the restrooms in the concession stand. I bought four more cokes.

We had a great time and took Bess home around 10:30. When we got to Nancy Carolyn's house, she pecked me on the lips, "No need to take me to the door. Mother left the porch light on. I'll see you tomorrow."

She bolted up her porch steps, opened the door, and disappeared.

"I don't think I have ever seen a person get out of a car and get into a house that fast," Roland said. "We flat tanked her up, but she held it. Like I say, huge bladder."

We did not pull that trick again, and Nancy Carolyn never went to the restroom on any date I ever had with her.

She was a wonderful person, and I loved her dearly. When I got my class ring, she took it off my finger, wrapped tape around the back of it so it would fit her finger, and we were pretty well engaged.

Unfortunately, a boy named Bobby Alexander came to town and asked her out. She dated him. I got my ring back and told her goodbye. No hard feelings, the relationship was over.

HUNTING

Troy Martin was a friend of mine.   His parents owned the Morgan County Credit Bureau. Sammy Prewitt, a local dentist, had shot Troy in the eye with an arrow when they were boys, and Troy was a little more than seven years old. Troy had a glass eye. He and his dad invited me to go goose hunting with them one cold winter Saturday.

All my life I had watched the honkers fly over Decatur heading south – Canadian Geese. Everyone wanted to kill a goose, but those birds were hard to get. I didn't expect to have any luck, but I agreed to go. Mr. Martin loaned me a 12 gauge pump shotgun.

We went way out in the country to a farm owned by a friend of the Martins. We then walked across a muddy field for half a mile. We stopped in a blind Mr. Martin had built earlier in the fall. We were less than 100 yards from the Wheeler Wildlife Refuge. I could see a ranger sitting, leaning up against a tree, waiting for us to set foot on the refuge.

Mr. Martin had brought some old white bed sheets, and we spread them out on the muddy field. Mr. Martin said that the geese would think that was fresh water and come in where we could shoot them.

"I'll tell you what," I spouted off. "I'll carry out any geese we kill because I don't think we will get a one."

I was so wrong. Within 15 minutes of putting down the sheets, a flock of geese came in for a landing. Once they saw it was not water, they began to take off again. We began shooting. We killed six geese.

Mr. Martin insisted that I carry them out. It was impossible. They were too heavy, and their necks were too limber. I couldn't do it, but I tried. Finally, the Martins felt sorry for me so we each carried two out.

Our family went to my grandmother's in Huntsville for Christmas. I took my goose, and her cook fixed it perfectly. It was all dark meat, and it was good. Preacher was a hero. However, I had no interest in ever going goose hunting again.

The week following our goose hunt, Troy took me duck hunting. We ran out of gas, got stuck in the mud, and, without a farmer's help, we would have never rescued my car. That was it for me; I didn't have to go duck hunting again.

However, I can prove there is no fool like a young fool. Troy talked me into going mountain lion hunting. It happened like this:

There was a mountain lion spotted near Priceville, Alabama. A lady claimed it jumped through an open window in her house and escaped out the open back door. Soon thereafter, calves began to be killed and partially eaten. There was a $25 reward for anyone who would kill the beast.

Mr. Martin had a farm in the area. The Martins called it their ranch. They had cattle, horses, and a ranch boss who lived in the ranch house with his family. One of the calves in the lower forty at the base of the mountain, had been killed, obviously by the mountain lion. It did not eat the entire carcass.

Troy called me and asked if I could go hunting with him to kill the mountain lion. He mentioned the reward. Like so many of my youthful escapades, it sounded like a brilliant idea to me.

Mr. Martin drove Troy and me out to the ranch. There, we saddled two horses near sunset. The ranch boss had taken a small tractor to the carcass and dragged what was left of it partially up the mountain to a relatively flat spot. It was in a small clearing in the deep November woods.

Troy had a 30.06 rifle and Mr. Martin loaned me a .308 with a scabbard. We took our bedrolls, some water, and headed out for the kill. We tied the horses about 50 feet from the carcass. We put our bed rolls up against a tree, checked our guns, and waited.

Near 1:00 in the morning I was in my bedroll dozing off when the horses neighed, broke their bridles, and headed for the barn at a gallop.

"It's in the area," Troy exclaimed.

He didn't have to tell me. I was already up, and I knew the lion had returned for his meal. We could hear his huge feet crushing the leaves, circling us, just out of our sight.

Somehow, we got back-to-back holding our weapons and circling with the sound of the leaves. It was safeties's off, finger on the triggerin the pitch blackness of the night.

Around and around it went, maybe four times, perhaps thirty feet away. I wasn't scared because I was going to shoot the mountain lion the second I saw it. However, I was very concerned that it might bound out of the darkness and attack Troy or me so fast we couldn't shoot it. It was nerves-on-end time.

Just then, it screamed! It was a blood-chilling scream, the likes of which I have never heard before or since. It sent chills up my spine, and my kidneys turned loose for the only time in my life. Every drop in my bladder emptied in my pants.

Troy fired a shot in the air, and I could hear the animal running away.

Troy said, "Let's get out of here."

It was hard for me to walk almost a mile in wet pants and shorts - at night. We made it a little after three in the morning. Troy woke the ranch boss, borrowed his pickup truck, and we went home. The insides of my thighs were raw due to walking in urine-soaked pants. In all, it was really a bad experience. I still hear traces of that scream, now and then, on very black nights.

Later in life, when I was working at B.F. Goodrich, the Union leased a hunting lodge at Boligee, Alabama. I believe it was called the Dollarhide. They were going to have a deer hunt. I was the only member of management that they invited, so my boss insisted I go. "Good labor-management relations."

Several of the men had spent the night. I got there before daylight. It was an organized hunt. After breakfast, I was loaded on a farm tractor-trailer, along with several other men, and taken to my stand. I was told that men with dogs would start about a mile away and drive the deer toward our stands. When we saw a buck, we were to shoot - no does and no fawns.

So I sat in the brush and waited while hearing the dogs barking some distance away.

Without a sound, the biggest deer I had ever seen in my life was standing about ten yards from me across the field road. I had a dough ball in my shotgun, and I shot the deer killing it. Some hunters on other stands came running, hearing my shot. They field dressed the deer as, I certainly didn't know how to do that job.   By the time they were through, the tractor came back after the driver heard the shot. It took five of us to load that animal on the trailer. Finished hunting, I rode the trailer back, and waited at the lodge until all the hunters were brought in. We killed six deer that day and they were all strung up on a cable rack out back.

I was the hero of the hour. I had killed a 12-point buck, the largest animal taken in that hunt. They said they would mount the head and put my name and date on a gold plate under it. They then poured a cupful of the deer's blood on my head and cut my shirttail off just below my shoulders. This was the initiation suffered by a deer hunter who kills a deer on his first hunt.

The butcher cut my deer up and gave me more meat than two large grocery bags would barely hold.

Celeste and I tried every way in the world to eat that meat. We went by every recipe we could find from deer hunters. Some were downright exotic. Still we couldn't eat it. The meat was too tough. Of course, I have had great deer meat from time to time, but this was not it. I concluded that the deer was an old buck, and he was just too tough.

At least I never had to go deer hunting again.

I had one final hunting experience -- coon hunting in 1965. Soon after we moved to Fort Payne, State Farm Agent Milford Kuykendall, a friend of mine, invited me to go coon hunting on Lookout Mountain. I agreed, and he picked me up in his pickup truck a little after 7:30 p.m.

It was already dark, and he drove us out into the deep woods. There, other pickup trucks were parked in a rough circle. They were positioned so that their tailgates faced a fire that had been built in the middle of the circle. Milford duly backed in and parked.

There were probably twelve or more men there. Everyone was very jovial, as they all knew each other as coon hunters. They then opened up the cages on the back of their trucks and let their dogs out. Most of the dogs were beagle hounds. I saw one or two blue ticks. The dogs jumped joyously off the tailgates of the trucks and waited for a signal. It seemed to me that all the dogs knew each other.

Milford said loudly, "Are we ready?" The men responded that they were ready. With that, Milford yelled, "Go!"

Away the hounds went into the woods, barking as they went. After the dogs left, the men went to their truck cabs and brought out plastic glasses, water, and whiskey.

Everyone stood around the fire holding their glass. Whiskey and water was passed around. When one bottle was empty, another bottle started around. After one drink, the men began to listen to the dogs.

"That's Jip," one of the men said. "She's on the trail. Listen to her. She's getting closer. I'll bet she trees that coon."

"Oh. Yeah," another hunter opined. "I hear Sparky. I think he's right in there with Jip. That's his tree bark. Yep, they got a coon up a tree."

I listened to the sounds of hounds running through the woods. The hunters knew each dog by the sound of the bark. Also, the bark told the hunters if the hound was chasing a coon and what the coon was doing.

As the whiskey was consumed, the more excited the hunters became involved with their dogs. Announcements of dog activity came so often some of the men had to yell over others.

"Hear that? That's Spot. He's working the trail."

"Sam is right in there with him!"

Although we could still hear the dogs in the distance, at a little after 11:00 p.m. one of the hunters suggested we call it a night. By then, everybody was either drunk or well on the way.

"Okay boys, let's piss on the fire and go home."

Urine-smelling smoke rose off the ashes as all of us circled the fire and urinated in unison. The fire was out. Milford and I went to his truck.

"What about your dogs? You just going home without them?"

"That's coon hunting," Milford said. All of the hunters will come back in the morning, and the dogs will be here. The dogs will run all night. It's what they do."

"Don't you want to catch a coon?"

"Hell, no. What would I do with a coon?"

Now I had been coon hunting. I concluded that it was an excuse to stand around a fire in the woods, tell embellished stories, listen to dogs bark, and get drunk. I figured it was not much different from those people who hang out in clubs and bars. At least I never have to go coon hunting again.

CHAPTER EIGHT
WINDING DOWN

It was the fall of 1951, sometime in September, and twenty former famous baseball players were traveling the country playing exhibition games – American League v. National League. All the while they were doing this, they were spotting talent everywhere they went. They invited all the American Legion and high school baseball players to come out and warm up against them.

Roland pitched against one of the players, and he knocked every strike Roland threw for a home run over the fence. The batter didn't fare as well when Bobby Freeman pitched. He got hits, but only two went out of the park. They had me catching one of their batters with a runner on first attempting to steal second. I nailed him.

The players, whom I believe were really scouts, were amazed at the size of my hands. All my fingers had been broken catching baseball, and my hands were not a pretty sight. Still, when the exhibition games were over, their manager came around and offered Bobby Freeman, Marvin Breeding and me a bus trip to Pensacola to participate in a major league tryout.

The three of us boarded an old Trailways bus, that didn't have air conditioning and took a trip to Florida. I don't know how many teams were represented at the tryout, nor how many potential players attended. It was a crowd. We stayed there the better part of 3 days, sleeping in the bus two nights.

Marvin Breeding got a callback as a shortstop with the Baltimore Orioles. He wound up playing there some 19 years. Bobby Freeman was a bit too wild and didn't get a callback. Rather than going to school his senior year, he transferred to Auburn where he starred at quarterback for three years. Later, he played pro ball for some ten years and returned to Auburn to coach. I heard that he had passed away in his early 70's.

I didn't get a callback. However, the Saint Louis Browns wanted to take a closer look at me. Finally, one of their guys found a flaw in my play. From a catcher's crouch, or standing up, I winged the ball to second base using a slider. My father had taught me his old trick of how to nail the runner from first to second – throw the ball with the middle and index fingers. A right-hander should throw the ball over the pitcher's left shoulder. The ball curves to the bag on second. It had worked well for me in American Legion ball. However, the scouts thought the ball took too long to get to second base. My baseball career was over before it started.

JUNIOR YEAR

I think I had just turned 17 in September. I do remember that it was soon after school started. Roland and Frank Paine were going to fight. Paine had said something insulting about Roland's sister, Rebecca. Both of us had sisters named Rebecca. The news went through the junior high school in a flash -- "Fight!"

We fell out at recess to see the fight. Roland threw a couple of punches, and Frank Paine began to land some good blows. He bloodied Roland's nose.

For reasons unknown, Roland said, "Yeah, you can do me this way, but you can't do Robert French that way."

Paine was still excited in the fight, turned around, saw me in the crowd, and hit me right in the jaw.

I pounded him until he yelled, "Uncle." I still find that entire encounter strange. Roland didn't even call me Herman. Further, I can't understand why Paine hit me. I had never crossed his path at all. I can only attribute his act to the adrenalin of the fight.

AN ACTOR AMONG US

I was working at V. J. Elmore's and going to school. I was in Miss Eich's home-room. She was the toughest math teacher in the school and a genuine perfectionist.

Each Junior and Senior Class was in charge of the weekly assembly on Friday. Usually, some talented kid would tap dance. One might play the guitar, another the piano, and one might do a reading. Miss Eich said her class would do a play. She had selected a play called, "Make Room for Rodney."

The play was about a boy who wanted his own room. His parents said he had a room. However, he knew it was his mother's sewing room. He set about to help his older sister get married. Then he would have her room. The play then concentrates on his efforts to marry off his sister. Each encounter ends in disaster. Finally, his sister fell in love with a beau, but they had an argument and broke up. Rodney tricked the suitor into coming over to look at his stamp collection. While he was there, Rodney let his pet snake get out. This frightened his sister, who ran into the arms of the suitor. The couple reconciled and married. Rodney got his room. Final curtain.

Various students volunteered for the parts of the mother, sister, boyfriend, and others. There was no one to play Rodney. Several students suggested that I do the part. Unfortunately, I had to work and would not have time to rehearse for the play.

Miss Eich believed I could learn the part. Each night, after work, Hester and I would read the script. She read all the parts and I did Rodney. Then I went to one rehearsal and the dress rehearsal. The play went down without a hitch. It was a great success.

Other teachers said Miss Eich was setting the bar too high. "Everyone can't do a play for assembly."

I did not have time for athletics at school, as I was working. I did make the golf team and played in two matches, Jasper and Florence.

The time came for the Senior Class Play, "Lunatics at Large." It was a murder mystery where Detective Britt had to solve a murder that occurred in a nuthouse.

Among the lunatics, Mr. Hyde was an insane villain. Priscilla was a bloodthirsty wench who remained expressionless during the most exciting moments. John Alden hunted Indians throughout the play, whereas Lady Macbeth was a solemn young woman who quoted Shakespeare.

There were many others down to Lt. Britt, who worked hard but was not particularly bright. The murder was solved by Wing, a Chinese worker, who was played by David Rowe. I was Lt. Britt. Edna Jackson was Lady Macbeth. Dean Drake and Allen Moody were the husband-and-wife team trying to make a getaway. Paul Marion was Mr. Hyde, and so it went.

I can't remember who all was in the play. I simply remember some of my lines.

Later, our Senior Class established a tradition at DHS - "Senior Scrambles." This is a two-to-three-night presentation where everyone in the senior class must do something. It is produced to raise money for the school and does very well. My part in 1952 was, "I Gotta Pass." I had to write the part. I developed it as a student worrying about his grades and what is going to happen to him when he fails to graduate.

I remember my best line: "They say college is a fountain of knowledge. I guess that's where students go to drink." It brought down the house.

I did not use any props and did the part in front of the curtain. Since I had written the thing, pretending to be nervous was easy. I was hoping the audience would like it. They did.

MOVING ON

Near the end of my senior year, I questioned Mr. Manker about my future with V. J. Elmore's. I asked him to get me a full-time job as an assistant manager. I was sent to Birmingham where I was interviewed by the personnel manager.

Two weeks later I was told that V. J. Elmore's had no interest in me as my draft status was A-1. There was nothing to do other than go to college.

I have always thought Mr. Manker didn't want me to go into merchandising as a career. He thought I could do better. He could have used his influence to get me the promotion. So I quit and worked as a sack boy at Kroger's for a few weeks, then went to work at Mr. Oliver's service station.

Mr. Oliver would not let Roland work for him, but I worked hard, and he seemed to appreciate it.

The first credit card I ever saw belonged to the Country Music Star Clarence "Hank" Snow. Mr. Oliver took one look at the card, ran it through the machine, gave it back to me and said, "You think he's moving on?"

I thought it was funny as that was the #1 record at that time. Mr. Oliver told me that the credit card was going to change the way the people of America did business. Time has proven that he was absolutely right.

Because I was working there, when Roland was off from work, he would hang out at the service station.

Two other guys worked there. Russell, a heavy-set man from Florida, who claimed to have been an alligator wrestler. The other fellow was Jewel, who was hairlipped, from Athens. They were both in their early 20's, and did not like each other. They were spoiling for a fight. It would have to be when Mr. Oliver was not there, and that was not often.

One night the three of us were working late. Roland came by. The station had a washing bay and a mechanic's bay. Mr. Oliver was installing a new hydraulic lift in the mechanic's bay. The one we had used consisted of steps down into a hole under the car to work. He had the concrete removed from the hole and was awaiting the parts to install the hydraulic lift. A gigantic hole occupied the mechanic's bay.

The four of us were standing, looking down in the hole. Jewel said, in his hairlipped voice, "I'd give three dollars to the man who could throw me down in that hole."

Obviously, it was a challenge to Russell. He put the three dollars on the top of an oil cabinet.

Roland nudged me; "Throw his ass in the pit, Herman."

I whispered back, "No, he'll beat me up. He whipped a squad of National Guardsmen."

"It's three dollars. Throw his ass in the pit. I'll grab the three dollars, and we'll get outta here. It's time for you to go home anyway."

Like the fool that I was, I grabbed Jewel by the seat of his pants and the collar of his shirt, spun around, and threw him headlong into the dirt at the bottom of the hole. Roland grabbed the three dollars, and we ran across the station lot to get into his car. I didn't make it.

Jewel got out of the hole quicker than we thought he would. He hit me with a flying tackle on the concrete. He then proceeded to stomp me. I was rolling around, and he didn't land but one solid lick, and that was on my head. I was almost unconscious, but I had enough sense to roll away again. This time, I got to my feet. He was ready to square up.

"You said you would give the money, and I earned it. If you didn't mean it, you should not have said it."

I pulled my knife out of my pocket. "You hit me again and I'll cut your throat."

"You ain't worth hitting. Stay out of my sight." He walked away.   Russell just stood in the door and watched us.

That night I had horrible dreams, and for the only time in my life, I walked in my sleep. My mother found me going out the front door at 3:00 a.m. and woke me up. That head lick had been bad.

Jewel was fine the next day. I took two of the three dollars for the stomping, and Roland got his share of the money.

A GARAGE CALENDAR

Later, that summer, I rode my bicycle to work, and Roland came over on his. Mr. Oliver told me to go to Mr. Lemley's Garage and get a used 1939 LaSalle fuel pump. We were working on the car and found the problem - a punctured diaphragm in the fuel pump. There was no way that part could be found in Decatur, Alabama. Mr. Lemley had a garage that was more junkyard than garage.

I rode over to Lemley's on my bike. Roland went with me. When we got inside the used parts department, Mr. Lemley was looking diligently for the fuel pump.

Roland and I noticed the naked woman on the calendar on the wall. Neither of us had ever seen a naked female before.

Mr. Lemley came out of the dark oil- stained interior and said, "Tell Melvin I don't have that fuel pump."

We thanked him and left.

As we were getting back on our bikes Roland said, "You reckon we can come up with an excuse to come back here next month?"

SCHOOLS OUT – WHAT TO DO NOW

The Korean Conflict was going full bore. Many of my friends and classmates were going into the Army. The members of the National Guard had mobilized and were gone.

I told Roland, "I may catch gonorrhea or pyorrhea, but I don't want any of that Korea."

Roland had already decided he did not want to be a theater manager nor a disc jockey, which is what he did after school was out in May, 1952. We decided to go to Florence State Teacher's College.

By then, I had a 1948 baby blue Ford, one of the best cars I ever owned. We drove over to FSTC and registered. We then had to register for the dorms. We were planning to room together. Helen Keller Hall was the place to live. Roland and I went in wishing to register. A Mrs. McFarland was the housemother.

She let Roland register, and looked at me. "When are you going to take that hat off?"

I realized I had on a wine-colored corduroy waistcoat and a matching hat. Smartly, I replied, "When I go to sleep tonight."

"Then you shall sleep in Florence Hall. You are not qualified for Keller."

Florence Hall was sometimes referred to as "splinter village." It was a white clapboard two-story building that had been a dormitory when the college had been built in antiquity. It was considered terrible to live in the "clap-trap." It didn't bother me. It was a mansion compared to some of the places I lived in growing up. And so, Robert and Roland arrived in college.

My family could not help me as the four girls were all in school. I think Rebecca had started to school in 1952. I was able to get a job at Kroger's in Florence to defray my expenses. Also, living in Florence Hall was cheaper than living in Keller Hall. I applied for a scholarship through the Daughters of the American Revolution. Because I had a number of grandfathers who served under General George Washington, I was approved. I really appreciated the DAR for their help.

We had to stay in the top 25% of the class and take ROTC; otherwise, our names would be called for the Korean Conflict draft.

Both of us enjoyed college. I wrote a comedy column for the school newspaper while Roland wrote for the sports page. Mostly, he wrote about the exploits of Harlon Hill, for whom the trophy as the most outstanding football player of Division II was later named. Roland was fortunate enough to be going to school full-time. I had to work as a stock and sack boy at Kroger's and go to school part time.

CHAPTER NINE
THE U.S. AIR FORCE

At the end of the second semester in college, I could see the writing on the wall. I was out of the top 25% of my class because of my work and enjoying campus life. I was going to be drafted.

I had to renew my driver's license. I went to the courthouse in Decatur, and as I was getting out of my Ford, a jet came over the building and went straight up. I went in, renewed my license, and joined the Air Force.

Mother was broken-hearted. However, she didn't want me going to Korea as a grunt. Roland wanted to know why I didn't tell him; he would have joined up with me.

"That's the reason I didn't tell you. You are still in the top 25%, and you are doing well in ROTC. Stay there and finish school. I'll finish when I get out of the service."

I had every intention of becoming a jet pilot.

On March 20, 1953, my darling mother stood at a spot below my window on the Greyhound bus bound for Montgomery. Tears were streaking down her face. She had missed her boy when he went off to college, but now, he was gone for good.

LACKLAND AIR FORCE BASE
SAN ANTONIO, TEXAS

The Air Force boarded all recruits in the same place for three days. All day we went through physical and mental examinations. By the time I left, I felt like they knew everything about me. They certainly knew that I wanted to be a fighter pilot. I put that on every document asking about my plans during the Air Force.

When they were finished with us, they bussed us out to Maxwell Air Force Base, put us on an old C-47 that had seats put in it, and flew us to Lackland. As we exited the airplane, we were directed to various busses that were there to take us to our respective flights. I got into my barracks a little before 4:00 a.m.

The first floor was packed out. The second floor of the barracks had beds in a line down the two long walls of the building. Each bed had an upper berth. The guy who drove the bus told us to find a bed and turn in. The only one I could find was an upper berth over a guy from Wyoming. He was sleeping away.

Somehow, I got into the upper berth, pulled the army blanket over me and promptly went to sleep. Less than an hour later, I heard somebody with a very loud voice yelling something I couldn't understand.

"Haul out! Haul out, I said!"

I put the blanket over my head and rolled over on my right side. The next thing I knew, I was flying through the air. The man doing the incomprehensible yelling had grabbed the end of my thin mattress and jerked it, along with me, off the bed, and onto the floor. I woke up with a giant of a man, dressed in olive drab fatigues, standing above me, yelling. "When I say, haul out! I mean haul out! Now, make up that bed, and haul out!"

Several of us were repairing our beds. Apparently, he dragged every non-responsive man out into the floor. I got dressed, put my bed back together, and asked a red-headed guy near me, "What was that big guy yelling?"

"I am really not sure. I think he was saying, 'fall out.' Anyway we need to get downstairs before he comes back up here."

Downstairs we were told to count off. There were 62 of us. The big guy began to talk in a very loud and concise voice.

"My name is Corporal Snyder. I am six feet four inches tall. I weigh 264 pounds of all bone and muscle. Take a good look at me. You will never call me anything other than Sir. Make a mistake of calling me anything else, and we will have go to the hospital to get my size 14 boot out of your ass.

"For the next nine weeks I am going to be your mother, daddy, brother, sister, and girlfriend. But, you will not fuck me. You, do you know what a hostler is?"

He pointed to one of us. "No, Sir."

"Who knows?"

My bunkmate spoke up. "Sir, a hostler is a person who breaks horses."

"Correct! I am a drill instructor, a hostler of people. I'm going to break every one of you, and when I am through, you will be Airmen, and worth something. Right now, you aren't worth a shit. Now, get your jackets on, Rainbows. We are going to chow."

By the time he had us all lined up six abreast, in columns, according to our height, it was breaking daylight.

"Try to stay in step. Otherwise, the guy behind you is going to step on your heel. Forward Harch."

We moved out.

"On my count, your heel should hit the pavement. Hut, hoop, three, four, your right, left, right. Get in step, three four."

We made it pretty good and did much better on our way back. He called us rainbows because of our colorful clothing. The rest of the day dentists, medical doctors, and barbers examined us.

"How do you wear your hair?"

"Some around the sides and a little off the top."

His clipper was so hot it almost blistered my scalp. He thought he was funny. He took his clipper and went around my head, "A little off the sides."

Then he went right down the center of my head. "A little off the top."

Then he practically shaved my head.

When I went outside, all the other guys had the same haircut – none. Beards and mustaches were gone as well.

We were then marched to the quartermaster where we were given our bedding, toilet articles, and clothing.

One of the fellows had enough courage to ask Corporal Snyder, "Sir, why did they cut off all our hair?"

"We're checking you for lice. It'll grow out. Shut up!"

The next day we were taught to roll our clothes, make our beds, and organize our footlockers. We were given a stamp to mark our clothing, and forced to memorize our serial number. The following day we would get our dog tags and be taught to shine our brogans.

After a week, we were all dressed in Air Force Fatigues, which looked like an olive drab mechanic's one-piece coveralls. We were taught how to wear our uniforms down to our caps.

We were slowly acclimating to Lackland Air Force Base, "A place where you can stand in mud up to your waist, and have sand blowing into your eyes."

It did take some getting used to. The wind never let up. Its constant blowing was difficult to deal with.

Corporal Snyder was a mean man. A guy from Iowa named Baimler was marching with us and asked Corporal Snyder if he could approach. "Granted."

He approached the DI and informed him that he had diarrhea and needed to go to the restroom.

Snyder told him to hold it or shit his uniform. Baimler couldn't hold it. Feces ran down his leg and into his brogans, and he still had to march.

When we got to the barracks, Snyder ordered Baimler to go into the latrine and wash himself, his uniform, and his brogans. Poor Baimler had marched with feces in the crack of his butt to the point it was so red it was bleeding. He put Vaseline on it and marched again the next day.

After about two weeks, they took me over to Randolph Air Base to be tested for cadets. I was thrilled.

It looked like I would be flying jets in no time. They tested me physically and mentally; I passed. They tested me psychologically because I had been knocked unconscious when I fell off the Clarence Campbell mule. They ruled no brain damage. It looked like I would be leaving basic training and enter Officer's Candidate School.

Not to be. I failed my very last eye. exam. They kept me extra time and checked me again due to how I did on everything else. The problem showed up again. I had 20-20 eyesight; however, there was a possibility that a cockpit strut might obscure my vision for a second.

I was sent back to Lackland. We began to go to class for five hours a day and train for four more. I enjoyed the classes on history, warfare, weapons, defense, hand to hand combat, marksmanship, and many other classes about the military.

I enjoyed the 14-mile hike, the bathing in a helmet full of water, and so on. The only hard part of the physical training was marching, obstacle course, crawling under barbed wire while a machine gun sprayed bullets above your head, and firing the big guns. I qualified as a marksman with an M-30.

No matter how well I completed any assignment, Corporal Snyder seemed to hate me. I was assigned the dirtiest details, put on KP, and cursed about something every day.

He wanted to know if anyone in the flight could catch. I said that I was a catcher. He had me fall out at 2:00 p.m. for a week and catch him trying to pitch. He failed to make the team. I think he hated me more because I was a much better catcher than he was a pitcher.

The squadron shipped out after nine weeks. I remained for five more weeks. I was never told why. I was assigned to train with another squadron.

I will never know why Corporal Snyder and another DI decided to beat me up. I did nothing to either of them. I was not under their command; I had earned my Airman Third Class stripe. Yet Snyder told me to meet them upstairs in an empty barracks.

I didn't like the set-up so I got there early. I found an extender for a bunk - the part that helps hold up the top bunk. It was a good steel club, so I hid it under a mattress where I was waiting for them.

When they arrived, Snyder began hollering at me about my disregard for the chain of command.

The other DI said, "Yeah, I've seen some of the stuff you turned in during classes, and it is obvious you hate the chain of command. What do you think of it?"

I thought, I'm going to have to fight these men over something like this. It didn't make sense. I reached under the mattress and pulled out the steel extender and said, "I think it is a bunch of red tape."

Snyder advanced toward me. "That's it, you are getting your ass whipped."

I pulled back my steel bed extender like a baseball bat. "Come on, big boy, I've been waiting for this."

Right then, the other DI grabbed Snyder by the arm. "Let's not do this. It is going to get messy. We will all be court-martialed, and he has nothing to lose. He's not worth it. Let's go."

Snyder stopped short, thought for a second, and said, "You're right. This piece of shit is not worth being busted."

I didn't say anything. I just watched them leave. When I made sure they were gone, I put the extender back under the mattress and left the building.

That was the last time I saw Corporal Snyder. A few days later I received orders to proceed to Keesler Air Force Base in Biloxi, Mississippi, and enroll in radio operator's school.

KEESLER FIELD

I took a 10-day furlough, as radio operator's school would not start for that length of time. I went home and discovered that my sisters, primarily Dot, had sold my Famous James, and she had wrecked my baby blue Ford.

I was being paid $80 per month. I sent it all home, other than $10. With what I had saved up, more than $100, I took the Ford to the shop and had it fixed for $90. Then I drove it back to Keesler Air Force Base.

Before I began schooling, they gave me an IQ test. I scored 143. They said that was very high so they tested me again. Same score. As a result of that score, they put a little green sticker on my file. I never did understand what that meant.

I was assigned to Squadron 3380. I did everything I was assigned, and I was promoted to Airman Second Class. Soon I became a flight leader.

I was determined my flight of 60 men would be the best in the Squadron. I hounded the men for perfect inspections. I made them march in precision. I checked their grades, made them get haircuts, took them to sick call, and even taught Sunday School. On occasion, I cut their hair. As a result, my flight was the best student flight on the base. I was raised to Senior Flight Leader, now in command of 360 men making up the entire squadron.

I then set about to make 3380 into the best squadron on the base. About this time, my mother advised me that there were men from the FBI asking questions about me all over Decatur. She wanted to know if I was in trouble. I was not in trouble, and I had no idea why they were investigating me. Later, I found out that they were clearing me for a very high secret clearance. Why? I would soon learn.

When I finished radio operator's school, instead of being assigned to an aircraft or another active base, I was told I would remain at Keesler and go to intercept school.

Now I knew why the FBI was investigating me. You had to have a security clearance to attend intercept school.

The first day of intercept school I was told that when I finished intercept school, I was being transferred to intelligence employing the knowledge I had learned in intercept school.

While I was doing the six weeks schooling to learn intercept, my First Sergeant came to me and said, "French, some of the staff here at the school believe you should go to West Point. You have the grades, the ambition, and the staff thinks you would be a good officer. If you know a congressman, ask him to appoint you to the Point. If you don't know one, the General will find one for you."

I knew my Senator, John Sparkman. I had met him in a high school panel discussion. Further, it was known in the family that he had grown up on one of my relatives' farm outside Hartselle, Alabama, where his father had been a share cropper. (When I was 78 years old, that farm was sold, and I believe I received $750 for my part.)

Anyway, I wrote a nice letter to Senator Sparkman about appointing me to West Point.

He had already issued his two appointments, but my Congressman, Bob Jones of Scottsboro, still had one available. He contacted Congressman Jones, and he wrote to me. He had used his West Point appointments but would appoint me to the Naval Academy. I was very happy. After all, being in the Navy ran in the family.

I was transferred to the Naval Academy Preparatory School in Bainbridge, Maryland. There, I met Larry Hill from College Station, Texas. He had been a football player for Texas A & M before joining the Air Force. He and I hitchhiked into Washington several times to see the McCarthy hearings ferreting communists out of Hollywood and the government.

I was in Bainbridge less than two months when Congressman Jones ran me down and said that one of the boys he had appointed to West Point had declined to go at the last minute. He would appoint me if I could leave within the next week, as classes were starting at West Point Preparatory School in Newburgh, New York.

I accepted and asked if he could help get Larry Hill appointed so he could go with me. Miracles happen. Somehow Larry got the appointment and left about the same time I did. We were reunited at Stewart Air Force Base just outside Newburgh.

I was thrilled to get to Newburgh. I was a cadet, and a poor boy from Austinville, Alabama, was going to get a high-flown prep school education. I loved the school.

Unfortunately, because I had to work, I had never had geometry nor a language. The professors assumed everyone had those courses, and understood the advanced classes they were teaching. It was very difficult for a Diversified Occupations student. I never understood geometry -- nor algebra, for that matter. I applied myself diligently and mastered the language part.

I knew I was looking at failing geometry and language so I worked very hard – studying late and often.

IN LOVE AGAIN

It was during this time that I fell madly in love with Patricia Sparhawk. I had met her in a diner where she worked and was a photographer's model on the side. I thought she was truly the most beautiful woman I had ever seen. She was gorgeous, and I saw her every minute I had away from studies or school.

One Saturday night, she was out of town, and four of us decided to go to town for dinner. Larry Hill, Gary Atkinson, Larry Boekman, and I enjoyed Newburgh a little too much, and we missed the last bus back to the base. We were all in uniform, looking sharp as possible, and we decided to hitch a ride back to the base.

We stood on a very well-lighted street corner thumbing a ride. A carload of girls came by and hollered at us. We begged them to stop. They drove around the block and came back. There were four student nurses in the car. They gave us a ride. Out of that ride, there were three marriages. Larry Hill and Celeste Mongiello hit it off right away. Liz and Atkinson later married. Boekman and another nurse married. Mary Clendenon was in the car, and she remained single all her life. While Larry was dating Celeste, I was dating Pat, and we had a great time.

I attended First Baptist Church regularly and asked Pat to go with me. She went one Sunday when they were serving communion. She thought that was the most hilarious thing she had ever seen. The Baptists were eating a small cracker that they called bread and drinking a spoonful of grape juice in a tiny shot glass pretending it was wine. She laughed loudly and uncontrollably. She embarrassed me to the point I could never return to the church.

Although I was having a difficult time adjusting to a northern girl, she was a great cook and fabulously beautiful. I sent her modeling pictures home for Mother to put up for me. She didn't; she burned them. I have only one portrait picture of her left.

Pat was a friend of the famous Mike Hammer author, Mickey Spillane. She, her sister, and I visited him at home one Sunday. We told him we were engaged.

During conversation, I mentioned that I did not watch TV. Spillane said, "Well, I know Pat loves TV. How are you going to deal with that?"

"I'll put the TV on the ceiling of the bedroom."

He thought that was one of the funniest things he had ever heard.

Things rocked on with Pat and me. She would have beer from time to time. I had never tasted alcohol and asked her not to drink. She said that she would not drink again. She wanted to have sex, but I wanted to save that for the marriage. She agreed, but she returned to drinking beer. I found out about it and broke up with her.

Losing Pat, I dedicated myself to my studies. Although I applied myself the best I could, I failed the entrance examination by two points on geometry.

For some odd reason, they allowed me to take the test again, and I flunked geometry again by two points. Sadly, my West Point career was over. Larry Hill flunked the language part, and they did not allow him to take the test again. He would have to wait six months. So I washed out of prep school, two points in geometry; however, having attended West point Preparatory School at Newburg, New York always looked good on my resume'.

Because of my secret clearance, I was assigned to Emergency Radio Teletype. Larry Hill was transferred to Maxwell Air Force Base in Montgomery, Alabama. He and Celeste broke up because he did not want a long-distance relationship.

Larry later married a girl from Montgomery and became president of her father's electrical business.

RADIO TELETYPE

Per my new assignment, I worked in what was called the RATT Shack, a 10' X 20' enclosure surrounded by a 12' high fence with barbed wire on the top. The shack was capable of fitting on the back of a pickup truck so it was small. Six men were assigned to man the RATT Shack 24 hours a day, 7 days a week.

We were a back-up to Colorado Springs, Colorado. In case of a nuclear attack on the East Coast and our electricity was down, we were to scramble the B-29's carrying nuclear bombs to retaliate. It was a highly sensitive job. We operated off gasoline generators and did a radio teletype check with NORAD every 15 minutes, around the clock. Our weapons were loaded, and we were ordered to shoot anyone who attempted to interfere with our work.

The airman coming off duty allowed the airman coming on duty to enter the gate and gave him the rifle. Thus, the loaded weapon was transferred at least three times a day. If there were people in the area, we did not approach the gate. The officers did not want regular personnel to know who the RATT men were.

We told people we were communications specialists or radio operators.

The fun for the job was on Saturday night, some of the regular airmen would get drunk, pound on our fence, and holler, "What the hell you sons-a-bitches doing in there?"

The sign on the gate was clear, "Highly Restricted Area, Unauthorized Persons Will Be Shot." We ignored the drunks, but they were entertaining.

We were on a RATT Net that went around the world. This was during the heart of the Cold War, while Eisenhower was President, and we were ready.

Naturally, boys will find something to entertain themselves when things get boring. Our orders were to remain in constant contact. This usually meant running a Radio Teletype tape through a highly secured transmitter every 15 minutes on a top-secret frequency.

We said, forget the tape. For 14 minutes, we would stay in constant contact by writing stories. Every 15 minutes we had to stop and run the one- minute check tape.

The other 14 minutes went like this: a guy in the Middle East might start it by writing, "There I was in the heart of the Amazon Jungle, armed with my trusty Remington, accompanied by my porter, Aqui, when all of a sudden...."-- Another guy in Thule, Greenland might pick it up and type, "I saw a huge saber-toothed tiger on a limb, 10 feet above me, ready to pounce. Quick, Aqui..."-- And then I might write, "Give me my Remington and be sure it is loaded. Quickly, man! And Aqui..."-- And where it might go from there could not be calculated. There were 12 stations on the net, and almost all of them participated in the story writing that could last an entire eight-hour shift. Sometimes the Airmen and Soldiers would create situations that the main character could not get out of, and the next guy down the net had to figure some way to save our hero. It was fun while it lasted.

CELESTE MONGIELLO

Then out of the blue, Celeste Mongiello called me. "French, Liz and I are throwing a party Saturday night and need some men for the student nurses. Atkinson is coming for Liz and Boekman is coming. I need you to come, and bring three guys with you."

I agreed and rounded up three of my buddies. On Saturday, we headed for Middletown State University. Celeste and I caught up on our activities for the past several months and became fast friends. We agreed that we would start dating.

I dated her in Newburgh and Middletown. We went up and down the cities along the Hudson from Tarrytown to Poughkeepsie and enjoyed ourselves.

Celeste graduated as a psychiatric nurse and began working at the mental hospital on Rikers Island in New York City. Her folks lived in Astoria, Long Island, and she lived with them off and on.

She had an apartment in Greenwich Village in downtown New York City that she shared with a married couple, Fred and Olga Policastro. She had lived with them in the past when she was an art student at CCNY, and worked on Wall Street as a secretary. They were called Bohemians then.

I never had the pleasure of meeting the couple because I always visited at Celeste's parents' apartment in

Astoria. However, we exchanged Christmas cards every year.

Our romance bloomed, and I came to Astoria more and more. We had fun in New York City. I became very close friends with her father. He worked as an electrician on the lights on Broadway. He had worked for Broadway Maintenance Company for more than 30 years. He was the Bocce Champion of New York State, and he had the Budweiser Trophy to prove it. An aside: All my life, my family had called me Robert. I acquired Herman as a nickname in Junior High School. When I got to Lackland Air Force base, I was no longer Robert nor Herman. I was Bob, a name I hated. I had fights in school with boys who called me Bobby or Bob. Now I was Bob.

I was on furlough home before going to Michigan. I stopped by to say goodbye to Celeste. On this occasion, Mr. Mongiello called me aside near the local Bocce court.

"Bob, you know I like you. Phyllis (Celeste's mother) likes you. Mike and Rene (Celeste's brother and sister) like you. The whole family likes you. But, Celesta, (using the Italian pronunciation,) is 21 years old. That's old for an Italian girl not to be married or have prospects to be married. We need for you to be serious with our Celesta, or move on, and let some other man woo my daughter."

I agreed that was fair. When I got home, I told my mother about the conversation.

She said, "Let's go to Rose Jewelry. This is the best news I have heard in a long time."

I think my mother was so happy I was away from Pat that she truly believed Celeste was right for me. As usual, my mother was absolutely correct.

It was 1955, and I bought a solitaire diamond for $106.00. I mailed it to Celeste in its jewel box with a note inside, "Will you marry me?"

She called me by telephone when she received the package and said that her answer was, "Yes."

Mother had never met her, knew she was a Catholic, but she was satisfied with my choice.

NEW ASSIGNMENT

After I had been a RATT man for several months, I received notice that I was being shipped overseas. I had less than 18 months to go on a 4-year enlistment. I thought sure I had avoided foreign service. I did avoid the normal overseas assignment. I was going for a year of isolation duty. That was a real kick in the head. I had been told to go to Selfridge Air Force Base in Mount Clemens, Michigan, just outside Detroit. I would receive my assignment there.

I checked in at Selfridge and waited. In a few days, I received orders to deploy to an isolated radar site where we were watching for the Russians coming over the Arctic ice cap. The brass was concerned that this was the shortest distance from Russia to New York and Washington. The U.S. had established the Distant Early Warning network, affectionately called the DEW Line.

Since I had a high security clearance with RATT experience, I was an apt candidate to be the radio operator in the "Chosen Frozen." Upon radar picking up the Russians, my orders were to scramble interceptor jets from Sault Ste. Marie, Michigan.

Of course, I had to do a year's tour of duty, and mine fell on leap year. Day 366 was the longest day of my life.

There was only one radio operator on duty per rotating shift. So you had to keep on your toes for eight or more hours. The worst thing that happened to us was a new Chief of Operations rotated in. The first thing he did was clean the coffee pot. From the time I arrived, I observed the custom of simply adding water to the pot with new coffee grounds. The pot was never empty, and it was so strong it would stain your teeth. This guy cleaned it out, and no one could drink coffee for a month.

About this time I went outside one morning when it was -32 and got the bridge of my nose frost bitten. It's still raw after all these years.

The average American citizen never realized the lengths the military went to during the Cold War. Alert was the order of the day, and sometimes it became very nerve wracking. Still, it was better than combat. Compared to what guys on the front lines were doing, my job was cushy.

The Russians would test our resolve by pretending to fly over the cap to see how fast we would react. So far as I know, there was never a time they could have succeeded reaching the U.S.

My main enemy was the mosquitos. Apparently, they thrived in the frozen muskeg of the tundra and grew large and vicious. We killed one that we put in a penny matchbox for burial, and he would barely fit. If you went outside, you had to have repellant on any exposed part of your body. Even with that, they would attack your lips and try for the eyes. I learned that people who got lost up North would sometimes go crazy fighting the mosquitos.

GETTING MARRIED

Celeste and I wrote to each other every day. We finally decided to get married when I could get a furlough down to Hearst, Ontario, the last city in Canada before Moosonee on the Arctic Circle.

Once you get north of Hearst, the only commercial establishment you will see is the Hudson's Bay Trading Company, established in 1670.

On September 23, 1955, I met Celeste at the most northern commercial airport in Ontario - Kapuskasing, Ontario. We were married that night in Hearst by a Catholic Priest with the City Clerk as our witness.

We spent our honeymoon at the Waverly Hotel where our fire escape was a rope near the window. The day after getting married, we found a couple, Hans and Grace Hitalla, who would rent us a room. With living quarters in hand, we went to the Hospital Notre Dame and visited with Sister Joseph Sarto, the administrator of the 20-bed facility. She hired Celeste as Director of Nurses.

Now we had a place for Celeste to live, and she had a job. Eight days later, I returned to the base.

I acquired a close friend who was a radar operator, Larry Kosker. We made a pact that the first one of us to get our picture on the front page of the *New York Times* would immediately contact the other to share the success. When I made it in 1963, I tried to find Larry. I'll tell you about how it came about later.

Any time I got free time and could arrange transportation, I would go to Hearst to see Celeste. We became. great friends with the Hitalla's and corresponded with them for more than 30 years.

We kept up with Sister Sarto until she died a few years later. She always wrote the sweetest letters.

At the end of my tour of duty, Celeste and I boarded a southbound train for the USA. We had saved our money, and we were going to Detroit to buy a car. We bought a '53 Packard and headed to Alabama for Celeste to meet the family. We broke down in Bean Station, Tennessee early on Sunday morning. The people there were so nice. A mechanic came out, persuaded his neighbor to open his parts store, and installed a new fuel pump on our car.

To say that Celeste was a hit with the family would be an understatement. Everyone loved her, including Roland. Daddy seemed to have recovered from much of his illness. He was not the way he was before the accident, but he was much improved and working regularly. Becky was 9 or 10 years old and the only child still at home. Dot,

Hester, and Daina had all married before I had married Celeste.

We had a delightful visit and then drove to New York to visit with Celeste's family. This was a very successful visit, and we had a great time.

Good times were over, and it was time for me to return to work. Near the end of my stint watching for the Rutskies, I had been transferred to Mitchell Air Force Base at Hempstead Plains, Long Island, New York. I was assigned to Military Amateur Radio Service (MARS). My job was to build a radio station to transmit messages for service personnel around the world. I had less than 6 months to go in the Air Force. Plus, I had applied for early release to start to school at the University of Alabama in January, 1957.

Lenny VanDewal and I were to build the station. He knew something about it, as he had been in radio maintenance. All I knew was how to operate the equipment once we had the station built.

We requisitioned all the equipment we needed, and built the largest station on the east coast. When we announced we had completed the job, the Major sent in experts to check our electrical work. Once it was up and running, I supervised the staffing, and we brought in only the best operators. We had more traffic than any station in the world because we were now the station for New York City.

Celeste and I had rented a two-room apartment in Roslyn, New York. After a month, things didn't work out with our landlord. He had never rented the apartment before. He stayed in our place about as much as he stayed downstairs.

We moved into the basement of the home of Renee and Frank's - Celeste's sister and brother-in-law. Their home was in Queens, Long Island. I was commuting to work.

We decided to buy a new Chevrolet. We bought a 1956 210 Chevy, Bama colors, of course. We acquired a Golden Retriever puppy from a couple at Babylon, Long Island. Since she was from the Middle East, we named her Cleopatra – Cleo for short.

While Celeste took care of the dog, I applied for admission to the University and was granted. I applied for the GI Bill that would pay me $127 a month while I went to school.

CHAPTER TEN
THE UNIVERSITY OF ALABAMA

We arrived in Tuscaloosa at 4 o'clock in the morning. We had one month's house rent paid on 303 Cedar Crest. We had $40 cash, a dog, and everything we owned on a U-Haul trailer. I like to say I arrived in T-Town with $40, a wife, a dog, and a car payment. It was shortly after the first of the year. We unpacked our trailer and set up our used couch, that made into a bed. We put some bed clothes on it and went to bed. We slept our first day in Tuscaloosa.

The following day we bought some groceries, ate a meal, and organized what we had of furniture. We spent the next day looking for jobs. Celeste was hired as an obstetrics nurse at Druid City Hospital, midnight shift. Two weeks later, I found work with Snipes Business Machines as a typewriter repairman and salesman.

On January 29, 1957, I entered the University of Alabama School of Commerce and Business Administration.

School was exciting, but waiting for Celeste to get paid and waiting for another GI Bill check found us flat broke. I had a full tank of gas, and Celeste and I drove to Decatur where my mother gave us $15.00. That was my family's total contribution to my education. However, I really appreciated it.

That small amount kept us from going hungry. In a few days, Mr. Green, of Green's Grocery, across 15th Street from where we lived, let me open a charge account. From then on, we were in fat city.

Just as in high school, I went to class from eight until noon. Then, I worked the rest of the day. I drove Celeste to the hospital at 11:00 p.m. every night and picked her up at 7:30 a.m. We began to do all right.

The first thing we bought was a window air conditioner to put in the bedroom so Celeste could sleep during those hot Tuscaloosa summer days.

I was repairing a segment bar on an Underwood manual typewriter. Electric typewriters had not made it to Tuscaloosa at that time. The bar was broken, and we did not have another in stock. I took brass, with a torch, and began to put the bar back together. The more I worked, the larger the lump of brass became on the small pencil thin bar.

Mr. Snipes came into the shop and looked at what I had just finished. The typewriter worked perfectly. Mr. Snipes wanted to see the bar.

I said, "It don't look like much, but it'll hold."

Mr. Snipes was clearly displeased. "Yeah, Bob, that's what the farmer said when he sewed a bull's ass up with a log chain. It don't look like much, but it'll hold."

I said, "I'll file it down."

"No, let Bill do it. I think you will do better in sales. So, dress appropriately tomorrow."

The following day, I began pounding the streets of Tuscaloosa. I went into each commercial establishment and offered to sell the manager a business machine or a box of carbon paper. Remember, everything I was selling was mechanical.

The adding machines and accounting machines were motor driven but manual in their calculations.

I took Salesmanship and learned a lot about my trade. I learned to sell features and benefits. I worked hard in the class and assisted the professor for a couple of semesters. In fact, I became quite good selling machines and carbon paper.

Underwood came out with a small adding machine called the Add-Mate. It was an adding machine the size of a telephone. I went out to sell them. If the manager allowed me to plug it in, he bought it for $165.00. I sold one to a cotton farmer in a pickup truck.

I sold so many of them that the President of Underwood, Mr. Beane, who had been a partner in Merrill, Lynch, Fenner, Pierce & Beane on Wall Street, came down from New York to congratulate me. He told me that when I graduated from the University, to come to Number One Park Avenue, New York. He had a job for me.

PAUL WILLIAM BRYANT

I rocked on through undergraduate at C&BA making high grades. My major was Trade Unions, and like every other commerce student, my minor was Accounting.

To make my major sound official, the University called it Labor Management. However, I went straight down a curriculum that dealt exclusively with trade unions. When I received the degree, I was the third student in University history to acquire such a specialized degree.

I think it was my experience with Mr. Cooper that influenced me to be so interested in trade unions.

When I became a senior, I sold a dictating machine to Professor Jay Murphy, a labor arbitrator as well as Professor of Labor Law and International Law. He suggested that I take my cognate electives in law school, so I could study labor law, legislation, arbitration, and other courses related to management involving trade unions.

After school started, Celeste and I became football nuts. We went to football games when "Ears" Whitworth was coach. He had played for Championship Alabama teams during the 1930's. Now we lost and lost. I later learned that Hank Crisp, as Athletic Director, never allowed "Ears" to have full control of the team.

For us, the most exciting thing about a football game was that the Spanish students bringing their guitars and playing flamenco music in the student section.

After Auburn beat us 40-0 on Legion Field in

Birmingham, it was time for action. It was so cold at the game that fans built a fire in the north end zone. Celeste and I were in the south end zone, dressed in arctic wear, and freezing. Ears took responsibility for the loss and resigned.

Celeste and I joined other students gathering at the Student Union Building at night and shouting, "Give us Bear or give us death!" By December 3, 1957, Coach Bryant signed a contract saying that he agreed to "Return to Mama."

He was very successful at Texas A & M with the Junction Boys and all. Now he was coming home to his alma mater. Our football fortunes would soon turn around. We would be Alabama again!

The guys at Snipes Business Machines said, "Bob, are you going to sell Coach Bryant a typewriter when he gets here?"

Underwood had just introduced an electric typewriter in competition with the only other electric typewriter - IBM. "If he's living, breathing, and walking upright on the blue planet earth, I will sell him an electric typewriter."

I kept up with when he arrived in Tuscaloosa. Early on, before Texas A & M played their bowl game, he came to Tuscaloosa and met with the players. I continued to check daily until his first day in his new office. I think it was Friday, January 3, 1958. I didn't want to bother him that day, so I waited until Monday.

His door was open. He and his secretary were unpacking boxes and hanging things up on the walls. He had moved an old ugly gray sofa next to the right wall to the left of his desk. He called his secretary a letter rather than a name. He saw me in the doorway.

I had never seen him before, and I could tell that he was a very large and forceful man.

"Miss A, see what that boy wants." He turned back to emptying a box on his desk.

I spoke up. "Coach Bryant, I'm Bob French. I'm here to help you by selling you an Underwood Electric Typewriter."

He turned and looked at me in amazement. "You are trying to sell me an electric typewriter on my first day at work?"

"Yes, Sir. I'm here to help. I have the best electric typewriter on the market. It's inexpensive and will shorten your workday."

He tried to ignore me, but finally he growled, "I'm an IBM man."

"Coach, IBM's are more expensive. We have local service. If you buy an IBM they have to service it out of Birmingham. We're as close as your telephone. You won't lose time, and you save money. It is to your great advantage to deal locally."

He was obviously not happy with my persistence. "Miss A, show the young man out."

As the lady took me by the arm, I said, "Coach, if you would just let me bring by a demonstrator, I think you will change your mind. Our machine is far superior to the IBM."

I then found out why they called him Bear. He raised his voice.

"This is my first day in Tuscaloosa! Can't you see I'm busy! Get the hell out, and stay out!"

Miss A gripped my arm more forcefully, pushed me out the door, and closed it behind me. A few days later, I ran into her on campus.

"Now that he's settled in, do you think I might see Coach Bryant?"

"Young man, you stay away from Coach Bryant. Furthermore, he has bought an IBM."

I figured that was that. I had given it my best effort, and the matter was closed.   I was so wrong.

At precisely 10:00 a.m., when it was not raining, Coach Bryant and members of his staff would walk from his office to the Supe Store (That's the Student Supply Store), in the Student Union Building, for coffee. This stroll was down University Avenue past the School of Nursing, the president's mansion, Denny Chimes, etc. The Coach would be accompanied by Carney Laslie, Sam Bailey, Ken Donahue, Howard Schnellen-berger, and others I can't remember. It was an entourage of the coaching staff.

Although Bryant would not come to Alabama as long as Hank Crisp was Athletic Director, I saw Crisp with them now and then. He had coached Bryant in the 30's as well. Bryant kept him on staff in some capacity.

At 10:00 a.m. I would walk from C&BA to the Farrah Hall the Law school, across the quadrangle, to take labor law and legislation. I walked on the sidewalk a couple of times, and each time I did, Coach Bryant would say, "Stay away from that boy, he's a high-pressure salesman who could sell tits to a boar hog."

I never understood what that meant. Perhaps it came out of Moro Bottom, Arkansas where he was raised. Later in life, I met a lady who said that her grandfather used to say "useless as tits on a boar hog." Anyway, that is how he warned his coaches about me.

Celeste and I were determined to go to the Bear's first game. It was in Ladd Memorial Stadium in Mobile. The opponent was LSU with Billy Cannon. My cousin, Bill Hasty, went with us. Somehow, I had scored two tickets from Jack Warner, President of Gulf States Paper Company, and they were on the 50-yard line 25 rows up.

We were doing pretty well holding our own in the first quarter. Coach Bryant kept quick kicking the ball back to LSU pushing them back. He was trying to control

Cannon. I think Gary O'Steen was the quick kicker. I can't remember.

Toward the end of the first quarter, I went down to the end zone and told Bill to come up and sit with us. We had a vacant seat next to Celeste.

Shortly after we became comfortable in the second quarter, the end zone stands collapsed. More than 70 people were injured. 17 ambulances hauled people away for treatment. The game was delayed for quite a span of time. More than 30 people were transported to local hospitals. In short, it was a mess, and thanks to Billy Cannon, we lost the game.

In later years I told Bill that I had saved his life by coming and getting him before the stands fell. It became a family joke.

Fast forward to 1964. Alabama was working on becoming the National Champion, and I was running for Congress on the Republican Ticket.

I was alone, standing looking in the window of Schwobilt Clothing Store in Tuscaloosa. I was lusting after a metallic gray suit in the window that I could not afford. Jim Martin, of Gadsden, a fellow candidate, had such a suit, and it looked fantastic on him. As I was looking and wishing, I heard a deep voice behind me.

It was Bear Bryant. "Aren't you that high-pressure salesman that can sell tits to a boar hog?"

I turned around, "Yes, Sir."

"Well, I want you to know something. Me and Mary Harmon have talked it over. We are going to vote for you. But if you tell it, I'll say it's a lie."

"Thanks Coach, I won't tell it." And, I didn't.

Many years later, in fact it was December 8, 1976, I was flying my Beech Barron into Mobile where I was defending former County Super-intendent of Education, Dan Alexander. He was charged with bribery and other crimes in office. He was being prosecuted by my old friend, Jeff Sessions, U.S. Attorney, who would later become U.S. Senator and Attorney General. We were going to the wall with it.

I had Jessie Myers, a jury selection psychologist from Washington, D.C., helping me during the trial. My investigator, Eddie Brown, was also on board for the trial. We were well prepared, and it was a big deal locally.

As I was on final approach into Bates Field, Mobile, I heard a plane behind me over the outer marker in bound. It was an Alabama jet. I landed, taxied to the ramp, took a few minutes to order fuel, arrange a tie down, and headed to the men's room. The Alabama jet had landed right behind us.

I'm standing at the urinal taking care of business when in walked a giant of a man to occupy the adjacent urinal. I could smell the sweet smell of vodka in the air when he spoke. "Don't I know you?" He asked in a low, familiar growl.

"Yes, sir."

"Aren't you that high-pressure salesman who can sell tits to a boar hog?"

"Yes, sir."

"Did you ever amount to anything?"

"Yes, sir. I'm a lawyer in Fort Payne, Alabama. I'm down here defending the Superintendent of Education. I've done very well."

"Humm. I thought you might, what with that gift of gab and being a politician and all."

With that, we finished our business and went out. He was in Mobile to attend the funeral of a former player who had been killed in an automobile accident.

That was the last time I saw Coach Bryant in person. He died a few years later. But.... I had one on him that he never knew about.

Celeste was the head nurse at the Student Health Service. When Bryant came to Tuscaloosa, the team did not have a doctor on staff. It used the Student Health Service. In a couple of years, or a little more, the school retained a team doctor.

However, early on, Celeste worked closely with Coach Bryant. He took a personal interest in any player who was injured or sick and often would accompany them to the doctor.

Sometimes he would send Quarterback Pat Trammel over with the player.

Coach Bryant had a great affection for "Mrs. French," and they got along fine. She gave him his flu shot every year and was at his beck and call if needed in the athletic department.

He never put it together that she was the wife of that high-pressure salesman who could sell tits to a boar hog. Sometimes I wonder how things might have changed if he had ever put us together.

ALWAYS A GENTLEMAN

If ever there was a gentleman alive, it was Bill Hasty. He was the epitome of a resolute gentleman. He dressed impeccably. He never raised his voice. He was always courteous and interested. He was humorous. In short, he was a man you would like to know and be around because he always did and said the right things.

A week after the early fall loss to LSU, actually the following Sunday-week, Celeste and I decided to visit my family in Decatur.

We invited Bill to go along. He was happy to go as he would like to see Uncle Robert, Aunt Nina, and any cousins who might be around

We drove from Tuscaloosa, taking the back roads, up Highway 69, through Black Warrior National Forest, to the City of Jasper. Then we went on through little places like Addison, Danville and other small towns into the backside of Decatur. The route was very sparsely populated and was mostly forest all the way. The trip took right at 2 hours. It was the same route we took from the D. O. Convention when we saw the tornado.

We had a great visit, lasting about three hours, and we headed back to T-Town.

Once you started an engine, Celeste had to go to the rest room. Then, about an hour into the trip, she would need another visit. I always said she had a bladder the size of an English walnut.

We were south of Jasper, and could see the tornado trail from high school. It was in the country – deep country – national forest type country. Celeste had to go.

I had not remembered any service stations between Tuscaloosa and Jasper. There may have been one at Oakman, but this was Sunday and it was closed. We drove deeper into uninhabited areas and luckily came upon a small country grocery store. It was open!

Celeste was in the passenger seat of the '56 Chevrolet. Bill was in the back.

She said, "Bill, would you mind going in there and asking if they have a rest room? I'm embarrassed to go ask with all those men in overalls sitting around the porch."

"Of course," Bill responded as he crawled out of the car and headed into the store.

About that time, I noticed the little brown shack out back. It had a well-worn outhouse path through the kudzu, that was plentiful, behind the imitation brick covered building. I wondered how Mid-town Manhattan Celeste was going to handle that. She had rolled the passenger side window down awaiting Bill's return with good news.

Bill came out of the store in his well-tailored suit and very expensive shoes, looking like the stereotype English butler. He came presenting a roll of toilet paper to Celeste ensconced on the middle finger of his left hand.

As he walked to the car to give her the necessity, she rolled the window up, and locked the door. Bill stood beside the car nonplussed, confused as to what was going on, and what to do next. Celeste waived him away.

Dutiful, as always, Bill returned to the store, thanked the owner, and surrendered the toilet paper.

The grocer, in the darkness of the old run-down store, said, "Too good for us, huh?"

Bill responded that she didn't have to go as badly as she thought she did.

"Thanks anyway." He made a hasty retreat.

As soon as he was back in the car, I left in a hurry. The people on the porch weren't too happy about a woman needing to go, and being too good to use the little brown shack out back.

Celeste said, "I'll die of internal drowning before I will go to an outhouse in this God forsaken place. I'll hold on until Tuscaloosa, but stop at the first service station you see."

B. F. GOODRICH

When I got my B.S., and I applied for work at various unions around the country. I was told by each union that their managerial people came up through the ranks. I then applied for a job at the local B. F. Goodrich plant.

I was interviewed by Mr. R.H. Young, Personnel Manager. I was so fortunate that he hired me as a personnel assistant.

It was a great job. I hired in at more than the Dean of the School of Commerce and Business Administration was earning. The job was made for me. I was in charge of the Suggestion System, the Work Simplification System, the plant newspaper, the dispensary, housekeeping, the safety program, and helping with arbitration and contract negotiation. On the side, I worked in discipline, employment, discharges, and worker's compensation.

I loved the job. On fair days, the golfers of BFG met at Meadowbrook Country Club and played in a golf tournament. This was usually five days a week, weather permitting.

Once I came in sweaty, sunburned, exhausted, but with a huge winner's grin on my face. Celeste met me at the door, hands on hips.

"I've had it. You have made me into a golf widow. It is either golf or me!"

I stopped short, unbelievable that anyone would mention my relationship with my beloved golf. I thought long and hard. "Pack your bags."

That was the last time Celeste ever mentioned my golf playing, other than to say, "It's a beautiful day, are you playing?"

It was a wonderful life. We had bought a home, finally had a child, owned a sports car, went to church every Sunday, and generally lived the good life.

I took my job seriously. I established the longest accident-free man hours record in the history of the rubber industry, a little over 6 million hours without an injury. That record stood for years until General Tire broke it. My newspaper won the Industrial Achievement Award. My suggestion and work simplification systems saved the company millions of dollars each year. I kept the cleanest plant in the company.

In short, I excelled at every task I was given. I even sold safety shoes and safety glasses. Whatever came up, I loved it.

I was fortunate to be the only member of management allowed to cross the picket line when the rubber workers went out on strike.

The powers that be in the company came up with a brilliant idea – they would harvest the brightest young man in the 32-country conglomerate, promote him to assistant to the president, and let him learn the administration of the company from the top down. They assigned the task of finding this young man to a fellow, whom I believe, was named Nirada from Akron.

Somehow, someway, Mr. Nirada visited the Tuscaloosa plant and told me that I was among the top three finalists for the job. My boss, Mr. Young, was ecstatic. He had never had someone in his office receive such an honor.

He and Mr. Lehman, our Plant Manager, took Mr. Nirada to dinner and learned that I was the front runner for the job.

The second day, Mr. Nirada came to me and said, "If you were to be offered the job of assistant to the president, J. Ward Keener, would you accept the offer?"

I asked him if I could have one day to consider the question and discuss it with my wife. He agreed to stay in Tuscaloosa one more day.

Celeste and I discussed the opportunity until the wee hours of the morning.

She finally said, "I spent a lifetime trying to get out of the dark, frozen North. If I gave up New York City, how on earth could I be happy in Akron, Ohio?"

I agreed. We would turn down the offer.

At a little after nine, Mr. Nirada appeared in my office and asked if I had made a decision.

I told him, "If I were offered the opportunity to accept the position assistant to the president, I would respectfully turn it down."

He said, "Young man, you are making the worst decision of your lifetime."

Again, I thanked him profusely. He left and went into Mr. Young's office. After about 15 minutes he left without speaking to me. Mr. Young called me into his office.

"Bob, you have just turned down the opportunity of a lifetime. You were the front runner. The job was yours, and you turned it down." Tears ran down his face.

"This may be the worst day of my life. You have no future with this company. I suggest you look for another job. I'm not going to discharge you for this, but your future here is no more."

When I got home, I told Celeste what Mr. Young had said. We had to do something. Our future was now.

"Why don't we load up and move to Birmingham? I can work at UAB Hospital while you study medicine and become a medical doctor."

"I don't want to be a doctor. I don't even like medicine. I have 16 hours of law school. I could go back to law school and become a lawyer. I don't like being a lawyer, but it looks like our only way out. Anyway, you can't support us because we have too much debt for your salary. We've got a house payment, a car payment, day care for Michelle, and then we have living expenses in this house. We can't afford law school, although I have two years left on the GI Bill."

"Talk to Mr. Young and see if you can work something out."

The next day, I asked Mr. Young if I could arrange hours so that I could go to law school 4 hours a day, if I could work it out.

He said, "Bob, you are the best young man I have ever had work for me. I don't want to lose you. See what you can do."

I visited the Dean of the Law School to see if I could work and go to school. Dean Harrison said that he would give me a waiver if the president of the University gave me a waiver. It would take two waivers.

I visited Dr. Frank Rose, the president of the University. He checked my record and agreed to give me a reluctant waiver.

He said, "In signing this waiver, I think I am simply signing for another student to flunk out of the University. But, I will take the chance."

The following semester, I enrolled in law school. I went to work at 5:00 a.m., worked until 7:45, drove to the University, went to class until noon, ate on the road, and worked until 6 p.m. I then went home, ate dinner, and studied until midnight. I slept four hours, and began the schedule again the next day.

If Professor "Black Jack" Paine, a rabid Democrat, had not given me a "D" in Wills and Trusts, I would have graduated with honors.

Because I had almost all "A's," he agreed to allow me to take the course over and give me whatever grade I made then. Fair enough. I took it over. He gave me an "F." There went the honors, Order of the Coif, all of it. I had enough quality points to graduate. So, with Law Review and the others out of the way, I simply concentrated on graduating.

Further, I was the only Republican in law school. It was full of future politicians who were aspiring Democrats. Many of my classmates became judges, senators, congressmen, and even governor.

Me? I was a politician, a Republican politician. I would never be elected to public office, but I would change history in Alabama.

Several years later, in June, 1969, an old friend, David Matthews, President of the University, wrote me a letter and said that in reviewing my record, it was discovered that while I was at the University, I had earned a Doctorate Degree in Law. Send $25 to pay for the printing, and I would receive my Doctorate. I was thrilled. Now I would have earned a B.S., L.L.B., and a J.D. Not bad for a country boy from Austinville. I told my secretary Fay Freeman, to send the U of A the $25.

When I received my sheep-skin, Fay cut me down to size. I was bragging, telling everyone to call me "Dr. French." I was having it framed and placed on the wall.

She said, "I wish I had $25 to throw away. If I did, I would get me one of those degrees."

Sometime later, I can't remember when, everyone graduating from a law school got a Juris Doctorate Degree. I could always say, "At least, I earned mine."

POLITICS – IN THE BEGINNING

During my second semester at Alabama, Celeste and I decided to become involved in politics. I genuinely hated the fact that for 112 years Alabama had been solidly democratic. I lived to see a two-party system in the state.

The Young Democrats and Young Republicans had announcements on the bulletin board as to the time and place of their meetings. Surprisingly, both met at 7:00 p.m., Tuesday night, at the Student Union Building. We decided to see what was going on with the Young Democrats.

The gathering of about 20 students let us know that we were not welcome. The chairman asked me what fraternity I belonged to. When I said none, he asked what was my business. I said that we had come to join the Young Democrats. He said to come back later when they were accepting memberships.

That was my first brush with "The Machine" that controlled campus politics. Seems the fraternities and sororities met each election, picked their candidates, and block voted their choices into the leadership positions of the Student Government. It had been that way since, "The mind of man runneth not to the contrary."

For that reason, as "Independents," Celeste and I were not welcome to become part of the Young Democrats.

We went across the hall where five young people were meeting. We were joyously welcomed to become Young Republicans. We attended a few Republican functions, but there were so few of us, it was barely worth the effort. Still we worked in Republican campaigns, and attended meetings during election cycles.

My next brush with politics was when I had been working at B.F. Goodrich for about three months in 1959.

Mr. Young came into my office. "Mr. Lehman wants to see you in the corner office."

Nothing good ever comes from a visit to the corner office at the plant manager's request. I thought, "Here I've got the greatest job a man can have, and now, I'm in trouble. I wonder what I've done."

When I got to the corner office, Mrs. Pollard, Mr. Lehman's secretary, told me to go right in.

Mr. Lehman had a bum leg from playing football at Carnegie Tech University. He hobbled around his catty-cornered desk, and looked me directly in the eye.

"You're a Republican, aren't you?"

I became very concerned. I thought, I'm about to be fired because of my politics. "Yes sir, I'm a Republican."

"Good! Take this card. It has an address written on it. It's the home of Herb Stockham, Jr., outside of Birmingham, in Mountain Brook. On Thursday night, at seven o'clock, I want you to be there representing the West Alabama Managerial Association."

"Sir, I'm not even a member of that organization."

"Bob, it doesn't exist. I just made it up. Doesn't it sound good and official? Go. I know you will represent us well."

He handed me the card.

"This guy, Greener, has been aggravating me, wanting me to come to the meeting. I don't have the time nor the interest. Report back to me on Friday."

On Thursday afternoon, I did not play golf. I drove to the address on the card. It was quite a home. Seems Herb Stockham, Jr. was the son, or grandson, of the founder of Stockham Valves, one of Birmingham's most successful steel businesses.

When I arrived, there were eight men there, excluding our host. I dutifully announced that I was there representing Mr. Lehman, Chairman of the West Alabama Managerial Association.

The other men there were John Grenier, Manyon Millican, Dr. Tom Brigham, Charles O. Smith, Wallace Stanfield, Homer Jackson, Jr., James Van Antwerp, Perry Hooper and myself, the youngest person there. I was 26 years old.

John Grenier and Dr. Brigham took charge of the meeting and, with Manyon Millican, carefully outlined a plan to defeat the Democratic Party in Alabama and in the South.

A little about the attendees: Charles O. Smith was from Russellville, in Northwest Alabama. He would later be a congressional candidate. He dropped out to let Jim Martin get elected when George Wallace redistricted the state 3 weeks before the election in 1964. Wallace Stanfield was from Florence. He was faithful to the Party the rest of his life. Homer Jackson, Jr. was a CPA in Birmingham, and a faithful treasurer of the Party, once we got up and running.

He was the second youngest person there. I became the only survivor of the original nine when Perry Hooper died in 2016. Hooper served Alabama well. He later became Judge of Probate of Montgomery County and Justice of the Alabama Supreme Court. His son became a State Senator. Jim Van Antwerp was from Mobile and served the Party faithfully until he passed away in July, 2009.

John Grenier explained why we were there. Dr. Brigham and Manyon Millican explained our operational plan to change Alabama. Grenier then extracted a pledge from each of us that we would devote our lives and sacred honor to the cause of a two-party system in the "Solid South." I believe all the men involved in the meeting did exactly as they had pledged.

For the record, I am sure there were other meetings held by these people. However, this is the one that I attended.

The following day, I reported to Mr. Lehman.

He said, "What kind of guy is this guy, Greener?"

"I think he is a Cajun. Although it's spelled 'Grenier,' his name is pronounced 'Grenyea.' He is the only man I have ever met who can strut sitting down."

"Maybe that's what it takes to change this state. Thanks for going."

It was Grenier's aim to take over the Alabama GOP by "packing" the convention with Young Republicans. He got himself appointed Young Republican State Chairman and began to organize Young Republican clubs in every county possible.

He called the GOP leadership in Alabama, "Post Office Republicans." They were satisfied losing every election, as long as they could appoint the federal positions in Alabama when a GOP national administration came into power.

In 1962, we packed the State Convention held at Garrett Coliseum in Montgomery. John Grenier was elected State Chairman of the Alabama Republican Party.

Meanwhile, Celeste and I were staying very active in local politics in Tuscaloosa. In 1962, I managed the Campaign of Charles Wilson, the first Republican to run for office in Tuscaloosa County in more than 100 years.

Wilson ran against the senior member of the Alabama Legislature, Temo Callahan. We fought hard while I was in law school and working at BFG. We lost, but those who followed politics closely could see the handwriting on the wall. We didn't lose as badly as we had in the past. We were coming. I thought the change would be soon, but thanks to George C. Wallace, it took 50 years.

YOUNG REPUBLICANS

In 1963, Jim Holliman, Dan Benton, Ed Nelson, Jimmy Graham, Jimmy Sizemore, John Posey and several other Young Republicans came to our house and sat on the living room floor asking me to run for State Chairman of the Young Republican Federation.

Grenier had taken all the leadership into the senior party, and the YR's were going to be history without a strong leader. They thought I was that leader.

If I didn't have enough on my plate --work, law school, church and local politics -- Celeste and I agreed to run for YR State Chairman if the people there would commit to help me. They committed, and there went my weekends.

Jimmy Holliman and Dan Benton drove me all over Alabama in my spare time talking to what was left of the Young Republican Federation of Alabama. We found that most of the "clubs" wanted to continue on but were devoid of leadership.

Ed Griffith of Mobile ran against me, as did a fellow named Johnny Townes from Huntsville. Townes dropped out when we captured the Huntsville YR club right out from under him. He never forgave me for that little move.

Ed Griffith was another matter. He had a large following among the senior party, primarily due to the support of Post Office Republican, Mary Ellen Miller, National Committee Woman, from Mobile.

We packed club after club by bringing new Young Republicans, as new members, getting ready for the coming Young Republican State Convention. Jimmy Holliman was so good at packing clubs for commitments that a saw was made up about him: "Bar the door, and latch the latchet. Here comes Jimmy with a brand new hatchet."

In a close election, we won. I was the new State Chairman of the Young Republicans of Alabama! I told Celeste, "I kinda feel like the dog that chased a bus until it stopped. He thought to himself, now that I got it, what do I do with it?"

Never one at a loss of ideas, I came up with a program for growth. We would organize a club in every county in Alabama. We would publish a monthly newspaper, "The Pink Pachyderm." We would recruit people to run for office, and we would give the YR clubs instructions as how to organize for victory.

David Oxford, another student in our organization, approached me, "Bob, there's a guy from the *New York Times* here in Tuscaloosa. He is looking for a Young Republican to have his picture taken near some ramshackled shacks, owned by Lady Bird Johnson. I thought of you. He's coming over in a few minutes."

The reporter arrived, and confirmed that Jimmy Holliman and I would follow him down into South Alabama to a town called Millry.

When we arrived, there were five or six old run-down shacks occupied by poor African-Americans. The reporter took my picture talking to one of the men, who lived there, in front of the shacks. My picture appeared on the front page of *The New York Times*.

I tried to find Larry Kosker. I found Larry Kosker in Washington, D.C. I called him. The conversation went like this:

"Hey Larry! This is Bob French. I'm calling to let you know that yesterday I made the front page of *The New York Times*."

"That sounds interesting, but you must have the wrong Larry Kosker. I don't know you. However, congratulations. Were you above or below the fold?"

"It was below the fold, but it was the front page, nevertheless."

No luck finding Larry.

Within one month all the houses had been rebuilt and bricked. The Black folks owed me. I was told that Lady Bird let them live there rent-free until LBJ went out of office.

Later, in 1963, we took a delegation to the Young Republican National Convention in San Francisco. Jack Warner, the President of Gulf States Paper Company, persuaded his brother-in-law to lend us his bus to drive across the country.

The motor blew up in the Superstition Mountains in Arizona. We got a tow to Perkins Diesel Service in Mesa, Arizona. We met Richard Timmons, a doctor who was the YR Chairman of Arizona. He organized a group of delegates to go to the Convention with us. We borrowed cars from his patients, and away we went.

I became a floor leader for Donald "Buz" Lukens of Ohio, who was the conservative candidate for National Chairman. Len Nadasdy, of Minnesota, was the chairman, who was running for reelection. It was a hard floor fight, but our two delegations made the difference, and Lukens was elected.

I was named the Outstanding State YR Chairman of America. Mr. Perkins gave us a great break on the repairs to the bus. We were only charged $1,200. We didn't have the money, but Jimmy Holliman's father, C. B. Holliman, raised the money for us through Marvin Mosteller in Mobile. Both of them had been "Post Office" Republicans. I still have the ashtray Mr. Perkins gave me to remember the occasion.

BEGINNING THE RACE FOR CONGRESS

The YR's around me said that I ought to run for Congress in 1964. At the time, Alabama had the 9 – 8 plan. We had 9 congressmen and had been redistricted to 8.

The democrats wanted to defeat Carl Elliot of Jasper, whom they considered too liberal. He had a storied past. He was the first student to defeat the Alabama Machine. He was elected President of the student body in 1936 running as a country boy from Alabama. He was one of the congressmen who had been shot in 1954 when a Puerto Rican Nationalist fired 30 rounds into the floor of Congress.

He was popular and could not be defeated in his district. However, he was not a supporter of George Corley Wallace. As a result of this animosity, George Wallace and his crowd came up with the 9 – 8 plan. All Congressmen would run statewide, and the candidate with the lowest vote count would be excluded. In their primary, their dirty tricks worked. The low man was Carl Elliot.

A smear sheet had been put out against him statewide one week before Election Day. It was signed, "Cecil Noel, Boaz, Alabama." I ran into Noel years later. I asked him about the little blue sheet. He said, "I'm not saying anything about that. But, it worked, didn't it?"

The remaining Democrats were going to run in new districts against the Republicans in the Goldwater Race of November 1964.

CHAPTER ELEVEN
POLITICS PICK UP SPEED

Leading up to the election, some of the YR's and I were elected delegates to the Republican National Convention in San Francisco. It was the first of five National Conventions where I would be elected to serve as a delegate.

Celeste and I went to San Francisco while Michelle stayed with my Uncle Gene and Aunt Nita in Albertville.

Leading up to the Convention there are always unbelievable parties for the delegates to socialize. We were invited to a reception at the Jack Tar Hotel. There were well over a thousand delegates, alternates, officials and guests in the room.

Ed Nelson had been elected delegate. He came over to me, "French, see that ice fountain over there?"

"Yeah. That's a fancy ice sculpture of a bunch of big fish."

"See that dirty water spewing out of that big fish's mouth? That's not water, it's Champagne and I have three plastic cups." He handed a cup to Celeste and me.

We immediately went to the fountain and began dipping our cups into the trough flowing around the ice sculpture. The rest of the Alabama delegation joined us.

While we were drinking ourselves silly, in walked Richard and Pat Nixon. He had just lost out in California and had told the press that they would not have Dick Nixon to kick around anymore. The media had viciously attacked him. The Democrats piled on. Republicans simply avoided him like the plague. We had been through a lot with Nixon beginning with the Eisenhower Administration when he was Vice President and the vicuña coat.

He and Pat went to a corner and sat down in some chairs. They were intentionally ignored. There was a wide circle of people shunning them.

Celeste said, "That's Pat and Richard Nixon. Look how they're being avoided like the plague. Let's go over and make them welcome."

As we went over, the Alabama delegation followed us. We began to celebrate the Nixons being there. As we enjoyed the Nixons, other delegations came over, and soon he and Pat were being venerated as celebrities.

As I was about to walk away, he looked back over his left shoulder and took my hand again, "I won't forget this." He didn't.

TIME FOR A FLASH BACK

In 1963, I had graduated from law school and had been admitted to the Bar. Sadly, I gave my notice to Mr. Young. He said that he had expected me to leave the company as soon as I got my degree. But, he had no regrets. I had been worth the accommodation, and he wished me well.

I have been forever in his debt. Without him, I don't know what would have happened.

I went into practice with Ralph Williams on the 9th floor of the First National Bank Building in Tuscaloosa. Ralph had a very distinguished resume. He had been the youngest colonel in the history of the U.S. Army – full bird colonel at age 19 – younger than George Armstrong Custer. He had been Alabama Director of Industrial Relations under Governor. John Patterson.

He had earned the reputation of one of the foremost labor arbitrators in the country. He was the man I wanted to work with. More than anything, I wanted to be a labor arbitrator. I had the education for it and the experience to go with it. Now I needed to learn how to do it from the decisionmaker's point of view.

We took in a man named McDuff and organized the firm of Williams, McDuff & French.

146

Ralph then set about to teach me how to practice law. One of his favorite methods was to send me to Tuscaloosa City Court each Tuesday at 12:00 noon. There, Judge Burns held forth with a courtroom full of people. They were always standing around the walls – 90% black people. I was learning criminal defense law.

Some of his rulings were strange. One couple came before him, and he asked the woman why she was back. She said that she wanted a divorce. The man was not faithful, and he had hit her. She wanted out.

Judge Burns said, "Crook your index fingers and join them."

The couple joined index fingers.

He hit them with a pencil and said, "You're divorced!"

The lady shouted, and said, "Praise the Lord!"

I went up after court. "Judge, I know I'm fresh out of law school, but how did you divorce those folks with a pencil?"

"They've been battling for years. They are in here all the time. I divorced them with the pencil because they have never been married."

Legal lesson learned – things at law are not always what they seem.

FIRST FREEBIE APPOINTMENT

Less than a month with Ralph Williams, Judge Reuben Wright called me to his office in the Tuscaloosa County Courthouse. He was a big man, about six-four, and weighing about 350 pounds. He had a big booming voice, long gray hair, spectacles, and an impressive nature.

"Mr. French, I have an appointment for you. You are to defend Oney Lee Martin, Capital Rape."

"Judge, I can't spell capital rape. I sure do not know how to defend one. Please get someone else."

147

"No. This is a horrible case, it could tear this town apart, and I have to be very careful with these appointments. There were five men involved."

"Involved in what?"

"They are five Ku Kluxers. A few Saturdays ago, they decided to go 'Nigger knocking.' They went to this lady's house, and raped her at gunpoint in the presence of her husband, her mother, and her children. They were dog drunk, and they all raped her. Because of holding the people at bay, and raping her, they are charged with kidnaping, the supporting crime, resulting in Capital Rape."

"I can't do this case. I really can't."

"It will enhance your reputation," he said with a heavy south Alabama accent.

"I need something to enhance my pocketbook. Judge, I can't do service to this case. I am just too inexperienced. You can't put this man's life in my hands. I don't care what he has done. That's just too much responsibility. I can't do it."

"You can, and you will! Now on your way."

I went to the jail and met Oney Lee. He had no defense, other than being a member of the Ku Klux Klan and being dog drunk. He didn't even know the family and could not remember the activities of the night. I assured him that the family would remember the night, and he was in a world of trouble.

I drove to the victim's home, and watched the activity going on. The victim was a very attractive woman with several small children. She and her husband lived modestly and kept their home immaculate. I continued to investigate the case and interviewed the other Klansmen.

The deeper I got into the case, the worse it became. These guys were going to the chair if an all-white jury didn't save them. The Civil Rights Movement was barely on the horizon. However, the Klan and White Citizen's Council were active.

Judge Wright was determined to get this case out of the way as soon as possible. The community demanded it. He understood the explosiveness of it. He called it for trial within two months.

It was summer, 1963, Tuscaloosa, and hot. The old courthouse had 12-foot-high ceilings and covered a city block. One side looked out on Greensboro Avenue and the other, I believe, on 25th Avenue. Don't hold me to that, because I can't remember. The courtroom was huge, no air conditioning, and oiled wooden floors.

Four lawyers had been appointed to represent four defendants at their own expense. This was my first indigent defense, at my own expense -- lawyers were expected to give something back to the community -- and there would be 16 more.

Mr. Ed DeGraffenreid, the dean of the Tuscaloosa Bar, had been hired to represent one of the Klansmen.

We went to a pre-trial conference and Judge Wright said that, to avoid the explosive trial that would attract national attention, all the men should plead guilty to simple rape and be sentenced to Life.

Fred Nichols, the District Attorney, did not like the deal. He thought they should get at least Life Without Parole. He wanted five capital convictions. He felt the victim deserved this. To make all of the mess worse, the victim was on her period when the five of them took turns raping her.

Mr. Ed didn't like it, and made himself clear about it.

"Judge, I've been paid well to defend my man. These other guys are appointed. I have to do better than they do."

Judge said, "We'll take it up again trial date." He set the date and we were on.

The day of the trial, there were at least 500 white people out on Greensboro Avenue or in the courthouse. There were almost that many black people on 25th Avenue. Judge had subpoenaed 152 potential jurors. So the courtroom was packed with potential jurors and spectators. Many observers were standing around the walls and sitting in the open windows.

Fred was at the prosecution table with his witness and assistant. We were at the defense table with our clients. The huge judge came out of his chambers in a flowing black robe. He walked to the Greensboro Avenue side of the building and looked out at the crowd. He clopped across the wooden floor to the other side and looked out. He walked back to the center of the courtroom and looked at us.

"All of you, come into my chambers. Leave the non-lawyers in the courtroom."

We went into the ancient office behind the bench and sat wherever we could find a wooden chair.

"Gentlemen, I will not allow my town to be destroyed. There is a riot standing out in the hot sun on both sides of this building. Depending upon the outcome of this trial, one side is going to be very angry. It will not be good for Tuscaloosa, or Alabama, for that to happen. You must settle this case. I propose that four of the defendants take life, simple life, I'm saying. They can be out in 15 years on good behavior. Since Mr. Ed has been paid, I suggest 15 years for his man. What about it?"

"I don't like it, Judge," the District Attorney responded. "However, there will be trouble no matter how this case comes out. The State will reluctantly go along with the settlement only for the good of the community."

The judge went around the room. "What about you, Mr. Woolridge?"

"I'll go along, Judge," Woolridge agreed.

He then asked the next lawyer and the next. They agreed to take the settlement. Then, he got around to me.

"What about you, Young Mr. French, you're on board, aren't you?"

"Judge, you put me here. I begged not to be in this case, but you made me take it. Oney Lee Martin will get 15 years just like Mr. Ed's client, or no deal."

The judge huffed and puffed, practically slobbering.

"You can't do that, Mr. French. The future of Tuscaloosa may depend on how this case is handled."

"My future depends upon how this case is handled. Get the same as Mr. Ed, or we go to trial. I'm ready to tee it up."

Judge Wright was flabbergasted. He turned to the district attorney and asked him what he thought about giving two of them 15 years and 3 of them life? Fred didn't like it, but he agreed.

"Done!" The judge walked out into the courtroom, explained to the jury that the case had been settled and they were excused.

With the courtroom reasonably clear, he sentenced the defendants and returned to his chambers. He called the DA to come in. I was packing my materials. My client had already been taken away. The crowd on the streets was disbursing, and I was leaving.

I heard the judge say, "God-damned Republican! I knew it was a mistake to appoint him when I made the appointment."

As I left the building, I realized that my reputation had proceeded me. I wondered what the future had in store. Within less than 30 days, I would find out.

Judge Wright called me to his chambers.

"Mr. French, you did such a great job for that Klansman, I am appointing you to another important case; you are to defend the Right Reverend P.A. Heaton."

I knew better than to try to beg off.   "What is he accused of doing, Judge?"

"Well, it seems this man of the cloth was tired of his mother-in-law living in the house with him and his invalid wife.   He decided to do away with both of them. He pretended to be working on the house.   Instead, he was nailing the doors shut with boards. He then went under the floor and set the house afire.   Fortunately, some prostitutes living close by, saw him scurrying about with five-gallon kerosene cans and called the police and fire department. The women were saved, but the house burned. He is charged with First Degree Arson."

I knew then that I had had the lick. Managing the campaign of Charles Wilson, and being active in the Young Republicans was going to cost me, and it did.

Ralph Williams gave me 24 hours to become a Democrat or get out. I got out and moved into my own office in the bank building near old classmate and long time U.S. Senator, Richard Shelby. He laughed at me and ridiculed me about politics until he saw the handwriting on the wall and changed parties.

The juries set the punishment back then. I jumped all over the prostitutes, the victims made bad witnesses, and Heaton got out with 10 years.

However, the appointments for freebies kept right on coming.   The worst case in Tuscaloosa County was going to Bob French.   It became common knowledge among members of the Bar.

CRANKING UP THE CONGRESSIONAL CAMPAIGN

When we returned from the Convention, my "staff" went to work. We rented a vacant building on University Avenue and set up shop.   Jimmy Holliman and I had recruited Jerry Barksdale to the Young Republicans. He

152

was now at the University preparing for law school. He was the campaign manager. Dan Benton, Jimmy Graham, Con Bolton, and Ed Nelson rounded out the campaign staff with separate tasks. Barksdale was in charge of the office and staff. Jimmy Holliman was in charge of the candidate. All the guys did a wonderful job.

When John Buchannan, a candidate from Birmingham, saw how smoothly my campaign was running, he asked if he could "borrow" one of my young men to head up his campaign in Jefferson County. Ed Nelson was the only one of the guys who was free to go. He moved to Birmingham and elected Buchannan. He became his Congressional District Field Manager. He was able to attend Cumberland Law School while running the Congressman's office.

Later, he married Linda Mayes, a staff member of the Congressman. The guys, Celeste and I, lumbered on through the campaign.

The Birmingham News picked me and Jim Martin as the strongest Republicans, and would probably be elected. George Wallace had other ideas.

Three weeks before the election, after we had been campaigning statewide for months, Wallace and the Alabama Legislature redistricted the state. I was given the Bessemer Cut-off, Tuscaloosa County, Shelby County, Bibb County, and 8 black belt counties. I didn't have a chance. I was now running against Armstead Selden, a 12-year incumbent black belter from Greensboro, Alabama. However, we fought on in desperation.

George Wallace came in and campaigned against me. Other Congressmen came to Selden's rescue. Bob Jones, who had appointed me to West Point, said that I was an ingrate and had married an Italian from New York City. He said "Italian" with a very long Southern "I." The Democrat-George Wallace organizations did not campaign against the other Republicans personally. As a result, all the other Republicans were elected to Congress.

AFTER THE LOSS

Celeste and I were devastated. We had worked so hard, and we had given up so much to lose. I lost by less than 1,200 votes. If my church, where we attended every Sunday and taught the Bible, had voted for me, I would have won. If the BFG employees had helped me out, I would have won, and so it went. All I needed was 600 votes and I would have won.

Later, we found out that my name was not even on the ballot in Green County. Democrats play hardball. We decided to leave South Alabama and return to my roots in North Alabama.

I looked at Huntsville. My Uncle Popeye now owned the old family home on Clinton Street. He offered to let me have that building for a Law Office. We seriously considered moving to Huntsville. However, at least 10 members of my graduating class had gone to Huntsville. Further, I was related to at least 10% of Madison County. We decided against Huntsville.

We went back to Decatur. I was the boy from the wrong side of the tracks there. It didn't feel right, and I didn't believe we could make it there.

John Posey's uncle offered me his practice in Haleyville. It was a great offer; however, Celeste didn't feel right in Winston County. It was the only Alabama county to stay in the Union during the Civil War. The rest of the state had very hard feelings against the Free State of Winston. So, we were very indecisive.

We went to a GOP State Executive Committee meeting. I was serving as Vice-Chairman of the Committee. John Grenier was Chairman. There was a lot of sympathy for my loss.

Milford Kuykendall and Wendell West, from Fort Payne, were there. They told me I ought to leave Tuscaloosa and come back to North Alabama, primarily Fort Payne. They said I could go into practice with the only Republican lawyer in the area, L. Clyde Traylor, an old classmate of mine. They brought Clyde into the room. He told me that he was overworked and needed help. With my name recognition, we would blow them out of the water.

Celeste and I agreed to visit small town Fort Payne. She, Michelle, and I were weekend guests of the Traylors, and we hit it off famously. Clyde and Nancy spent the weekend giving us a tour of the beautiful mountains, lakes, waterfalls, and the other tourist attractions of the area.

We loved it because we had always wanted to build on the edge of that hill above the town. Later we learned it was Lookout Mountain. Earlier, we would drive through Fort Payne each Christmas going to New York to visit the family. We always admired the "hill" with the star on top.

Funny story about the star. Mr. Hansard was working for the City. He persuaded the powers that be to let him build a star and put it on the brow of Lookout Mountain above the city.

He constructed a five-point star, a little more than 15 feet, from point across to point. He then lined the cross members with lights. Each Thanksgiving the City lights up the "Star in the East." It is a wonderful tradition.

Roland was driving to Atlanta one Christmas season. I'll let him tell the story: "I was coming into downtown Fort Payne. It had been so foggy on Sand Mountain that I had to drive 15 miles per hour. It was still foggy as I came into town. Then! All at once the fog lifted, and I looked up and saw that star!

I said, "My God! It's the end of time and I'm not ready!"

CHAPTER TWELVE
PRACTICING LAW

I went to see my banker in Tuscaloosa, George LeMastre. I told him that I thought I would leave Tuscaloosa, but I needed money to relocate.

He said, "Bob, I'll let you have a $5,000 loan. Go ahead and leave. I've been here 32 years, and I am still a stranger among strangers. You will never be accepted here."

I called Clyde, and he found us a house to rent on Alabama Avenue. We moved to Fort Payne with the determination to build a home on that hill near the star. I reported to work with Clyde on Monday, April 12, 1965. That adventure is covered in my book, *The LAWyer*, page 170.

Clyde and I did very well. We were Traylor & French. I tried to persuade Clyde to take 55% of the partnership, and he refused. He wanted 50-50. I had been through problems with Ralph Williams, and I thought one of the partners ought to call the shots, but we remained equal. We worked 14 to 16 hours a day, 5 days a week, and sometimes 6 days a week.

We began to grow and needed more room. After due consideration, we built an office building on Nancy's property right at the courthouse. Clyde and I designed the building. It was exactly what we wanted. We put an extra office in it for Barksdale, whom I had promised to bring into the practice when he graduated from law school.

I practiced with Clyde until 1968. We dissolved over the fact I could not acquire any ownership in the building while I was paying half of the price of it. Nancy had financed it, as she was very wealthy being a Lennox Heating and Air Conditioning heir. The long and short of it was Clyde just couldn't stand to part with any piece of real estate.

Later, he became a judge and spent the last 20+ years of his life on the bench. He did a good job, I might add. In the meantime, I rented a small office across from the old Opera House and practiced there until I could buy a house on Alabama Avenue behind the courthouse. I planned to convert the house into an office building, and I did so later.

A lot of my early years in Fort Payne are described in my book, *Beaten, Battered and Damned, The Drano Murder Trial*. That book covers much of the price I paid for being a Republican.

SOLE PRACTITIONER

When I pulled out of the partnership, I was saved by Dave Tingle, Credit Manager of the Tennessee Corporation, a credit card company for farmers. It was also connected to City Service Corporation. Dave gave me the accounts that had been written off as uncollectable. I took them on a one-third contingent fee. There were millions of dollars involved, and I hired a girl to help Fay Freeman. She had been my secretary at Traylor & French and left the partnership when I did. We became bill collectors.

Fortunately, for us, the Tennessee Corporation big wheels did not realize that most farmers are honest as the day is long. They had been having some rough weather resulting in crop losses. They relied on their credit cards to finance the next crop, rather than relying upon the bank as they customarily did after a bad crop.

I wrote the debtors kind letters, understanding their predicament, while holding the possibility of a lawsuit that might cost them the farm over their heads. I was kind and worked out payment plans for them. I began collecting hundreds of thousands of dollars a year. The French family was doing well off collections. Everything else in the law practice was fluff.

Like every good thing, it is always too good to last. The President of the Company noticed that a non-descript lawyer, in podunk, was making more money a year than he was. He took the written off accounts in-house and failed to collect hardly anything like the success I had developed for his company.

Jerry Barksdale came to practice with me, but the building was too small. When Clyde and I had dissolved, I took our office building in Rainsville, while he took our stock in the new nursing home.   Rainsville   was begging for a lawyer, and Jerry moved into the building out there. The same day he opened our office, John Baker, from an old Democrat family, opened an office in Rainsville. We had competition from a well-known name. His father had been our State Senator. After a year or so, Jerry returned to Athens, his hometown, and opened a law office where he did very well. We have remained best friends all of these years.

The Tennessee Corporation had been a good ride for a little more than three years. By then, I had built up my practice so that I could convert the house into an office building. I had bought the property on credit right behind the courthouse. Somehow, someway, I got on the national circuit with fancy, big named lawyers, traveling the country. I began to take in large fees.

INDICTED!

About that time, the late 1960'S, the feds, primarily the revenuers, started an operation to stop illegal white whiskey in Alabama with the North End of Sand Mountain being directly in their sights. It was called, "Operation Dry-up."

It's signature Yellow and black bumper sticker was the words "Moonshine Kills" in the shape of a corpse lying on his back with a daisy sticking upward in his hand.

The revenue agents went to work with a vigor. The Great Cumberland Plateau had been known for its whiskey making since the white man came through the Cumberland Gap headed West. Until 1966, most people on the North End thought making whiskey was legal. They made it near their house and sold it in "town," Chattanooga.

Now the government was going to stop the illegal spirits once and for all. Earlier, when old time whiskey makers were caught, which was rare, they were slapped on the wrist and told to quit making. Now, if they were caught and convicted, they were going to federal prison.

During the crusade, I was fortunate to represent seven whiskey men. Each of them was a story unto itself. Usually, when the dogs barked, the bootlegger ran away from the still as fast as he could, and hid in the bushes of the forest. The Feds would chase them on foot if they could see them. Otherwise, they poured out the whiskey, sour mash and then dynamited the still. The bootlegger then had to visit another client of mine who made pots out of sheet metal and 2 X10's to start again. Most of the moonshiners bought their sugar from a merchant in Ider, Alabama, or from a wholesale company in Chattanooga.

Macon Weaver was the U.S. Attorney for the Northern District of Alabama. He and his staff tried all the whiskey cases. I don't believe he ever tried one by himself, but he did look in on every trial and sit at the prosecution table for a while.

My *modus operandi* in defending the whiskey makers was a detailed interview, a visit to the site of the still, find something totally insignificant that the revenuers missed and build a case out of that. Often the officer knew the bootlegger, but could not swear it was him at the still. Others chased the whiskey maker through the woods for a quarter of a mile and could not say who he was. Often there was mistaken identity that was fun to work with.

Then there was one little thing, "Officer. who was wearing those wavy soled shoes that left tracks that looked like a tractor tire?"

These were distinctive shoes at the time and if he couldn't remember the shoes, how could he possibly remember the man running from the still?

Or, my favorite, "Officer, I found where you folks were hiding in the old chicken house to observe the still. Which one of you had the peanut butter and jelly sandwich?" I had found the wrapper, and the agent could not remember who was eating the sandwich. And so, it went.

Macon Weaver said that no lawyer had ever beaten the government seven times in the Northern District of Alabama. I thought they were just fair game, good lawyering, luck, and sympathetic juries. Wrong. They never forgot.

Fast forward to the 1990's. The revenuers, now the high-sounding DEA, came after the dope dealers on Sand Mountain. The whiskey men had learned that it was easier to carry marijuana and cocaine somewhere than manhandling 100 pound bags of sugar through the woods. Whiskey making went out of vogue and dope dealing was the latest illegal money maker.

Being enterprising sorts, the marijuana dealers on Sand Mountain learned that wild hemp grew on the side of the road in ditches in Kansas. The difference in this hemp was that it did not contain *cannabis sativa L*, the ingredient that reacted on the septum of the brain and gave one the euphoric feeling. That didn't stop the Sand Mountain boys. They dispatched crews to Kansas to "harvest" the hemp growing road side, bring it back, and blend it with the hemp they had to pay for up the line. This doubled their profits.

Dope dealing became an epidemic. Sand Mountain dope dealers were supplying Chattanooga and somewhat in Atlanta. The Government had to do something.

Robert McGregor, Assistant U.S. Attorney in Birmingham, devised a program to put all the dealers out of business – "Operation Sand Storm." He ran undercover agents into the area, he made secret arrests and compromised the dealer to snitch out other dealers. Then, he secretly indicted Bob French. That was more than 10 years ago and I still do not know the grounds of the secret indictment.

Darrel Collins, Captain of the local Drug Task Force, told me that after he retired, he would tell me what went into my being indicted. Unfortunately, shortly after he retired, he passed away. So, I still don't know what happened. However, I do know why it happened.

McGregor and the FBI Agents were concerned that Bob French would defend the dope dealers and get some of them off. "Plus, he is hard to make a deal with because he does not represent informants."

Each time the agents arrested anyone, they would ask, "What lawyer are you going to use?"

If the perp said, "Bob French," the agent would say, "you're wasting your money there. We have him under indictment and he will be in prison before you are."

It worked like a charm. I did not get a single dope case during Operation Sand Storm. More than likely, their little trick cost me near half a million dollars in defense fees. Many old clients, who were out on bond, told me that they did not hire me because they feared I would be going to prison, and would not be able to defend their case.

When Operation Sand Storm shut down, McGregor dismissed the secret indictment against me.

I still have no idea what charge they used to get a secret indictment. I don't care. I beat them seven times in a row and it took them 30 years to get back at me.

I BELIEVE IN MIRACLES

In 1965, right after I partnered with Clyde, Walter Weatherly, a local banker, walked into my office and said, "Bob, I've checked you out. You are a man who is honest and willing to take a chance. If you ever need money, call on me for a loan."

I thanked him, as I did not need any money at the time. Not so, two days later. Eugene Crow came into my office and wanted to know if I knew anyone who might buy his lots on the brow of Lookout Mountain. There were six of them going down to a feather edge following a 40 line. He was asking $2,500 for them. We went outside the office, and he pointed to their location on the brow.

I told him to come back the next day and I would buy them.

I called Walter, and he loaned me the $2,500. I bought the property, and Celeste was so happy. Unfortunately, the best lot we bought only went back 219 feet from Scenic Road, not enough to cut some trees and have a view. But the Lord works in mysterious ways.

The next day, Ray Martin, a local jeweler, came into the office to make a deed to 100 feet on Scenic Road and a 40-acre tract down the mountain. He was disappointed that he did not have enough road frontage, but he was going through with the deal. He was buying it from Mr. Street, whose son had designed the Hyatt Hotel in Atlanta, which was revolutionary for its day and age.

I fixed the deed, Mr. Street signed, and I told Ray that I would give him 106 feet on Scenic road if he would give me 500 feet down the mountain. He agreed.

Celeste and I then owned 400 feet on Scenic Road and 719 feet down the mountain. We would have a view! Plus, we bought 212 feet north of us, giving us some 660 feet on Scenic Road. That property had 400+ feet down the mountain.

So, in less than a week, the Lord had provided our future home site.

In 1967 both the Martins and the Frenches built their houses on the brow of Lookout Mountain. We had a 30-mile view above the town. It has been like living on a Christmas tree. Celeste and I enjoyed it totally until she passed away in December, 2001. Since then, I have been living in a very large house with a standard poodle. It takes me two and one-half days to clean it every three weeks. I would not live in any other place in the world.

I still thank the Lord for blessing me with it on a daily basis. Because of the view, landscaping and additions, the house has increased in value more than 20 times what it cost Celeste and me to build it. Plus, the sunsets are indescribable.

MR. CIVIC MINDED

When I arrived in Fort Payne on April 12, 1965, lawyers could not advertise. They became well known through church or civic work.

Within a matter of weeks, I was teaching the Baraca Bible Class at First Baptist Church. The class had 120 members at the time. I taught it for 35 more years.

Dr. G.I. Weatherly invited me to a meeting of the DeKalb County Tourist Association. I didn't know it was election night and I was elected Chairman.

I mobilized the group and we were able to build the first Visitor's Welcome Center in Alabama. We put it where the Hampton Inn is now.

Because of that success I was elected President of the Northeast Alabama Farmer's Produce Market without being a member nor attending a meeting. The market was in a state of collapse due to internal fighting between the farmers and non-farmers. We took control of it and in two years had it back on its feet. In fact, we almost cornered the national super select cucumber market.

For these two great successes. I was named as one of Four Outstanding Young Men of Alabama by the Jaycees and listed as an Outstanding Young Man of America. So I was on a roll.

Fort Payne is one of the older Alabama Towns. Although John C. Payne built the Fort in 1838, Hernando de Soto had passed through the area in 1540 and Sequoyah had developed the Cherokee Alphabet in Wills Town, that would become Fort Payne, in 1821.

The town lays in a valley between Lookout Mountain and Sand Mountain. Between the two is Shinbone Ridge. From the air at night, the Fort Payne area looks like a giant scorpion.

The town is separated in almost one-half by the Norfolk-Southern Railroad. When rail transportation was the popular mode of travel Fort Payne was a hustling-bustling area.

When passenger travel stopped, the railroad station stayed vacant for years and eventually became a museum. Freights continued to lumber through the town honking and blowing as they thundered north or south.

Being young and energetic, I immediately noticed two things that needed to be rectified for the benefit of Fort Payne. 1. We needed to get rid of "Joe's Truck Stop," and 2. We needed a railroad overpass.

Alabama Highway 35 comes down Lookout Mountain and does a 90 degree right turn at the bottom of the grade. The road is steep and trucks with faulty brakes, or negligent drivers, cannot make the direct right turn at the base of the mountain. Trucks would wind up hitting the home of Joe Faulkner and his family located a little to the right of a direct line down Highway 35.

Eventually, Joe built a cement barrier about 4 feet high and 5 feet wide with steel girders implanted along its course. Once that was in place the runaway trucks would collide with the barrier with the usual result of the truck being destroyed and the driver either seriously hurt or killed. After I had seen two or three wrecks, I decided to do something about it.

Several times I saw ambulances waiting for the train to pass or move in order to get someone to the hospital.

During the Boom Days, when the town was settled the more affluent people located west of the railroad tracks. They built fine homes and the downtown area was located there. The professional people and the hospital was on the west side of town. The mill hands and less affluent folks built on the east side of town. When a train was parked on the tracks they were blocked off from city services. I decided to do something about that.

Sometime in 1967 I approached H. E. Collins, an Alabama State Trooper, who had connections in Montgomery. I proposed to Trooper Collins that the Alabama State Highway Department re-route Alabama Highway 35 to do away with Joe's Truck Stop and build an overpass over the railroad. Although it was an old idea, he thought it might work this time.

After several months, Trooper Collins called me and said, "Come see what I've got."

I met him at the railroad station. He had several rolls of prints from ALDOT (Alabama Department of Transportation). These prints showed Alabama Highway 35 coming off the mountain at a less steep grade and cutting across town behind the old hosiery mill over a railroad viaduct.

I could not believe it. "How on earth did you do this?"

He just grinned, "I have my ways. Now all you have to do is get permission from the railroad to go over their track, put the money together and the town is rid of Joe's Truck Stop and the trains that bring everything to a crawl."

I was thrilled. I drove down to Attalla, Alabama and met with the Division Superintendent of the railroad. I gave him our proposal to build a viaduct over the railroad.

The Superintendent liked the idea because it reduced the railroad's liability for people crossing the tracks when trains were coming. He would get back to me after he talked to the higher ups.

A couple of weeks later, I received a letter stating the conditions that the railroad would have to have to give the city permission to build the viaduct. Nothing there would prevent the project.

Collins had to return the drawings. However, I made a rough sketch of the project and with it, and the letter from the Superintendent, I went to the Mayor's office.

Mayor Purdy heard me out but he had little interest in the project.

"Bob, everyone has wanted a viaduct over the railroad for more than 50 years. We have never had the money for such a project."

I had anticipated that excuse. "I know, Mayor. That's why I have gone through our Senator in Washington and I have here the application for a government grant that will pay for 80% of the construction from the top of the mountain to the end of the viaduct. All we have to do is come up with 20%."

"And where are we going to get the 20%?"

"I suggest you pass a two mill sales tax and float tax free municipal bonds for the money."

"That's a great idea, but we have more pressing needs than a railroad viaduct. We need our sewage plant moved out of town. We need our water supply purified and upgraded. And I can go on and on. Your viaduct is low on our totem pole of needs."

I was so disappointed. But, being one who never gives up, I decided to change city hall.

At the time, Fort Municipal Elections were by party. They were always decided by the Democrat primary.

I recruited Jim Ellis, Frank Martin, Ed Westmoreland, Mary Nell Isbell and Ernest Thurman to run for City Council. I recruited my next door neighbor, Ray Martin to run for Mayor. It was a great ticket and our candidates ran hard. Our platform was the end of Joe's Truck Stop and a viaduct over the railroad tracks. Our motto was,

"It'sTime   For A   Change."

On August 13, 1968, we lost. Only Ernest Thurman was elected. I was so disappointed. Hoyt Wilson was elected Mayor.

That was the last city election based upon party lines. Subsequently, municipal elections were nonpartisan.

Now when a train is blocking the city for hours on end, or I hear a truck crash into Joe's Truck Stop from my deck on Lookout Mountain, I remember those days and think of what might have been.

THE OPERA HOUSE

I started devoting my civic work to saving the old Opera House. It was built in 1889 and was falling apart. My law office was directly across the street from the old building. Inside there was Black's Upholstery Shop, among other uses. It had a leaky roof and walls lacking plaster.

Paul Crow owned the building and was willing to sell it to me for $60,000. I had it appraised and it would take $30,000 to restore it. I didn't have that kind of money. Declining to buy it, I sat across the street and watched as it deteriorated.

The building was too beautiful to fall apart, but there was no way I could save it. Not with my Republican reputation.

I recruited my old friend, Betty Noel, and convinced her to head up the project. She said that she couldn't do it, but her mother, Lula Spears, a former school teacher, and Vera Beck might be persuaded to undertake the project.

Mrs. Beck, the wife, daughter and mother of prominent lawyers, was one of the most beloved women in Fort Payne. Along with Mrs. Weatherly, Ms. Spears, and some other interested ladies, Mrs. Beck began to recruit people to save the old building.

Walter Weatherly, James Ray Kuykendall, Hoyt Durham and others devoted time and energy to saving the old building. Eventually, they became a 501(c)(3),being "Landmarks of DeKalb County."

Betty Noel persuaded the owners of the Alabama Theatre in Birmingham to give the opera house its seats, stage sets and curtains when it was renovated. These items, along with some interior repairs and murals painted on the walls brought the old building back.

I take absolutely no credit for the restoration or saving the Opera House. All I can tell you is that in 1967, when I moved across the street from it, the building was falling apart. In 1970, it opened to the public almost completely restored. Some local folks worked very hard to save that building. I was not one of them.

In honor of my idea, Betty Noel and Lula Spears presented me with a huge tassel off the curtain of the Alabama Theater. That was reward enough.

COAL MINING

Roy Strickland, of Mentone, came into the office to organize a mining corporation. He and a friend had found a small seam of metallurgical coal on the East side of Lookout Mountain. They had been mining it by hand using rail and handcar. They were selling the coal for $12 a ton. They thought it was time to become a corporation.

I quoted a fee that he said was too high. Instead, he said that if I would organize the corporation, I could have one-third of the company. I agreed, and organized Lookout Mountain Mining Company, Inc., LMMC, for short.

The guys and some more men mined the coal. I kept the books and kept us legal. In order to do that, I had to acquaint myself with mineral and mining law. I went to every CLE available. I studied the subject voraciously, little knowing it would change my life.

Phillip Hale and his wife, Dorothy, were in the saddle making business in Henagar, Alabama. They walked into my office.

"Mr. Bob, me and Miss Dorothy want to go into the coal mining business, and we understand you know something about it."

I gave them a very lengthy interview. At the conclusion, although I advised against it, I agreed to draft a coal mining lease for them. I went to work on the document, and by the time I had covered all the bases, the lease ran more than a dozen pages.

Phillip Hale leased land everywhere he could find it. He then sub-leased to miners and people with heavy equipment. He single-handedly started a coal boom in Northeast Alabama, and it blew wide open.

I became the coal mining guru of the area. Every local lawyer, who was ever employed by a mining company, copied my lease.

Phillip and I bought rail property, built a 52-car siding, installed scales, a crusher, elevator, and other equipment. We were in the coal processing business, loading coal for international markets. Most of the coal we processed came from Phillip's leases; however, I was making a fortune from it.

The coal came across our scales, went to the crusher, was elevated into rail cars, and shipped to the State Docks in Mobile. There, it was dumped into ocean- going vessels and traveled to its final destination.

Phillip was a funny man. He sold a boat load of coal to the Government of France. He asked me to accompany him to New York to get his money. We went to the French Ligation near the very top of the World Trade Center. The officer in charge said that she would have a check cut for $6,000,000. Phillip said that he preferred cash.

The French said that they could not do that. Phillip said that we would wait. Four hours later, the lady counted out six million dollars, and we left New York with it in his briefcase. I expected to be robbed at any time. Fortunately, we made it to the airport and home without incident.

LMMC had closed down due to the seam narrowing down to nine inches. However, by this time I was representing the Cullinan Brothers out of Houston, Texas. Their Grandfather, was Buckskin Joe Cullinan, who had been a partner with John D. Rockefeller in founding Standard Oil of New Jersey.

After becoming filthy rich, he sold out to John D. and went to the Republic of Texas. As a geologist, he was convinced that oil could be found under a salt dome. He bought or leased every acre of land available in Texas. Spindle Top came in with a gusher.

Buckskin Joe went to Austin to organize an oil company. He discovered that the Texas Legislature had passed a law that all the minerals in Texas were the property of, and owned by, The Texas Company.

170

Unfortunately, the lawmakers never organized the company. Buckskin Joe did. Hello Texaco.

Of course, the powers that be negotiated with Buckskin Joe. He kept the name and one heck of a lot of mineral land in Texas. Later, he developed the first pipeline to carry oil. He developed the first tankers to carry oil by water. And, while he was at it, he passed through Northeast Alabama in a motor car, and thought there might be valuable minerals here.

He hired a crew, came in and bought 178,000 acres of mineral rights. He was then involved in litigation concerning the mineral rights for about 25 years.

The best I could tell, he wound up with clear title to 132,000 acres of mineral rights. I was hired by his grandsons, Joe and Craig, to administer those mineral rights. Thank the Good Lord, I was back in the big money again.

Their father had organized The American Republix Company, Maya, Corporation and many others. The Cullinans sold Texaco to "Bet-a-Million" Gates in, I believe, 1939. Joe, Jr., continued to operate the pipelines, rail lines and ocean-going vessels while Joe, II, and Craig became young men of leisure. Joe, II, lived on a yacht for more than 40 years. Craig busied himself around Houston dabbling in numerous businesses, but mostly playing golf at the Houston Country Club, where he was president now and then.

On one of my many trips to Houston, Joe took me to the Petroleum Club and Craig took me to the polo club. The Houston Polo Club may have been the most hoi-hoi place I had ever been in up to that point. Craig and I also played golf at the Houston Country Club – fancy, but no Polo Club.

An aside: Once, I was called to come to Dallas to do some work for Lamar Hunt. I believe he owned the Kansas City Chiefs football team at the time. Now, he had to turn his attention to some mineral interests of H.L. Hunt Oil Company. We were meeting in the Dallas Petroleum Club on the top floor of the First National Bank Building. You could smell money in the air. Another Hunt brother joined us, and Peter Hunt was supposed to be in the meeting.

Lamar said that his brother, Peter, was too busy attending to the hot food line of the club. There was something wrong with a steam table. Millionaires at work.

Anyhoo, we were working when a well uniformed man came to the table. "Mr. French, you have a call." He handed me the telephone.

I recognized Joe's voice, "Where the hell are you?"

"I'm in Big D."

"What the hell are you doing there?"

"I'm doing some work for the Hunt brothers."

"Them farts. You better watch 'em. Call me when you're clear."

I thought that only a man who would have huge shrubs planted in his front yard to avoid seeing Governor John Connally's home would have the tenacity to call the Hunt brothers "farts."

ANOTHER BRUSH WITH THE LAW

On New Year's Eve, 1979, I received a call to come to Mobile to represent some people who had been arrested for running a sloop loaded with marijuana aground in Pirate's Cove in Baldwin County.

I flew in to Bate's Field on the day after New Year's Day, and rented a car. I arrived in Bay Minette in time for the nine people captured to appear for their initial bond hearing. I learned that I would be representing 7 of the 9 people arrested. All of them were charged with various drug offenses. They had bondsmen from Miami on site to make their bonds.

172

Seems this sailing sloop had left Columbia with more than 7 tons of marijuana on board. The captain the vessel, named the Cher, was Danny O'Leary. Two of the others arrested were members of his crew. Laurette Martin, Raul Oyarzun and a few others were just around the site when the officers seized the vessel. I did not represent Ms. Martin, nor the alleged king pin of the operation, Michael Sava.

Michael Sava made bond and disappeared. Seems he was wanted for other bond violations in Florida.

I defended 7 of the 9 and won all cases except the last one where the state offered to let the defendant plead guilty to simple possession.

Judge Harry Wilters was so fed up with me and my courtroom antics that when he called my 6th defendant, Howard Clark, I answered.

"Judge, we're ready. I have a motion."

"Mr. French.. I fin d you in contempt of court. Sheriff take him to jail!"

The packed courtroom was stunned. I went with the Sheriff. When I got to the jail and met the jailer, a fat deputy who wore a belt and suspenders, I knew I was in trouble.

He scowled at me and said, "Sit down and shut up."

Around 3:00 p.m., some lawyers told Judge Wilters that they were going to sign my bond and he released me. The case was moved to Mobile and I won the case.

Clark, like Oyarzun and Martin, was just at the Holiday in to have breakfast.. Although they knew Mike Sava, they were not involved in the smuggling operation.

Danny O'Leary was convicted and I appealed his case all the way to the U.S. Supreme Court where we won it.

Oyarzun was a psychologist for the State of Alabama. They dismissed the charges against him.

Laurette Martin got a hung jury and the state declined to prosecute her.

The Sheriff and District Attorney stole a lot of the marijuana taken from the Cher, were caught, and both sent to prison.

Fast forward several years, more than 10 years, when I received a call from a client in North Carolina. I had been up there representing the inventor of the plastic zip lock bag. His invention had been stolen from him. We were unable to get his invention back for him. Now, a man with an unfamiliar name wanted to see me.

The potential client had come up with a unique idea. He built a three story office building in Wilmington that housed 20 or 30 offices. The offices surrounded a large open area. In the center of the open area, there was a secretarial pool, attendants, and whatever necessary to run an office. Thus, an Electrolux Vacuum Cleaner salesman could rent a one room office. The receptionist answered his calls and took messages. The secretary typed his letters on his letterhead, and a gentleman would accompany visitors to his office. It was a great idea and immediately successful.

In addition, the unfamiliar named person was in the solar power business. His company urged people to install solar units on their homes and claim a $1,400 tax deduction which the government had put in place to encourage solar energy.

The building management had an office on the second floor while next door, the solar power company had an office.

I went to the office building and met the gentleman in the conference room. He needed legal help because customers of solar units were complaining that the government was not giving them their $1,400 deduction. It was his opinion that they were filling out their tax forms

174

incorrectly. The president of the solar company would be my client.

I went up to the solar office and met the president of the company. We discussed problems and he showed me the papers that he had been served. He had a hearing coming up later in the week.

There was a local lawyer hired on the case and had done all the work. "But, Mike wants you to try the case."

"I don't know Mike."

"Yes you do. The man you have been talking with is Michael Sava. He just uses phony names."

I was floored. I had never met Michael Sava. I had seen him in the jury box with other defendants the day they made bond in Bay Minette, Alabama, but I did not remember him.

Long story short, Buford, the manager, went to court with me and the other lawyer. We tried the first case. I made the plaintiff admit he had not filled out his taxes correctly to get the deduction. The judge threw out his case and several more that were pending.

I was paid a nice fee and went back to Alabama.

I'm sitting in my office fat, dumb and happy when the phone rings. It was Laurette Martin. She had married and was living in St. Augustine, Florida.

After preliminary pleasantries, she said, "That guy Buford, you met. He reported Mike to the feds, and Mike is in custody facing a minimum of 10 years. He took his phone call to call me to tell me to get you to go to his office building in Wilmington and destroy all his records before the feds raid the office."

"I'm not about to destroy any records, but I will meet you in Wilmington this afternoon and see what we can do for him." I knew she would have to charter a private plane and I would fly my Baron up there. We could get together by 2:30 p.m.

Laurette met me at the airport in a rental car. We drove directly to the office building.

She said, "I have a master key. Do you want to go into Mike's office?"

"No, but I would like to go into the solar energy office."

We went into the office and, just as I thought, thinking like a criminal, I found all of Sava's files in the solar paneling file drawers mixed among solar file folders.

"Get a garbage bag."

She got a big black plastic garbage bag. We loaded all of Sava's files into that bag. She drove me back to the airport and I landed in Fort Payne with the files.

No. 1, I was betting that the FBI would not have a warrant for the solar energy office. Later, it was proven they didn't. No. 2, if they contacted me demanding the files, I would claim attorney work product as I needed them to defend any other solar claims. I might eventually lose the battle, but what did they need his solar files for if he was arrested as a fugitive from justice? They had no evidence that he had been doing anything illegal while on the run. He couldn't afford to.

It was winter time and we had a fire in the den fireplace. I told Celeste of my trip and showed her the garbage bag of files.

She said, "Bob, I don't like this a little bit. Let's not look at those files, but rather burn them. That way, we know nothing about what was in the files."

We burned the files sight unseen. I figured Sava didn't need them anyway. They would all be out-of-date by the time he got out of prison.

Two years go by. Sitting in my office, you know the score, FD&H, the phone rings.

Laurette Martin is on the other line with her lawyer and the FBI. She is being detained for something to do with her husband, Bruce Walther. She tells me that I am being recorded and the FBI wants to know what happened to Michael Sava's files. I told her to tell them whatever the truth is, but I am not talking with them. She said that she had already told them that I got them. I told her that she could tell them whatever she pleased. Good bye.

A couple of days later, I received a call from the Wilmington Office of the FBI. Agents would like to come to Alabama and talk with me. I told them, I would save them a trip, I would come to Wilmington.

We met in a vacant room with a table and six chairs. Four agents were going to question me.

The Agent in Charge said, "You are Robert B. French, Jr., and you live in Fort Payne, Alabama?"

"Yes, and before we go any further, I am going to place my tape recorded in the center of this table so there will be no mistakes as to what my answers to your questions are."

I started my little tape recorder and put it in the center of the table. Two other agents took their tape recorders out of their pockets and placed them close to mine.

After some preliminary generic questions, the agent got down to business.

"When were you last in Michael Sava's office?"

"I've never been in his office."

"You were in his office on such and such a date and you took his files out in a black garbage bag."

"I will tell you once more. I have never been in his office."

"Do you know the geographic location of his files at this time?"

"I do not."

"Do you have the files or know who has them?"

"I do not."

"If I get a warrant and search your property will I find those files?"

"You don't need a warrant. Come search away. You will not find any files other than mine."

"If you do not know where the files are, how do you explain Laurette Martin saying that you and she loaded them in Sava's office and you flew off with them?"

"I have never been in Sava's office."

"Have you ever reviewed Sava's files?"

"No."

That was it, short and sweet. I sure was glad Celeste insisted on burning the files without looking at them. That way, every word I told the feds was the truth.

Later, they sent an agent to Fort Payne to sniff around and see if he could locate any information that would tie me to Sava. Of course, there was none. But, we do exchange birthday and Christmas cards every year.

JOHN WAYNE

Jay Curtis, an attorney from Salt Lake City, Utah, represented Utah Light and Power Company. He had been down in Northeast Alabama trying to determine if a spin-off mining company might have any interest in mining in Alabama. He disappeared for a while, then out of the blue, he called me.

"Bob, John Wayne, the movie star, needs mining advice. He only trusts Mormons, and he called one of his bear hunting buddies, the President of Utah Light and Power, for advice. He immediately saw an advantage for their independent mining company. Therefore, I can't help him.

"Mr. Wayne said that if a Mormon he trusts couldn't help him, he would like a small town Southern lawyer. I thought of you. Can you go out to his home in New Port Beach, California, and meet with him, the mining company, their lawyer, and enter into a lease?"

178

Of course, I agreed. And the next thing I knew, John Wayne's agent, Curly Powell, was on the phone, arranging for me to come out to California.

The private jet landed in the snow for the first time in 50 years in New Port Beach, California. I was met at the airport and taken to the home of John Wayne. It was a non-descript looking house from the front, but once you were inside, it was unbelievable.

The house had a foyer that led to a theater on the right. He had every Winchester rifle ever made hanging on the walls. It was a very comfortable theater with the screen coming down out of the ceiling. It would seat about 40 people. His Oscar was on a stand in the front of the room.

To the left of the foyer was the bedroom wing, and straight ahead was the living room. It was huge, all glass, looking out on his mine sweeper, anchored in the bay. To the right of the great room was a botanical garden dividing the house from his offices. Sitting on the couch one could watch the people working in the other wing of the house. In the front of the theater was a door leading to a huge pantry. Going down the hallway to the right was the kitchen, dining room, etc. A hallway to the far right led to his business offices.

I never did see the entire house. Arriving at night, I met Mr. Wayne. He was not as tall as the movies seemed to portray him, and he was mostly bald. When I got up early the next morning, I went into the theater. The people from Utah were already there, as well as their attorney and a local attorney to kinda keep Mr. Wayne up with what was going on.

After a short breakfast, we went right to work. Mr. Wayne had discovered a huge rock-like formation on his ranch in Nevada. I understood he owned 35,000 acres. This seemingly rock was more than a quarter of a mile long and was submerged in the earth more than 250 feet. It was larger than Alice Rock in Australia. Curly Powell had the chalky material engineered, and it would not burn at 3,000 degrees. When ground into a power and mixed with water, it became a glue-like substance.

Mr. Wayne had been allowing an excavator to mine a little of it. They called it Acra-Lite. The miner had been selling his production to miners to spray on the top of underground mines. It kept down falling debris from the roof of mines. He also sold it to highway departments to hold the debris back from the main traveled paved portion of the roadway.

The dark substance holding the cut debris back is concrete. The very white substance is Acra-Lite. You'll see it. It is everywhere.

We were deep into minimum tonnages per day, advance royalties, accrued royalties, payments, reclamation, you-name-it. We were negotiating a mining lease.

John Wayne said, "I need to talk to my lawyer. Alabama Bob, come with me."

We went into the pantry.

He said, "Do you know Bear Bryant?"

"Yes, sir."

"Do you know what he drinks?"

"Screwdriver."

"Correct, and so do I. How about you? If I say I need to talk to my lawyer, will you join me for a pull off the jug?"

I said that I would.

He contacted someone who came to the other end of the pantry. "Fill up a jug of Salty Dogs."

We went back into the negotiations, and in a few minutes, Mr. Wayne needed to converse with his lawyer again. We went into the pantry and he poured me up a Salty Dog in a glass autographed by Mary Pickford. We repeated this procedure one more time before breaking, and going to the John Wayne Country Club for lunch. I rode with him in a Buick Station Wagon, custom built, so that he could wear his cowboy hat when he drove.

He got no peace through the meal. Dozens of people came over wanting autographs or just to say hello. However, he was congenial and did not turn anyone away. He'd just lay his fork down and take care of whatever was going on -- a very gracious man.

He let me hold and examine has Oscar. It was heavy.

By mid-afternoon, we had the lease hammered out to everyone's satisfaction. A lady dressed in black leather took our work to the office to put it in final form.

After another Salty Dog, the entire group went to await the clerical work in the living room. We are sitting around the spacious room talking when John Wayne jumped up.

"Damn! That dog is shittin in my botanical garden! I'll kill that son-of-a-bitch!"

I looked out and there was a German Shephard, named "Dog," relieving himself among the botanical plants.

Away John Wayne went to the foyer. He grabbed the first walking stick he could out of a canister of them. The one he selected was pure jade, carved with dragons, up and down. It had been given to him by the Emperor of Japan.

He ran out the door toward the garden, around the corner, trying to kill Dog. It seemed Dog might have seen this act before because he took off toward the ocean. John Wayne flailing away with the jade walking stick could not catch him.

Curley Powell said, "Gentlemen, kindly observe an American Legend chasing a shittin dog with a $30,000 jade walking cane. You won't see this often."

When I was completing my representation of John Wayne, everyone was celebrating that the transaction had been completed, the documents signed, the advance royalties had been paid, and it was time to leave. It had been a very successful trip. My pilot was ready to fly me home.

The president of the new mining corporation, that had signed the lease to mine the minerals on Mr. Wayne's Nevada ranch said, "Gentlemen, we thought this might be a successful negotiation. In celebration of this event, we had Cartier, of New York, strike seven solid silver belt buckles. I want to give one to Mr. Wayne, I'll have one, and our officers will have one."

John Wayne interrupted, "Give Alabama Bob one of those buckles."

I couldn't believe it. The buckle was an original silver eagle, struck especially for the occasion, never to be repeated. It was a very large piece of silver, perhaps 7 ounces, with a unique eagle head displayed, and "Cartier" stamped on the back.

The president of the new corporation looked over at me and pitched the light blue flannel Cartier sack containing the silver buckle to me.

I had an idea of the value of the buckle, and I knew the importance of the lease we had just signed, to I thanked him profusely. I thanked Mr. Wayne for considering me, and I looked at the magnificent buckle.

The buckle became my most prized possession because John Wayne had thought enough of me to get one of the very expensive buckles for me. I prized it so much that I very rarely wore it because I was afraid something might happen to it.

Several years passed by. My dear friend Jerry Barksdale came over to see me. At that time, we were pilgrims on the spiritual path, and very seriously pursuing the spiritual life. Somehow, we found ourselves in Eddy Brown's bedroom, on Sand Mountain, above Trenton, Georgia. We began discussing the aspects of the spiritual life. I was deep into writing my book explaining the Gospel of John at the time. I would later publish it as *An Adventure with John.*

I pointed out that quality is how slowly a thing wears out. Everything a person owns is wearing out – some more slowly than others. Yet, all possessions demand attention constituting an impediment on the spiritual path.

Jerry agreed with me. "If that is the case, and I truly believe that it is, then one might make great strides on our journey, if one could divest himself of the thing he treasured most. Because, as you say, that possession is draining our attention every time it crosses the mind, or must be attended to. What's your most prized possession, Bob?"

thought long and hard. I had many treasures, a Porsche, an airplane, property on an island in the Gulf, a great law office among others. I could do without all those things, but my most prized possession was something very few people knew about – my John Wayne belt buckle.

"My most prized possession is the 7-struck Cartier belt buckle given to me at John Wayne's house in Newport Beach, California."

"Could you part with it if it was hindering your progress on the spiritual path?"

"I believe I can do it. It will be very difficult, but I'll give it to Eddie."

"That's mighty strong, Bob. I don't know that I could do it, Jerry responded.

Brown interjected. "In that case, I will give Jerry my most cherished possession."

He went to his gun cabinet and brought out a Browning .44 magnum 9" pistol. "This has never been fired," he said handing the pistol to Barksdale.

Jerry admired the pistol. "Are you sure you want to do this, Eddie?"

"If French can give up his buckle, which I have never seen, the least I can do is get rid of this jewel, because I love it, and have never seen one like it."

Jerry said, "I'm sorry, I do not know what my most prized possession is. Right now, I don't have one. Perhaps this pistol Eddie gave me will become mine."

We left, and I was feeling released from the selfishness that caused me to look at that buckle now and then, and admire it, and be happy to own it. I was determined to deliver it to Edie Brown.

A couple of days later, I was going to see Eddie. I decided to give him the buckle then. I took the buckle from my jewelry box and admired it. I couldn't give it up. I looked through my buckles and found a very nice eagle buckle. I put it in my pocket.

When I saw Brown, I said, "Hey Eddie, here's my most prized possession." I handed him the buckle.

"That's a beautiful buckle, Bob. I really appreciate receiving your John Wayne buckle."

He took off his buckle, put it in his pocket, and put the new eagle buckle I gave him on his belt, and cinched it up.

We went about whatever we were going to do. However, I knew that he knew that was not the John Wayne buckle I had given to him. That bothered me. I was a fraud and a failure on the spiritual path. I was not only too attached to a physical item, I had lied about it. Horrible.

A few days later, I was with Eddie again. "Here, this is the real John Wayne buckle. I'm giving it to you. Give me my old buckle back."

Brown laughed and admired the silver eagle he was holding in his hand. "I knew you did not give me the John Wayne buckle. Now I have the real thing. It's beautiful. Thanks. I'm not going to put it on. It's too nice to wear with jeans."

Time went by. I felt better about the entire situation. I saw Brown again. He was wearing the old buckle.

"Hey. I want the old eagle back. You have the John Wayne buckle."

"No. You gave me this phony buckle, and every time you see it, I want you to remember your weakness when it came to parting with a prized physical possession."

Lesson well learned. It has now been 25 years. Brown still has both buckles, and still wears what he calls, "Bob's weakness buckle." I doubt he has ever worn the John Wayne Buckle. However, I did notice, the last time he showed it to me, that the light blue flannel Cartier sack it was carried in was worn threadbare. He must Look at it and show it a lot.

Barksdale gave the Browning pistol to his best friend, Glenn Duncan of Laramie, Wyoming.

Taking away my most prized possession had benefits. At the time, I was living a monk's life, meditating at dawn and late in the evening. I did not smoke, drink, nor eat heavy meals. I was running almost 4 miles a day, studying spiritual masters, going to spiritual conferences (As far away at Hawaii), and writing spiritual essays.

One morning I went into an especially deep meditation, into a separate reality, where I experienced the afterlife. I was in a silvery-blue environment. I was nothing, not a spirit, a body nor anything other than an awareness. I knew all my loved ones and friends, but did not see them, nor care to see anyone. It was just a very joyful existence.

I was aware there was a guide for me. I communicated with the guide, "What do we do here?"

The invisible guide said, "In the distance, there is a beautiful light?"

I could experience the most beautiful light imaginable in the distance. It lit up everything.

"The Light is God. You are in the 4th Heaven. Here we seek to merge with the Light and become part of the Creator creating everything."

Once I came out of the meditation and returned to the reasonable, rational world of the senses, I was forever secure in knowing my fate. I had never thought that death is all there is here because God does not create waste. Further, I am a devout Christian and a follower of Jesus Christ. Now, I was totally secure. I had seen the other side, and I realized that my soul had forever been, is now, and will forever will be. Comforting.

Another morning I was in deep meditation, very deep meditation, and I had another earth shattering experience. Out of nowhere I heard the sound of the universe. It was the most beautiful sound I had ever heard. I can't describe it. It was exquisite and lasted about 30 seconds.

After hearing that sound, I went to the books to see if anyone else had ever heard such a beautiful sound. I found that many writers had experienced the joy of the sound.

They called it, "The Sound of The Universe." One writer said that it is the noise made by time cutting through space. Very few people ever hear it, but it is there, 24 hours a day 7 days a week, always was and forever will be.

I not only survived the lesson of the buckle, I genuinely profited from divesting myself of my most prized worldly possession.   Question - is it failure to hope Brown will give it to my grandson after I'm gone? Maybe.

NELSON ROCKEFELLER

I got a call from my old friend, Charles Wilson.

"Bob, Governor Nelson Rockefeller would like to meet with you."

"What on earth about?"

"I have no idea. He called me and asked if you could meet his 707 in Rome, Georgia tomorrow, and fly to St. Louis with him. He needs your advice."

The following day, I watched the 707 land at Russell field in Rome. The stairs were in place, and up, and into the airplane I went. It taxied away and took off. A young lady ushered me into the Governor's office. To say it was fancy would be an understatement. He was sitting behind his desk. He got up, shook my hand, and motioned for me to sit down. Although he is long gone, I will honor his memory by failing to discuss our business.

However, I will say that when we had concluded what I was on board for, we were nearing St. Louis. There was little else to talk about.

So, I asked him, "Governor, what's it like to be one of the richest men in the world?"

"Well, Bob, how many rooms does your house have?"

"Sixteen, if you count the foyer."

"At Hyde Park, my house has 32 rooms. How many rooms can you be in at once?"

"One."

"Funny thing. I can only be in one at a time, myself. How many cars do you have?"

"Four."

"I have six favorites. How many cars can you ride in at one time?"

"One."

"Funny thing. I might have 10 or 12 cars available to me, but I can only ride in one at a time. So, you see there is very little difference between you and me. Perhaps it is a matter of degrees. But in America, almost anyone who will try, can live like the richest man in the world."

We landed in St. Louis, said our goodbyes, and I disembarked the 707, to be met by a pilot of a Leer Jet, who would fly me back to Rome. As I sat alone in the beautiful little private jet, I thought, "Yeah, it's only a matter of degrees." Is this country great, or what?

CHAPTER THIRTEEN
BIG TIME POLITICS

At the 1968 Republican National Convention in Miami, I was director of transportation for the entire Alabama Delegation. That meant I got to breathe a lot of diesel fumes.

Celeste, Michelle, and I also got to experience great adventures in Miami, particularly with the wild and crazy anti-war demonstrators. I was also a delegate leader for Richard Nixon and worked with his inner-circle pretty closely. Many of the insiders were old Young Republicans I had known in 1964.

We went to the nomination, and Nixon won. Then, we went into the election, and he won again. Now he was back! He was President of the United States! A lot of my friends were grabbing for positions in the new administration.

FOGGY MOUNTAIN BREAKDOWN

I received a personal invitation to attend President Nixon's inauguration. I didn't want to go, but it was an honor, and I had been given a personal invitation to attend. By the time it was time to leave, I had the flu. I was so sick I could hardly move; however, he had our reservations, airline tickets, the works, and everything ready to go.

I barely made it to the Birmingham Airport, then I could barely take our ride to the Marriott in D.C. We were on the 6th floor, and I went right to bed. I couldn't hold my head up. I'm laying there asleep, sick as a mule, and the fire alarm went off!

Celeste ran out into the hallway. She was told to go down the steps to the lobby. The fire was on the third floor.

Celeste came back into the room.   "Bob! You've got to get up and go down to the lobby. The building is on fire!"

"Celeste, I can't. I just don't have the strength. I can't get out of bed."

She was frantic. She ran back into the hallway. She met two men in the room next to ours.

"Please, sir's, my husband is very ill and he cannot go down the stairs. Would you please help me?"

The men said that they would do their best. They came into the room, and stripped the bed with me on it. They took two sheets, one on the other, and laid me on the sheets. They then proceeded to carry, and drag me to the stairs, and then down to the lobby – bump, bump, bump -- six floors down.

When they got me on a couch in the lobby, they were wringing wet with sweat and exhausted. They collapsed in some chairs nearby.

There were firemen everywhere with hoses running up the stairs. Cops were directing people where to go and what to do. I was practically in a trance.

After a few minutes, Celeste went over to the men who had saved me, and asked their names. They were Lester Flatt and Earl Scruggs of country music fame. Thankfully, I was saved by banjo pickers.

The third-floor fire was put out, and I struggled to the elevator, wrapped in the sheets. Celeste re-made the bed, and we were just about as well off as we had been.

The following day was the inauguration. Celeste went with some friends and marched in the parade and took in the inaugural address. I stayed in bed. That night I forced myself into my tux, and we went to the inaugural ball at the Smithsonian. We were with all the ambassadors and foreign dignitaries. The President and Pat came by, he waved, and I was ready to go home.

Of course, we had many other adventures on the trip, but I learned one thing: A person has to go to only one inauguration. No one can force you to go to another one.

A couple of days later, Bill Timmons, an old Young Republican with Bill Brock out of Chattanooga, called me.

"The President wants to know what you want?"

"Good government."

"No, really. Do you want to be a department head? What do you want? I'm working in the White House. Our other friends are taking over big jobs with 700 or more employees. What would you like?"

I saw that the conversation was going nowhere.

"I'll tell you what. I want a pair of those gold Presidential seal cufflinks. That'll be enough reward for me."

Timmons said, "Okay. That's mighty light, but you'll get them."

A few days later, I received one of the treasures of my life – Presidential golden cufflinks. Funny thing – when President Nixon was reelected, he sent me the tie clasp to go with them.

The President was not through with me. He had people contact me about judgeships, U.S. Attorney jobs, and other Federal appointments, I didn't want any of them.

I was happy to get a Christmas Card. Before it was over, I had received, I think, 18 White House Christmas cards. I still have them somewhere.

BREAKFAST IN THE OVAL OFFICE

During President Nixon's first term, I was sitting in my office, fat, dumb and happy, when the phone rang.

Fay Freeman buzzed me. "The Post Master General is on the line."

I had known Winton Blount from years back. Celeste and I had attended functions in his Montgomery mansion. He had sent me stamps commemorating the moon landing. He included exclusive photographs of the astronauts on the moon, along with a very nice letter.

I picked up the phone. "Yes, sir?"

"Bob, the President wants to see you next Thursday. He did not say what about. He just told me to contact you and escort you to Washington. A jet can't land at Fort Payne; the runway is too short. How about meeting me in Rome, Georgia at 3:00 p.m. next Thursday?"

I agreed, we said our goodbyes, and I wondered what was going on.

At the appointed time, a West Wind, a fairly large private jet, landed at Russell field. The stairs came down, I went up, and I met the Post Master General of the United States. We visited, had a drink, and flew into Dulles in D.C. We disembarked in a governmental hangar, boarded a long, black limousine, and I was deposited where else? The Marriott, of course.

At 7:00 a.m. the following morning, the limo was waiting for me when I exited the motel. The Post Master General was in the back seat. We were driven to the White House, and directed to the Oval Office. The President was there along with Attorney General John Mitchell. There were one or two others there that I did not know.

The President welcomed me like long-lost buddies and introduced me to the men I didn't know. I knew Attorney General John Mitchell as we had worked together at the Convention in Miami.

The President said, "Bob, we have some business to attend to, but first let's have breakfast."

He pushed a button, some people appeared from the kitchen staff, and they rolled in metal tables with breakfast on them. Chairs were produced, and we had breakfast. I thought it was quite an experience and wondered if it happened often.

After breakfast, everyone left the room other than John Mitchell, Red Blount, the President, and myself.

The President began, "Bob, I'll get right to the point. Several years ago, maybe 1957, the Congress created a Civil Rights Division of the Justice Department. This department has finally been funded, and the pressure is on for it to be established.

"Now that we are in the throes of the Civil Rights movement, the pressure is on the White House to implement the law and create the division. I have thought long and hard about it, discussed it with John and Winton, and we would like for you to be the Deputy Attorney General in charge of the new Civil Rights Division of the Justice Department."

I was more than flabbergasted. I was amazed.

I said, "Mr. President, I am not capable of such a job. I am really just a small-town southern lawyer from Fort Payne, Alabama."

He responded, "That's exactly why we want you to have the job. We expect substantial problems in the South and I need someone who knows the lay of the land."

"Sir, that is a big undertaking. I will have to talk with my wife about that. Can I have 24 hours?"

John Mitchell chimed in, "Oh, we didn't expect an answer today. Just let us know if you will take the job in the next few days."

Somehow, I managed to keep from passing out, and put on my best act of being totally in control of my emotions. We said our farewells. Red Blount took me to the limo, said for me to think long and hard about serving my country, wished me well, and I was off to the airport.

Celeste was all excited when I got home. I told her about the trip, word for word. She thought about it.

"That is a signal honor. I am so proud that you were considered for the job. However, remember this, if you take the job, we can never come home.

"We will have to move to Washington. That means taking Michelle to a new school, selling our home, and buying something in D.C. Further, this job is going to require enforcing the Civil Rights Laws against the South. You will never be able to come home again. Let's think about it overnight."

The following morning, Celeste said, "Bob, we can't do it. We will be totally relocating for perhaps a little more than 3 years. We have no guarantee President Nixon will live out his term or that he will be re-elected. We just can't do it."

I agreed. For the second time in my life, I had turned down the opportunity of a lifetime. I called Post Master General Blount, and asked him to convey my fondest appreciation for the opportunity that I had been provided, but I must respectfully decline.

Winton Blount was disappointed. However, he said that he understood.

The President made one last offer – a federal judgeship. I declined and did not hear from him again. Had I taken the job, Watergate would have ruined me. Again, the Lord works in mysterious ways.

ARNOLD PALMER

Sometime in the spring of 1970, Roland called me and wanted to go play a golf course he had discovered in Orlando. One of Roland's great adventures in life was finding out-of-the-way golf courses to play. His favorite was Hidden Hills in Jacksonville. We played there many times. He discovered EagleVail in Colorado, and then we played Sawgrass before it was Sawgrass. Now he had a new discovery, so we loaded up in his airplane a little before dawn, and away we went.

We rented a car at the airport and drove on Doctor Phillips Drive, through what I thought was a never-ending orange grove. We arrived at a nondescript white clapboard, concrete block, clubhouse. A small sign said, "Bay Hill Country Club." I thought, "Yeah, some country club."

Still, it was a golfing adventure.

We couldn't locate a pro shop. So we went into the white concrete block building and discovered it was a small restaurant. We paid our green fees at the cash register and ordered breakfast. There were only four, perhaps five, tables in the place. To call it sparse is generous. It was practically vacant.

Our breakfast came, and we were prepared to dig in.

Just then, Arnold Palmer walked in. Since we were the only people there, other than the cashier, he came over.

"Mind if I join you guys for breakfast?"

I thought Roland was going to wet himself with joy. "We'd be honored to have your company, Mr. Palmer," he gushed.

"Call me Arnie. You guys got a game? You are the only ones here."

"We have a tee time in 35 minutes. We've never played here before and are looking forward to it," I responded.

"What about me joining you? I have driven out here just to look around, but since you are here, we might as well tee it up."

Of course, we were overjoyed to have the opportunity to play with the Number One Player in the World.

Roland could hardly contain himself. "It would be our most distinct pleasure to play with you!"

The three of us finished our breakfast, had another cup of coffee, and went to #1 Tee.

While at breakfast, Arnold Palmer had told us that he was about to sign a lease-purchase agreement on the course. Seems he had played it several times in the past and enjoyed it. In fact, he had played Jack Nicklaus and beat him here. He had also won the Citrus Open in Orlando earlier.

It seems that he had committed to lease the course for some five years and, if satisfied with it, he would buy it at a predetermined price. He felt like he might accelerate the lease and buy it earlier as he had envisioned great things for the place once he had it the way he wanted it.

We talked about the purchase and his plans as we played. I let Roland drive his cart and ride with him because I knew it meant more to him to be with the legend.

We came around to #5. This was a par 5-hole green that you could see from the tee box. However, the alluring green was across a lake. Arnold said, "Don't be fooled by that view, boys. You can't cut across that lake until your second shot. It looks tempting, but it is an optical illusion."

With that, I teed it up, and drove one about 280 yards tracking the lake while remaining about 10 yards from the water. Roland and Palmer drove down the center of the fairway. They were away looking across the narrow spit of water that we now had to cross. They hit their second shorts, and came over to watch me hit mine.

While I was lining up my shot, a mallard duck flew over and landed in the lake. I stopped, and the three of us watched the duck begin to swim. Just then, there was a big squawk, and feathers flew everywhere landing on the surface of the lake. Then, we saw him for just an instant. An alligator had grabbed that duck!

We were amazed, and talked about that experience for several holes. Neither of us birdied that par

5. However, we all had pars. We kept looking for that alligator.

As we finished the 18 and were removing our clubs from our carts, some men involved in leasing the property to Arnold Palmer came out of the club house.

One rather larger business suit said, "How'd you shoot, Arnie?"

"Not too good. I once shot about a 65 here, but today's was more like a 75." Actually, he shot a 73, but who's counting?

"Oh, that's not bad," the big guy replied. "If I could shoot a 75 here, I would be very excited."

Arnold turned a little sour. "The only excitement I had out there today was I saw an alligator eat a fucking duck."

With that, we said our goodbyes, loaded up, and left with a lifelong memory. Interestingly, every time we saw Arnold Palmer after that, he always pointed his finger toward us.

After he bought Bay Hill and improved it, Roland and I made it an annual ritual to go down there at least one weekend a year. One or two years, we took our families.

Shortly before Roland died, we made our last pilgrimage to Bay Hill. It was now a 4-star resort, and we enjoyed it greatly. We asked about Mr. Palmer and were told he was flying in later in the morning from Latrobe, Pennsylvania.

Tiger Woods was there hitting practice balls. The Saturday shootout was ready to start. There were about fifty golfers gathered around the first tee, including Roland and me.

We would soon be divided into foursomes for the competition. It didn't matter who you were or how you played, you were designated into a foursome by the starter. If you were a professional, you were penalized a certain number of strokes to bring you down to the average golfer in the shootout. Everyone turned in their handicap, and the shootout was very fair.

Everyone was anxious to get started when Arnold Palmer arrived. Roland and I heard him say to the starter, "Joe, can you get me off early? I have business later today."

The starter, a big black guy dressed in Bay Hill coveralls and cap replied, "Mr. Palmer, you can start anywhere and anytime you want to; you own this place."

Everybody laughed, hoping Palmer would join their foursome. That was the last time I saw him and the last golf game Roland and I played together. We tried to play a round at Plantation in Scottsboro, but he couldn't last. I still miss him greatly.

REPUBLICAN PRIMARY

Although this is mentioned in my other book, BB&D, it will bear repeating here. It was later in 1970. Dick Bennett, the Republican State Chairman, called me.

"Bob, we have got to have a primary. People in Alabama will never understand our convention system. The Democrats laugh at us and say we select our candidates in a phone booth. People think when they vote in the Democrat primary voting is over. Alabama has a very low turnout in November. Of course, it has been this way since Reconstruction. Now, if we are ever going to be a viable party, we have to let the people vote in a primary.

"The only way we are going to get a primary is to run somebody statewide and garner more than 25% of the vote. The Steering Committee thinks you are that candidate."

I told him that I was shocked to hear that the Party wanted me to run. "What would I run for? I'm not going to get 25% of the vote against the George Wallace Machine."

"We thought about that too. We want you to run against Jere Beasley for Lt. Governor. This is a sort of nondescript race, and we believe you can pull it off."

I told him that I would have to talk with Celeste about it.

He said, "Qualifying ends tomorrow at midnight. So please make a quick decision. At this point you are still one of the most well-known Republicans in Alabama. Please do it if you can."

Celeste said, "Bob, if you have any political future in Alabama, it will be ended with this race. So you have to decide: do you want to run for elective office in the future, or are you through? It is going to be time consuming, and you have no chance of winning. I do believe you can get more than 25% of the vote. So that may be considered a success. At least you are sacrificing for the Party. You really don't need to be Lt. Governor."

By about three in the afternoon, I decided it would be worth it. The Party would never grow without a primary and we needed one now.

Dick Bennett called me, and I told him that I would make the race.

He flew his Twin Comanche Airplane into Fort Payne at a little after 11:00 p.m. Celeste, Michelle, and I, met him at the airport. I signed the qualifying papers at five minutes before midnight on the wing of his airplane.

I was the lone Republican candidate on the statewide ballot. I was running against the ticket of George Wallace for Governor, and my old classmate, Jere Beasley, for Lt. Governor.

My long-ago classmate, Bobbie Mae James, ran for the State Board of Education from Opelika.

After a long, hard-fought campaign, we were able to get 28% of the vote. The Alabama Republican

Party now had a primary, and we were competitive -- finally.

Having the GOP primary changed the complexion of the state. Voters now had to choose which party primary they would vote in to select candidates. Slowly we educated the electorate. And slowly, Alabama decided it was Republican.

It was a long way from 1959 to 2016 when the Republicans won every statewide race. It was a long fight, Maw, but it was worth it.

Sometimes I am really not so sure. All the old segregation Democrats became Republicans. The same old crowd from South Alabama controlled the House and Senate. The State voted straight Republican, and we were a one-party state once more. To hopelessly quote Walt Kelly's *Pogo the Possum*, "We have met the enemy and he is us."

I did have the joy of supporting Ronald Reagan when he lost in 1976 and when he won in 1980. I supported father and son Bush. Then, I just held my nose and voted Republican, until Donald Trump. Then I thought, it may have all been worth it.

CHAPTER FOURTEEN
INFLUENTIAL MEN

Looking back on my life, I have tried to determine who had the most influence on what I was doing and where I was going. Certainly, my mother and my wife were the most influential people in my existence.

The men in my life would have had to have been my father, first and foremost. He didn't intend to influence nor guide me, but by being my early responsibility, he certainly did. Then there was Corporal Snyder in boot camp. He certainly put his mark on me permanently. After him, I would say that early on it was Mr. Manker at V. J. Elmore's; Mr. Young at Goodrich; Professor Jay Murphy, who talked me into taking the cognate electives in law school; and finally some clients in my law practice.

J. E. HAMMONDS

Edgar Hammonds, of Ider, Alabama, a red-headed, fair-complexioned man, walked into my office shortly after Clyde Traylor and I had completed our building at the courthouse. He had some minor business problem that we solved in a matter of hours; however, that meeting resulted in a relationship that lasted more than 18 years, until he died in 1984.

Edgar was an unbelievable man. He started out as a young man in Valley Head, Alabama, with his brother selling tires, mostly used truck tires. After a couple of years, each went their own way, and Edgar matriculated into the over-the-road trucking business with one truck. He built that individual business into National Truck Service, Inc., a nation-wide freight hauler with more than 300 trucks.

I represented him in numerous truck wrecks. Sometime in the 70's, I believe 1971, I represented two of his drivers against White Freightliner. We claimed a defective weld on a torsion barn induced a truck wreck in New Mexico. We tried the case in the U.S. District Court in Gadsden, Alabama, and got a verdict in excess of $198,000. That, at the time, was the largest damage verdict in the history of North Alabama.

A funny thing about that case. We brought the attending physician in from Albuquerque to testify. I asked what was the first thing he did when the men were brought into the emergency room. He said that he tested them for syphilis.

I said, "You have two patients who have just been in a truck wreck, they're all banged up and injured, and you test them for syphilis?"

He said, "Yeah, we have a lot of that out here, and we need to know if we are dealing with it before we do anything else."

Later, I represented Edgar with John Morgan and Bobby Lee Cook in a truck wreck in Chattanooga. We lost and never should have lost it. I thought that there was some very poor lawyering involved. However, I was the low man on the totem pole, and Morgan and Cook held forth as to which of them could outshine the other.

Lesson learned: Trial law is an art, and there are very few artists. Most lawyers are totally incompetent when it comes to the courtroom. They allow their ego or personality traits to cloud their vision.

A trial is nothing more than a glorified debate with some very archaic rules. The lawyer's art comes into play when he tells his story convincingly. This is done by using the witness as little more than a relay as the lawyer unfolds his story in accordance with the law. On cross-examination, the attorney can make his closing argument to the jury or judge through closed questions to the witness. Then, in the final analysis, the lawyer should adhere to the six most important words in the English vernacular: "What is in it for me?"

No one is really interested in the client's problem nor the lawyer's presentation. Underlying every decision, consciously or unconsciously, those words prevail. That's salesmanship, features and benefits. Why buy this refrigerator? It keeps my food better than the other brand. It has more features that benefit me.

MAGNATOMETER

Although we didn't intend to, Cook and I did make our imprint on the country.

Mickey and Kirk McBryar worked out a job with the president of the bank at Stevenson, Alabama. They were going to hold up the bank, and it would be an inside job.

The brothers put on their masks, went into the bank, and announced the holdup. It had been arranged that the bank would have extra money that day. They took their time and put all the money that had been laid out in two duffle bags. They got away and stashed the two duffle bags in a pond. It was near their dad's house on Sand Mountain, above Trenton, Georgia.

The FBI put the pressure on the banker. He caved, and implicated the McBryars. The law put a diver in the pond and got the money back.

Mickey hired me, and Kirk hired Bobby Lee Cook. We could not work out a plea deal and had to go to trial in Federal Court in Birmingham.

When we reported to Judge Frank McFadden's courtroom for the trial, the place was covered up with FBI agents. I told Cook, "All these guys can't be witnesses."

"Nah," he replied. "There has to be something going on here. I've counted 23 of them so far, and they appear to be in a near riot."

I asked Mickey if he knew what was going on. He said he had no idea. Having been around for a while, I didn't believe him.

Officers came in and took Mickey and Kirk back to the holding cell. We were told to go into the judge's chambers with the U.S. Attorney and his prosecuting witness.

The walls were lined with FBI agents. The Judge began, "Gentlemen, we have encountered a problem with trying this case today. It seems, and we have it on good authority, your clients have hired some men from Chattanooga, referred to as 'Gators.' Three of these men came to Birmingham last night. Today, they were arrested coming into the courthouse with automatic weapons and hand grenades. Their purpose was to kill whoever was necessary and take the McBryar brothers out of here as free men."

Looking at Cook and me, "Do either of you lawyers know anything about this?"

Both of us denied any knowledge of the plan or implementation of same.

"Okay. Let's go back into the courtroom. We can't try this case this morning. Plus, there will be additional charges brought against your clients."

As we awaited the judge, I said to Mickey, "They are on to your game. Did you really mean for those gators to roll hand grenades into the courtroom?"

"Yeah. They were supposed to do that."

"You son-of-a-bitch. You were going to kill me for nothing?"

"Oh no, Mr. French. I was going to tell you to duck."

"Duck, my ass! You haven't seen the hand grenades I have seen."

The Court continued the case; the McBryars were taken away; they were denied bond; and one or two gators were charged with them.

Both Cook and I declined to go forward representing either of the McBryar brothers.

Within 10 days, magnetometers were installed in every federal courthouse in America. The case bothered the judge so much that he resigned from the bench and returned to private practice.

For several years, every time I went into a Federal courthouse, and had to empty my pockets and go through a magnetometer, I told the officers that they owed their jobs to me.

After that debacle, I needed a pick-me-up. Celeste agreed that I could spend some money for something extravagant. We had property on an island in the Gulf of Mexico. I had a new twin engine airplane. We had a beautiful home. In short, I had everything other than a Rolls Royce. That's what I needed, a new car. I bought a Rolls from Bill Florence of the dealership in Atlanta.

Owning the fine car was wonderful. I drove to Decatur, picked up Roland and let Mr. Oliver drive it. That was the only time he had ever ridden in a Rolls Royce. He loved it.

TWINS!

It was Wednesday, around 10 a.m. Edgar called me, "Hey Bob, how would you and Celeste like a set of twins, a boy and a girl?"

"That would be nice, but I'm pretty well sterile. We had to go to the Fertility Clinic at UAB to get Michelle conceived."

"No, let me tell you what's going on. One of my drivers, and his wife have twins, a boy and girl, nearly three years old, dropped off on them by their family from Minnesota.

"The kids are playing in a truck tire in front of my maintenance garage. Their aunt works here in our office, and her husband is one of my drivers. She had some sand put in the tire and brought the children to work.

"unfortunately, the Department of Human Resources is going to pick them up Monday and place them in foster care. They'll be separated and the aunt doesn't know what to do with them.

"The mother and father are from Florida and have divorced. Apparently, nobody can care for these children. The grandmother, aunts and uncles have given it a go at taking care of them, but they can't do it. They passed them on to the girl who works here. Sadly, the entire family is at a loss. I thought of you and Celeste. You all might want the children.

"If you and Celeste are interested, you are going to have to move in a hurry. Time is running out."

"Let me talk to Celeste. I'll get back to you. Don't let anything happen to the children."

I went home for lunch and met with Celeste and Michelle. We had always wanted more children, but no luck.

Celeste said, "You know that I am all for it; however, Michelle has the most to lose. What do you think?"

Michelle said, "If you can't do anything for the least of these, you can't do anything at all. I say adopt me a brother and sister."

I called Edgar and told him that we would take the twins. "Please send the aunt down here to go with me to get permission to adopt the children."

When she arrived, I loaded her up in the Baron, and we headed to St. Petersburg, Florida to see the mother, who was a police dispatcher. She called ahead and we met with the mother. She hated to give up the children, but she could not afford to keep them.

Their older brother had been blinded by two sexual perverts. He was 11 years old. She had all she could handle single, with a blind child. Her mother was helping her with the son. She signed consent to adopt.

We flew to Atlanta and found the father and grandfather. The father was willing to allow the children to be adopted, as he had no home, was driving a truck, and had no way to care for the twins. On his father's recommendation, he signed the consent.

Thursday morning, I filed a petition to adopt the twins with the parental consents.

Friday, the judge signed the order, and all at once, Celeste and I were the mother and father of children we had never seen. Michelle had a brother and sister whom she did not know.

We went to church Sunday, and the aunt dropped the children off at the office right after church. They were beautiful children, a little boy and little girl. They had no possessions. Their names were Tammy and Tommy. We had already considered changing their names and decided against it due to their age.

We loaded them up in the Rolls Royce and away we went to eat lunch.

Monday morning I called one of my Case Worker friends at DHR and told her that the children now had a home and a loving family. The CW was glad.

Long story short, we raised them as our own, put them through college, and they rewarded us by following our lead. Tommy became a great lawyer and Tammy went up the chain to management at The University Hospital at University of Alabama Birmingham. Both gave us fantastic grandchildren.

We had a wonderful time raising our children. Celeste and I had only one fight in 46 years and 4 months.

It lasted 35 years. It was, how to raise children. She wanted them raised like rich kids, and I wanted them to be raised in somewhat of the hardscrabble raising that I had. Still, all our children were a great joy.

The Lord works in mysterious ways.

MEDICAL COMPUTERS, INC.

Later, the week after the adoption, Edgar called me all excited. "I have a great idea. I'm coming down to talk with you about it."

A few minutes later he came in and sat down.

"Here's an idea. There's a guy named Holter who has invented and merchandised a device called the Holter Monitor. You strap this thing on your arm and wire it up to your chest for 24 hours. At the end of that time, you hook it to a computer and print out an electrocardiogram of the person's heart.

"Here's my idea: I know Dr. Maurice Rawlings at Memorial Hospital in Chattanooga. He is one of the foremost heart doctors in America – written books – lectures – all that stuff. So, I think we ought to organize a corporation, and put people in the field with these Holter Monitors. They can go into every doctor's office in the area, work out a deal to attach a Holter Monitor to their heart patients, and we will transmit the data by telephone to Memorial Hospital.

"Dr. Rawlings will interpret the EKG and recommend whatever treatment the patient needs. We should do pretty well until everyone buys Holter Monitors and computers to read them – which, by the way, have not been invented yet. So, we have about 5 to 10 years to do well. What do you think?"

"I think it's a great idea. What area do you want to work in?"

"We need to be where there are very few, if any, cardiologists. I think we ought to begin in West Texas to the west and West Virginia to the east." I see the need for about 11 representatives and maybe a two-girl office staff near Memorial Hospital."

I ran the idea by Celeste at lunch and she loved it. She thought we had a real winner. I called Edgar, and told him I would organize Medical Computers, Inc.

He began to set up an office and recruit a staff. This was something Edgar was very good at. Fortunately, he hired Ann Womack, my original secretary at Traylor & French in 1965. She had divorced and had moved to Chattanooga. She took control of the office, the bookkeeping, employment, the works. She and Edgar hired a retired doctor to travel around our territories and help our representatives market our product. I can't remember this doctor's name, but he was a great guy.

MCI began blowing and going. It was bigger than Edgar had envisioned. Of course, we had every problem one could imagine with such a far-flung business and an inexperienced sales force. Still, we showed a profit right off.

Dr. Rawlins became the third owner of the corporation. After about six months, we called a sales meeting in New Orleans. I loaded up our staff doctor and Edgar in my little Mooney and flew us into Lakes Front in New Orleans. We had a great sales meeting, and everyone left the three-day conference fired up and ready to attack the world – mainly because we had sweetened up their commissions.

THUNDERSTORM

We left the Crescent City just before dark to fly back to Fort Payne. Bad mistake. There was a line of thunder storms moving into our route of flight. However, they were scattered, and I could pick our way through them. We took off.

Near Meridian, Mississippi, the Air Traffic Controller handed me off to Meridian Approach Control. When I reported in, I asked Approach to vector me around the thunderstorms in the squall line as I did not have radar. A Bonanza was also on the Meridian frequency asking for a vector at almost the same time. He was going to Pensacola, Florida. Unfortunately, it was the controller's first day on the job after coming out of training. She gave the Bonanza my vector and gave me his vector. The result was that both of us went into the heart of two towering thunderstorm cells at night in single engine airplanes.

When I knew we were in severe turbulence (I thought the fillings in my teeth were going to come out.), I let the storm have the airplane. I had been taught to never pull an airplane apart fighting a cumulonimbus. We were at 7,000 feet. All at once, we were caught in an up-draft, and up we went to 18,000 feet. The lightening was fierce. As it reflected off the clouds I noticed that the light was not blue, gray or black, it was pink. I had never seen that before. The entire sky would light up pink, almost red. The thunder was deafening – like it was inside the cockpit. I guess it was.

Then, down we went! Sometimes the tail of the Mooney was far below the nose. It was like we were free falling backward from the top of a tall building. Then the storm would whirl us around and we were plunging straight down as if we dove head first off the tall building. The main problem was when we were almost up-side down. There was such a temptation to try to right the airplane. I didn't. I continued to give it to the storm, and let it have its' way with us.

I had never heard metal cry before. It was a strange sound as the metal covering the aircraft frame whined and cried like a new born baby. I thought the rivets were coming out of the skin.

And then, Wham! We bottomed out at 5,000 feet. It was like we had jumped off a roof top and splattered on the ground. I thought the little Mooney's wings would surely break off. I think that any other single engine private plane would have lost its wings right then. I praised Art and Al Mooney for devising a single steel spar through the little ship to fight vicious Texas winds. The airplane actually sat on the wing spar. Salvation!

I was trying to simply maintain attitude while praying a lot. The clouds were so thick, I could not see the propeller. Just then, the Saint Elmo's fire appeared on the prop. I could see the static arc through the clouds. If you have never seen that blue circle of electricity on your prop, you don't want to see it. It is a wild sight of electric blue. I was afraid it would start an engine fire.

Before I could gather my thoughts, we were in another up-draft. This time the altimeter unwound like a fly wheel, and up we went to 21,000 feet. I thought we would be spit out of the anvil, that indicates the top of a thunderstorm. If this happened we might be blown into the calm air like a leaf in a wind. Then again, we might be thrown into another squall line super cell.

Then I remembered that we were probably in a towering cumulonimbus, rising 50 or 60 thousand feet. We stopped, dead still, a long pause, and down we went again – faster and stronger. This time we bottomed out below the storm at 1, 300 feet.

I thought we were safe below the monster, but no, now we were in its' hail storm. The hail was worse than a drum roll on the airplane. You could barely hear yourself think. I knew the vicious hail was going to beat the sealer out of the windshield, let the water in, and short out the instruments. Then, we would be dead. This called for drastic measures.

I radioed Meridian. "Meridian Approach, this is Mooney November 7115 Uniform, landing Meridian, five miles from the outer marker, in-bound."

"Negative, One Five Uniform, Meridian is closed, airport is obscure. Thunderstorm in progress over the field."

"Meridian, One Five Uniform. You vectored me into the heart of the line. I'm not going back into it. I'm landing Meridian."

"Negative. You are denied access."

"Lady, will you at least turn on the rabbit? I'm landing one way or another. You have almost killed us, and we may not make it yet. I'm in intense hale. I will lose my instruments. I am landing Meridian, now!"

"You are denied access. Proceed at your own risk. The Approach Lighting System is engaged."

"Thanks."

It was solid black. The Saint Elmo's fire had dissipated due to our lack of speed. Still, I could not see the wings. It was like being in a Link Trainer. I retarded the throttle, went full prop, and set up for a normal instrument landing as I descended on the approach, final to land. At 120 mph, I deployed the landing gears, and engaged 15 degrees of flaps.

I told Edgar, "Look out the side window for lights in a sequence leading to the runway. That's the rabbit. I've got to have that to know where I am in relation to the runway." We were indicating 800 feet above the ground.

I told the doctor, who was in the back seat sweating profusely, "Look at this altimeter, every one of these marks is twenty feet. When I get below 500 feet, call out every mark. The field is 298 feet above sea level and we've got to fly it to the ground. There is no visibility!"

The week before the trip I had read an article in *Reader's Digest* about a military pilot who had landed a C-130 in zero visibility. I figured that if he could do it with that monster, like flying an apartment building, I could do it with the little Mooney. Regardless, we were not going back into the squall line. It was succeed, or crash and burn, and I planned to walk away,

Edgar had his nose glued to the window looking for the rabbit, while the doctor was calling out the 20 foot increments of descent. I was on short final descending at 60 mph. Neither of us could see the wing tips, nor the prop.

As the doctor called out 360 feet, Edgar shouted, "I see the rabbit."

Through the intense fog, I could see the aurora of the rabbit in the clouds, flashing in sequence, leading me to the runway. When we reached the end of the rabbit, I knew that we had plenty of runway before us, so I let the plane settle in – slowly, slowly, nose up, a little power, and I felt contact! We rolled out to a safe stop. I thanked the Lord profusely. However, we were still sitting in a blinding fog and hail. I could not see the runway lights.

I said the most appreciative words I have ever said, I keyed the mike and told the tower, "Kill the rabbit."

As we sat there with the engine idling. I thought that the plane was all dimpled from the hail. However, we would fly it home no matter its' condition. After almost 40 minutes, the fog lifted, and I taxied to the ramp.

By the time we were at a tie-down, the rain had passed through and the sprinkles had almost stopped. I went straightway to the tower. I was going to have it out with the approach controller who had almost killed us. The door was locked. I beat on the locked metal door.

A male voice from the other side said, "Go away. You know this is a restricted area."

"I want to talk to that controller that vectored me into the squall line."

"Look, this was her first shift in ATC as a controller. She mistakenly gave you the vector of a Bonanza. Obviously, you survived. The Bonanza, that caught your vector, didn't make it. A doctor, and his three family members, crashed near Gordo, Alabama. You landed. Now, go away."

I felt sorry for the doctor and his family. However, I was so thankful to survive the harrowing experience we had just been through.

We went to the fixed base operator, called a taxi, went to a motel, caught a night's sleep and flew home the following morning. Fortunately, the plane had only one dimple in the wing. I know for a positive fact that the Lord preserved my life that night. I still tremble writing about it.

I sold my interest in the company to my partners a little over two years later. Edgar and Dr. MauriceRawlins operated MCI for more than 10 years before they sold out. It was a good company, making good money, but I didn't have time to bother with it. Managing the staff of salesmen was like herding cats. Edgar could do that because he was used to dealing with hundreds of truck drivers. Life was just too short for me to continue to be involved.

I still look back on surviving that thunderstorm and I cannot understand how we made it. The experience was the most fearful thing of my life, yet I remained calm throughout the flight. It didn't stop my flying, but it made me a much more careful pilot.

TRANS-WORLD ASSOCIATES, INC.

One day, Edgar walked into my office with an idea to change the world. We would build one-mile square cities in Africa. We would surround these cities with 12' high, barbed-wire topped, chain-link fencing, with a gate on each of the four sides. These gates would be locked at night and have armed guards around the clock. We would build houses on 100 X 150-foot lots. They would all be the same with only the outside being cosmetically different. Each house would be built on a Moslem motif with a toilet just inside the front door. They would be mass produced to fit on a concrete slab and cost $30,000, lock and key.

The commercial hub would consist of a shopping center specializing in local food stuffs, dry goods, sporting goods, and four miscellaneous shops.

There would be a city hall, a 45-bed hospital, a local TV station, radio station, utility offices, a school, and a mosque. There would be a small Christian church or Jewish synagogue, depending upon the population. The able-bodied men, who were not employed by the city, would work at farms, oil refineries, or mines nearby.

What did I think about it? He had "studied" this idea for a while. He calculated it would require 30 million dollars to build the city, gravel the roads, sell the houses, rent the shopping center, and move on to the next one.

Once constructed, when the homes were sold, the developers would keep the utilities, TV, radio stations, and the shopping center. The hospital and school and everything else would be donated to the city.

"It will get the people up out of the mud – out of the jungle – and into the modern age. What do you think?"

"That's too hard for me to digest at one time. Let me get back to you on it."

I thought about it and was thoroughly intrigued. The idea of changing the world certainly appealed to me. Plus, helping all those poor people appealed to my Christian side.

A few days later, I called him and told him that I was on board. If he would pay the expenses and give me enough to pay overhead at the office when I was on the project, I would start to work. He agreed, and I began planning.

First, we had to organize an international corporation. We picked Trans-World Associates, Inc. and organized it in Monrovia, Liberia.

Soon thereafter, Edgar met an international crook named Herbert Alphonso Steed. He dressed formally, wore spats, carried a cane, and sported a derby. Steed was from Lagos, Nigeria, and appeared to be a man with connections.

We met him with Joe Trotter from Memphis and Eddie Brown in a motel room in Atlanta. He was trying to persuade Edgar to build an RC Bottling plant in Nigeria. We listened to his presentation.

Trotter said, "I'm out of the project. This guy is an international con-man who is after Edgar's money. I want no part of him."

Steed denied that he was a crook. However, it would take money to make the project go. Edgar asked how much, and he wanted $30,000 up front for "expenses."

Eddie had been paring his nails with his 8" Puma pocket knife. In one swift move, he vaulted across the bed, almost like a cartwheel, and put the knife to Steed's throat. "You steal one penny from my friend, Edgar, and you are a dead man!"

Steed started sweating and begging Eddie to put the knife down. He thought he could manage the start-up money on his own.

When things calmed down, Edgar, as he always did, came up with a way to use Steed. He told Steed his ideas, and Steed got on the telephone immediately to some of his friends in Nigeria.

A few days later, TWA had acquired an option on a square mile of land near Kaduna. It was directly across an unimproved road from a Humble Oil Refinery. The property was exactly what we were looking for.

I met with the managers of Kingsberry Homes, a pre-fabricated home manufacturer. They had a plant in Fort Payne, but had moved most of their facility into the Mid-West. They put their drafting team to work to design a house that they could mass produce, and deliver to Nigeria, erect it on-site, lock and key, for $30,000. In a matter of weeks, they had designed our beautiful little home.

The next thing we needed was a plan for the city. I contacted the Deltona Corporation, who had developed Marco Island, off the coast of Florida.

A real genius in their architecture department designed the city we were looking for. All four quarters of the city were mirror images of each other; all roads interconnected with the commercial hub in the center of town; and everything was within walking distance.

I contacted an ocean-going freight line and acquired an agreement to ship our pre-fab buildings to Lagos, Nigeria, at a very favorable rate.

A building contractor had completed his project in Nigeria and did not want to pay the expense of bringing some 5 million dollars' worth of heavy equipment back to the U.S. I made a deal to take the Caterpillar tractors, scrapers, diggers, you-name-it, for $3,000,000. He agreed to hold it for us.

After our initial effort, we needed some foreign investment, maybe as much as $10,000,000. I ran the plan by some executives of Wells Fargo. After a study, they conditionally committed to the project.

Although it took a little more than six months, I was surprised at how well things came together. The captains of industry were anxious to participate in an earth-changing project that would benefit so many people, while making a tidy profit, at the same time. The entire package took almost a full filing cabinet drawer.

We were finally ready to go. Herbert Alphonso Steed arranged for us to meet with a lower financial official of the Nigerian Government, ostensibly to talk about a Royal Crown Bottling plant in Kaduna.

Edgar, Ed Brown, and I flew into Lagos. Steed was already there. We met with the minister, and he began the meeting by saying, "I really do not have time to waste talking about some sugar water project."

I said, "Great! Forget the bottling plant. Let me show you what we really came here for."

I unrolled the map of the city, the drawings of the homes, and on it went.

He was visibly impressed. "I must bring other people in to see this."

He left us in this vacant room. Soon he returned with the Interior Minister and the Secretary of the Treasury. I made a full presentation with Edgar participating as my wealthy American investor who would make it all happen.

"What will it take to make this work?" The Secretary of the Treasury asked.

"The best we can calculate, we are going to need thirty million dollars, US, to finance the houses for the people buying them.

"We are prepared to finance the initial site preparation, construction of the fence, and transporting all materials to the site. As we have commitments to buy the houses, we will need financing for the purchasers.

"I propose to set aside the thirty million in a Nigerian bank, in trust, co-signed by ourselves and a government designee. We will draw down on the fund as mutually agreed. This is sort of like the FHA in the U.S. The home-owner will be responsible for repaying the government for his home. We will repay the government for the construction costs of the utilities, hospital, school,

TV and radio stations, the commercial hub, and places of worship."

They loved the idea. Little did I know that they immediately planned to move entire Hausa Tribal Villages into the city. They took it to the President of Nigeria, and he approved their going forward with the plan. It was easy since they were floating in oil money.

Edgar, Eddie, and I flew to Kaduna where we met a lot of wonderful people and visited the site we had under option. We saw the Humble oil refinery and closely inspected the equipment we were purchasing. It was all in good shape, and everything indicated the future was bright indeed.

The Government insisted that we take in some Nigerian partners. We took in Elijah Mohammad, one of Nigeria's wealthiest individuals. He was one of the sons of the Hausa Chief. He was a very devout Muslim, a very honest man, and a sterling character of an individual. Among other things, he owned the Mercedes dealership of Nigeria.

Elijah could open any door. He was so happy to be participating in a project that would, "Get my people up out of the dirt."

Some of the Nigerians told us that as soon as this city was operational, they had another site for another city. We felt like we were earth movers.

We were going to change the world for the good!

The three of us returned home, and Edgar and I refined the plan. It took about 6 weeks of constant communication with the Nigerians to get everything ready to move. We returned to Nigeria to close the deal.

We went directly to the Secretary of the Treasury's office. Edgar signed the necessary documents that I had drawn, and had been approved by the Nigerians.

The Secretary then slid the check, drawn on the Central Bank, across the desk to me.

I reached out for it.

He slid it back and talked very fast.

I noticed that it was for thirty-six million dollars! That was even better.

He slid it across the desk to me.

I reached for it and he slid it back jabbering in Hausa.

I didn't understand what was going on. Elijah punched me on the shoulder and motioned for me and Edgar to come out into the hall.

"He wants you to agree that he can keep $360,000 of the money. He has people he has to pay off."

"I can't do that, Elijah. That is called a corrupt practice in America. I could go to prison for 10 years."

"That's the only way you are going to get the money, Bob. That is the standard way we do business over here. He is not charging what I thought the government bureaucrats would demand. He has been instructed by the President to do us a favor. Everyone thought you knew how the game was played."

"I'm sorry, but I can't participate in paying a kickback."

Edgar chimed in, "You stay out here. I'll go in and make the deal. I'm willing to take the chance. This is how it's done internationally, and nothing is going to happen."

"Not while I'm here, you won't. I can't be a co-conspirator in a corrupt practice. If you insist on doing it, let me go home, and know nothing about it."

Elijah returned to the room, talked to the people in his native tongue, they folded their papers and didn't shake hands. They left in a huff.

As we taxied to the airport, Edgar said, "So much for changing the world."

Edgar continued to try to do business with the Nigerians. He did some minor dealings in coal and failed completely in oil transactions. See *BB&D* for the oil deal.

Edgar came to my office and said, "I put a lot of money into that Trans-World Associates. I paid for a lot of travel and defrayed your expenses. I would like to have the file of the deal."

I packed it up and gave it to him, little knowing what he might want with it. I later learned that he turned it over to Herbert Alphonso Steed. I was told that Steed sold all my paperwork, all my legal documents, proposed letters of credit, contracts, leases, you name it, to some people in London for six million dollars. I always wondered if Edgar got any of the money to repay him for all his expenses. Odds are, he didn't.

BACK TO NIGERIA WITH EDGAR

Edgar stayed in contact with Elijah. They were fast friends. Elijah and one of his wives came to Ider and visited Edgar and Pauleen. Of course, Elijah had family in the oil business. He enticed Edgar to consider buying some Bunny Lite, the world's best oil.

Edgar came to see me and discussed the deal. He wanted to know if I wanted in on the same terms and conditions as before. If I did, we had to go back to Lagos. I suggested we take Eddie with us.

When we landed in Lagos, the port authority detained Eddie. Of course, they were trying to get a payoff. We waited them out for three hours and left the airport around midnight.

We hired a pigmy cab driver to take us to the Eko Holiday Inn via his Peugeot. Shortly after we left the airport, we were stopped by a military patrol. We were ordered out of the car. They proceeded to search our luggage and our person. One soldier put an Uzi in my chest and looked me dead in the eye. I looked back, and there was no body home. I was in a world of trouble.

I thought, "Here I am in a foreign country about to be shot by a guy who doesn't know where he is."

Right then, Edgar stepped up. He held up a twenty-dollar bill. "Would this help?"

The officer in charge of the detail grabbed the money, jabbered in a foreign language, and the detail got back into their personnel carrier and sped off. Close, but not out of trouble.

Edgar was in the passenger seat, and Eddie was in the left rear. I noticed that we weren't going the usual way to the Eko. I saw a dead body on the side of the road, and it looked like we were going deeper into a slum. Eddie saw another dead body and thought the same thing.

"We're being set up!"

Eddie pulled out his trusty pocket knife and put it to the drivers' throat, "Turn around and get us out of here, or you are dead!" He cut the guy enough for blood to run down his shirt.

Just as we were in the middle of about a dozen men in a vacant spot, the pigmy wheeled the car around and sped out. He took us to the Eko, still bleeding.

We got our bags without giving him a tip. Eddie put the knife up to his temple as he sat in the car, "You ever try that again with an American, and you deserve to die."

After three days, we returned home without closing any deal. Forever after, Edgar said, "Bob French may think he's something, but his life is worth only twenty dollars, American."

Edgar continued to try to do business with the Nigerians. We went back over there for a total of four trips. One of the trips is detailed in my other book when we went after the Neelley trial. See *Beaten, Battered and Damned.*

Our last trip, only Edgar and I went. We slept in the same bed in the Eko Holiday Inn. We enjoyed their casino there and won more Kobo's than we knew what to do with. I think the kobo is equivalent to our dollar.

We slept in the same bed as it was the only room available. Edgar snored like a freight train. I had to catch his rhythm in order to get any sleep at all.

Then, all at once, the snoring stopped. I bolted wide awake. Almost three in the morning, and no more snoring. In fact, no breathing.

I lay there --- waiting – and waiting – nothing. I timed it. After three more minutes, I jumped across Edgar's body, sitting on his stomach, "Wake up, white man! You can't die on me in darkest Africa. I'll never get your body home."

Edgar stirred, "Why are you sitting on me?'

"I thought you were dying. You stopped breathing."

"Well, I'm breathing. Get off."

I was glad to do so.

Everywhere we went with Elijah, trying to put an oil deal together, a young attractive black girl followed us. After about two hours of this, I asked Elijah, "What is this girl doing following us?"

"She's a girl from the village that my brother sent out. I have a vacancy for a wife, and he has decided I should marry her. She is following me around to become acquainted with me. Tell you what, you can do me a favor. Take her to your room tonight and sleep with her. Tell me in the morning whether she is any good in bed. I've got other wives here, and they are not going to be happy with me taking on a young girl. They'll overlook it if she suits my fancy."

"That's a mighty good offer, but I have a wife, and she would not take kindly to me having an affair in

Africa. I am going to respectfully decline. However, I think you should keep her. She is young and beautiful."

"Yeah, but they grow up and plump out."

After four visits, I tried to look to the bright side of Lagos. I wrote the following poem:

LAGOS IN DECEMBER
By Bob French, Dec. 1982

Nameless Millions, lost in the
routine of Lagos.
Bartering, buying, selling,
trading, everywhere all the time,
The desire for money is the God
of Lagos.
Lagos swells accepting them
and rests when they are silent.

Dust, heat, taxicabs, dirt, trash,
garbage, sewage,
Stench, crowds, ever honking
horns of a million cars,
Thousands teaming in every
direction,
Lagos swells accepting them
and rests when they are silent.
Policemen, Government
workers, farmers, bankers,
Old rusty burned-out car bodies,
garbage on the side of the road,
Open sewage ditches lying
stagnant and smelling
Amid old buildings deserted by
the British Empire,
Lagos swells accepting them
and rests when they are silent.

Tin shanties, shacks, cardboard
homes.
Stacked against each other so
thick there is hardly room to breathe.
The smoke of burning animal
carcasses drifts across the shacks in the
lowlands. In the huts, one can breathe it or
die. Polluted waters, sandy beaches, dirty
waterfront, rusting hulks of old ocean-
going vessels wearing away in the sun,
dead fish, oil, dead birds, and shells.
Lagos Swells accepting them
and rests when they are silent.

Traffic jams and traffic cops
called "Yellow Fever" working for bribes.
Four-lane roads turned into eight-lane
catastrophes, defensive drivers with razor-
sharp reflexes circumnavigating the city
where there are no rules of the road.
Oh, the horrible wrecks of
Lagos, but worse – the exhaust fumes
Of one million reciprocating,
internal combustion engines hanging low
over the city, Lagos swells accepting them
and rests when they are silent.

With it all Lagos lives, Lagos
lives a serious life,
So serious nothing is ever as it
appears,
There is always more than
shown.
One forms the habit of looking
for something

Not shown to understand what is
seen.
        This suspicious, silent side of
Lagos accounts for
        The open happy side of the ant
hill called Lagos.
        It is the acceptance of "what is"
that keeps Lagos
        looking for the unknown. And
in its way, Lagos is beautiful.
        Lagos swells accepting them
and rests when they are silent.

        It is a beautiful statuesque West
African Lady,
        Dressed in her favorite color of
cloth,
        Walking on the horizon at dawn,
        A load balanced on her head and
her child on her back,
        She is the mother of the nation.
        And Lagos lives, in the heat of
the sun and the rain of the clouds,
        And Lagos lives in the
consciousness of seven million people
        Who band together with more
and more people to share
        The common consciousness
called Lagos.
        Lagos swells accepting them
and rests when they are silent.

HELLO ISTANBUL

Edgar got with Phillip Hale, and somehow, they went into the coal business together. Edgar mined a boatload of coal that I was happy to process for him, and he sold it to the Turks.

We had met Jeff Kokdemir, the nephew of the General of the Army of Turkey. Through his uncle, Jeff had arranged for the Government to buy a boat-load of coal.

Edgar saw a bright future in selling coal to the Turks. However, the plant manager of the largest steel mill in Turkey, located at Karabuk, a Black Sea town high in the Ural Mountains, near where Noah's Ark was found. They wanted him to come to the mill and negotiate face to face. He would take all the metallurgical coal Edgar could mine.

There was nothing to do but load up and go to Turkey. Jeff Kokdemir was going with us to interpret. He was living in Miami at the time on a green card.

We flew into Istanbul, and the pilot taxied the huge passenger plane to the government hangar where the three of us disembarked to be met by the General of the Armies. Fortunately, I had brought him a bottle of Jack Black. We got along well.

We were driven to the Istanbul Hilton where we had reservations. Later, we had dinner with the general, and we met a real live Turkish belly dancer – I still have the picture – beautiful woman. And she could ring those bells on her fingers.

The following day, we had a Fiat automobile loaned to us by the general. Jeff was driving and said that we would cross the bridge over the Bosporus that separated Europe from Asia.

I asked Jeff to stop and let me urinate off the bridge. I carefully informed him that urinating off famous

227

bridges had been a hobby of my lifetime. I started with the Helen Keller Memorial Bridge in Decatur, moved on to the Tennessee River Bridge at Florence, the Whitesburg Bridge at Huntsville, and from there, the world was my urinal. I did the Golden Gate in San Francisco, the George Washington in New York, the Verrazano Narrows going to Staten Island, the London Bridge, the bridge near the Eifel Tower over the River Seine, in Paris, the Marathon Bridge on the way to Key West, and others.

Jeff said, "Absolutely not. This bridge is highly guarded from the shorelines by soldiers with orders to shoot to kill. You'll be seen and shot."

At that point, we encountered a shepherd with a huge flock of sheep, each with a red or blue spot on their back.

"I can do it here," I exclaimed and jumped out of the car among the sheep. I urinated off the bridge as hundreds of sheep were pushing me almost over the edge. Ah, success is sweet! Now you know that I am crazy.

We drove all day and into the night. We did not sleep. As we drove, there were literally hundreds of huge German trucks hauling goods to Iran. They were bumper to bumper each way for hundreds of miles.

Finally, we turned off into the mountains. It was time for breakfast. Jeff stopped at an isolated café. In the café, they had coffee and scrambled eggs in goat cheese and milk baked in the oven. I thought it was pretty good. Edgar took one bite and gave me his. I ate it. Bad mistake.

We arrived at the steel mill around 11:00 a.m. something I had never seen before. The entire town was the steel mill. Everyone lived around the mill, and everyone worked in the mill. All the commercial establishments were owned by the mill. The manager of the mill ran the town.

We were shown into a large conference room. The staff came in and we hammered out a contract. The problem was that the specifications for the coal exceeded any coal we might find in Northeast Alabama. However, Edgar was not deterred. He told me privately that he would buy very high grade metallurgical coal and blend it down to specs.

While we were negotiating, the goat cheese breakfast came back on me. I had to go badly. The plant manager pointed me toward the to management men's room. There were no commodes. There wereporcelain foot pads over holes in the floor. Okay, no hill for a climber. I began to open my fly. An elderly lady walked in with a babushka on her head. She held a roll of toilet paper and stood by the place I was going to squat.

It took a minute for me to realize she was not going to leave. She was a men's room attendant, and she was going to stand near me while I did my business, then, hand me the paper.

"Ain't no way!" I zipped up my fly, determined to hold it until we could get out of Karabuk. I wondered what she would do if a man was constipated.

I just about died, but I held on until we cleared the city limits. Then I crawled down in a ditch and found relief. I was happy I had an expendable handkerchief with me.

We spent two more days in Istanbul. We visited the famous Blue Mosque, which had once been the capital of Christianity until the Arabs took Istanbul from the Romans. We saw the harem and other interesting rooms in the facility.

We saw the old city wall built by the Romans and links of the famous chain used to keep ships out of the Black Sea. It was interesting that wherever we went, we saw people wiping their cars. Once a driver stopped his vehicle, he immediately got out and cleaned his car with a cloth.

We flew back to the U.S. Try as he might, Edgar could never get the right blend of coal for Turkey. He tried for months and finally gave up.

The trip to Turkey was as close as I would ever get to the Apostle Paul and Noah's Ark. Next stop, South Africa.

JOHANNESBURG

Somehow Edgar became involved in business with a mining family in South Africa. Due to business constraints, he could not go to Johannesburg and negotiate a contract involving diamonds, gold, and coal. He asked me to go and negotiate for him. I had no idea it would be that difficult.

The do-gooders in the U.S. were trying to force the South Africans into giving up apartheid. This was a racial segregation system far more severe than segregation in the United States. We had been through the Civil Rights Movement, and now the Civil Rights leaders were leaning on the powers that be to force integration on South Africa.

South Africa had a much different history than the U.S. When the Dutch and Moors settled in South Africa, there was no native population. The land was devoid of the human species. After the white people settled the land and began to build, Africans migrated into the country. The whites tried to send them back home but were unsuccessful. So they developed a system of occupying the same land but never mixing. The liberals in the U.S. didn't like the system and brought sanctions against South Africa.

I was unaware of the severity of the problems when I tried to get a visa to go to the country. I had to go to Paris and meet with the South African Ambassador and get permission to enter the country. It was a bit difficult, but after several days in the City of Lights, I made it, and flew into Johannesburg. Plus, I got the bridge over the River Sèine.

In Jo'berg, I rented a car and drove on the wrong side of the road, using an automobile with the steering wheel and brakes on the right side. I had a map and made my way to the Hilton. I called my contacts, and they came down and took me to dinner at the Country Club. They lived on #5 fairway, if my memory serves me correctly. We were going to do business the next day. They would pick me up at 10:00 a.m.

JOHN LENNON

The following morning, I fell out at a little after 7:00 a.m. and went downstairs to have breakfast. I was wearing a gray/red pin-stripe suit Celeste had picked out for me. As I was crossing into the lobby, I noticed the same suit in the window of one of the shops. I stopped to look at it.

As I was looking at the suit, a woman said to me, "Did you buy your suit here?"

I turned and noticed that she looked familiar, "No, I'm an American here on business. I'm just surprised to see a suit like mine 2,500 miles from home."

"Oh. Would you care to join us for breakfast? I'm Yoko Ono and my husband is at the table over there. He's John Lennon."

"Why not?" I joined them.

She was very friendly, and he was friendly enough. However, for the next better part of an hour, he held forth on a variety of subjects without any interest in whatever anyone else might add to the conversation. He was not interested in who I was, where I was from, or anything about me.

He discussed world affairs according to his point of view. He was highly critical of the South African government. I doubt I said a dozen words during the breakfast. He did pick up the tab.

The parties came by. We went to their offices and discussed a variety of situations. It was finally decided that they might be interested in importing coal. However, they were in the process of migrating to the States as they wanted to get out of South Africa before the system collapsed.

They had seen what happened in Rhodesia, and they did not want to have any part of the South African government going the way the Brits went in Salisbury.

The following day, I flew back home. I reported to Edgar, and he and the South Africans continued to talk about a deal. In a few weeks, the oldest son of the family came into Fort Payne. He told me that he was looking for a place to relocate the family.

I took him to see Edgar, and they talked about importing coal through a family friend. Nothing ever came out of it. The family moved to Texas, apartheid collapsed, and the rest is history.

FLYING THE CONCORDE

I am now going to tell you a story that I hesitate to tell. First, it is totally implausible. Second, it was illegal. and third, if the circumstances had not changed, I would never tell it.

Edgar and Eddie had gone to Europe to travel on to Geneva and open a bank account. They went by way of Paris, France. They got into some kind of impasse and needed me to come to Paris and join them immediately. Edgar called and told me to fly to Washington and catch the Concorde to Paris so I could be there the next day.

I flew the Baron into Dulles, parked at the FBO, and bought a ticket to Paris via Air France on the Concorde. I caught the evening flight out of Washington.

I noticed the speedy SST was a lot smaller than I had thought. Plus, it had very little wingspan. However, the seats were comfortable, and the stewardess came by and served Champagne and hors d'oeuvres while we were sitting on the tarmac.

I'm sitting there in my usual trance – fat, dumb, and happy – when the young lady serving the goodies stopped at my seat. In a very heavy French accent she said, "Are you a captain?"

"No, Ma'am. I'm a civilian. I was a sergeant once."

"No, no, no. I mean, are you a pilot? Fly an airplane, you know?"

"Well, I am a pilot. Have been one a long time."

She disappeared into the forward area and stayed a few minutes. As the plane taxied into position and hold, she returned.

"The Captain of the Concorde would like for you to be his guest on the flight deck of the Concorde."

I followed her up the aisle into the flight deck. The pilot, co-pilot, and flight engineer were in their appropriate seats. I was amazed at the instruments, knobs, buttons, dials, you name it.

However, standing there looking at them, I could identify almost all of them. The co-pilot motioned for me to sit on a small jump seat across from the flight engineer and buckle up.

We began to roll, were airborne, and up we went. I thought we were going pretty slow for a supersonic transport. The climb was placed on autopilot. The pilot got up and motioned for me to sit in his seat. I buckled in and acclimated to the instruments.

I think the crew intended to impress me with the flight deck for a minute or two and return me to my seat. However, I thought we weren't climbing fast enough, I had a competent co-pilot, so I thought I might as well fly the sucker.

I reached over, gripped the throttles, and pushed them to the firewall. The pilot grabbed my hand and retarded the power.

He said in a heavy French accent, "Too early. We must observe noise abatement. We cannot go full power until we are through 25,000 feet and 25 nautical miles offshore."

So I sat. When we went through flight level 250, I pushed the throttles again. This time the co-pilot smiled. "Cruising altitude?" I asked.

"6-2-0," came the reply.

I couldn't believe it. We were going to 62,000 feet. That's more than five miles up -- on the edge of space. Oh well, she was still on auto-pilot with her nose pointed toward the stars. I sat back and enjoyed the cockpit.

As we approached flight level 6-2-0, I gave the crew an order. "Level at 6-2-0, orient on course for Charles de Gaulle, Paris, France."

"Roger, wilco." We leveled her out, the flight engineer trimmed the huge engines back to their best operational speed, and the co-pilot pointed toward the switch that raised the nose cone.

I raised the nose cone and asked the standing pilot, "What do I do now?"

"Keep the cone temperature at 315 degrees or below. Do not let it increase more than that."

Once we had her trued out, running like a sewing machine, headed across the ocean for Paris, France, I checked everything once more. Our speed in MPH was 1,262. We were going more than twice as fast as the speed of sound, faster than a .22 rifle bullet. We were riding a rocket. I could see the curvature of the earth and the terminator where light and dark divide. It was quite a wild ride.

The pilot enjoyed himself watching me fly the ship. I would take nothing for the experience. In right at three and one-half hours we were descending into Charles de Gaulle. We started our descent 200 miles out. I thought the pilot would run me out of the seat, but he stood there grinning.

I had a great co-pilot and flight engineer, so if they would risk me landing it, I was ready. The co-pilot set up the approach and handled the radios in English sometimes and in French at others.

I asked the pilot, "How do I land this baby?"

He said, "Landing the Concorde is sort of a modified crash. You must fly it to the ground. Cross the fence at 160 knots, keep power on, and let her settle in."

I did exactly what he said, and it was a piece of cake. The three crew members, and the young lady from the cabin, clapped as I rolled out. The co-pilot had followed me through on everything I did, so there was never any room for error.

The pilot motioned for me to get up and took his seat.

I had a hard time believing it. I had flown the Concorde!

Edgar moved on to greener pastures. He developed oil wells in Kansas and had other projects. I did not lose track of him, but our world traveling days were over (and I didn't even tell you about Paris, London or the Netherlands.) All these cities figured in some kind of international law, but nothing much exciting happened in any of them, just legal drudgery with a few small adventures dialed in.

Interestingly, I was listed in *Who's Who in International Law*.

CHAPTER FIFTEEN
FRIENDS

I lost my best friend when I lost Celeste December 22, 2001. Celeste was my head cheerleader while being my severest critic. We were a matched pair. She was beautiful, a talented artist, dancer, and anything else she wanted to be. Her children would say that she was the best mother a child could have. She survived cancer, but a glioblastoma, phase 4 took her out in 79 days. I still miss her every day.

Next to Celeste, I guess I miss Roland as much as anyone. We were friends more than 66 years. We got into everything and got out of everything. We played golf with Arnold Palmer, Bob Toski, Tom Kite, and other famous professional golfers. We raised our families together, and I miss him each day. I still quote his famous sayings at least once a week. "Let's don't and say we did. Absence makes the heart grow fonder for somebody else. All work and no play makes Jack a dull." And, so on.

I have finally realized that almost everyone I know is dead.

EDDIE BROWN

Eddie Brown probably should have his own chapter. He has been an unbelievable influence on my life without ever trying to be. I guess his wife Charlotte characterized our relationship best. She said we were nice guys alone, but together we were horrible. He took up in my life where Roland left off. Of course, Roland never left, but we did drift apart due to geography, children, marriages, jobs, you name it. But we were never far from each other.

I can't remember exactly how I met Eddie. I know that he was Hoyle Stevens' nephew. In my book

THE LAWyer, he is "Ernie Brock." In *BB&D*, he's "Eddie." So, if you think he is interesting here, pick up the other books and learn more about him.

I think he got into some kind of trouble, and his Uncle Hoyle Stevens sent him down to me. I know that I was practicing in the little building across from the Opera House, having just left the partnership with Clyde.

There are two early memories of Eddie. The first is he was charged with automobile theft in Jackson County. He, along with Glenn Hicks, were accused of stealing and stripping a new Mustang. I was hired to defend them both.

The case came on for trial in Scottsboro. A jury was empaneled, and Chief Deputy Sheriff Robertson was the State's primary witness. Of course, they had the person who owned the car, the wrecker driver who towed what was left of it, and the seller, to testify as to the value of the stolen car. The only eyewitness was the Chief Deputy.

Robertson testified that it was below freezing on Sand Mountain in January. He was on routine patrol and discovered a new Mustang in an unfamiliar place. It was pulled up under some trees, off the highway, with a motor crane in front of it. That was strange. So he decided to park his car down the road and walk back up to the Mustang and see what was going on.

As he hid in the bushes, in the dark, he saw Eddie Lennar Brown and Glenn Hicks dismantling the Mustang. First, they took out the radiator. Then, within a matter of minutes, they lifted the motor out of the vehicle. They stripped the seats, the side paneling, even the glove compartment.

They put all of the parts on the back of an old pickup truck. They jacked the hull up, removed the wheels, including the spare tire, threw them on the truck, jumped in, and away they went.

"It took those two three hours and forty-five minutes to completely dismantle a brand-new Mustang and drive away with the parts. The only thing left was the sheet metal hull.

"Because I was away from my vehicle, I could not give chase nor did I get the license plate. It seemed they got away clean. In a few days, they tried to sell the parts to a known stolen parts dealer who owned a junk yard. I watched his place, and when it looked like he had a bunch of new parts, I threatened to arrest him. He snitched out Eddie Lennar Brown and Glenn Hicks."

The junk dealer refused to testify, and Brown and Hicks denied ever having anything to do with the matter.

It was a simple defense. Not a single juror would believe that two 18-year-old boys could dismantle a new Ford Mustang in three hours and forty-five minutes. Impossible. I didn't put on any testimony.

The jury came in, "Not Guilty."

And so began my relationship with Ed Brown that goes on until this day.

Brown came down and wanted to work for me as an investigator. I thought that might work, as I had developed a large criminal law practice. I figured that a criminal might help me investigating crimes.

One of our first cases was in Columbia, Tennessee. We were defending a guy accused of being a cocaine dealer. The State's only witness was an FBI agent. At that time, he had not had the equipment to test the white powder and prove it was cocaine. Instead, the judge allowed him to testify as to what his expert opinion was regarding the contraband. The State went forward and qualified him as an expert. Then:

"You examined the white powder. What was it, in your opinion?"

"In my considered opinion, it was cocaine."

"You had seen substances such as this before?"

"Many times. And, in my opinion, it was cocaine."

I thought we were dead. How was I going to overcome that testimony? I looked back at Eddie; he motioned for me to come over. He whispered in my ear, "An opinion is like a belly button. Everybody has one."

I went back to the witness. "You know that to convict, you must prove that the substance was cocaine?"

"Yes, sir. And in my considered opinion, that was exactly what it was."

"You will agree that this case rises or falls on your opinion?"

"Yes."

"Would you agree that everyone has an opinion about almost everything?"

"Yes."

"So opinions are like belly buttons; everyone has one?"

"Yes."

"And that's all you have, a belly button. Uh, I mean, opinion?"

"Correct."

"Belly buttons can be an innie, or an outie; right?"

"I guess."

"So, belly buttons and opinions can differ, can't they?"

"Yes."

"And, all you have is a belly button-- uh, an opinion, to put this man in prison?"

"He's put himself in prison."

I had gone too far. I went to the court reporter.

"May I borrow your dictionary?"On her stand, she had a little black pocket dictionary. I looked up 'opinion.'

"Read Webster's definition of 'opinion.'"

He began to read, "'Opinion,' what one thinks, a judgment, a guess.'"

"A belly button. No further questions."

It was easy from there. Brown and I had completed our first successful defense.

Eddie has hung out with me for years and years. He is one of the very few who still does.

MILLARD FULLER AND MORRIS DEES

I went to school with a number of talented people. Millard and Morris were two of a kind. I first met them when I was still selling business machines for Snipes. They had somehow originated a brilliant idea.

They had a mole, probably one of their wives, working in the University Registrar's Office. The mole provided them with the names, birthdays and local as well as home addresses, of all students. Millard and Morris, operating out of the law school library, wrote to the parents of each student having a birthday, suggesting that the parent give the student a birthday cake honoring the occasion. After all, the student was away from home and would appreciate his or her parents thinking of them.

They made a deal with a local bakery to bake the cakes for $10 and sold them to the parents for $25. The cakes were dutifully delivered to the students on the date of their birth.

The operation worked well until some well-meaning parent congratulated some member of the administration for being so thoughtful. Wham! The University closed down the birthday cake escapade.

That did not stop Millard and Morris. They had associated themselves with a local printer named Arthur Nottingham. Through him, and their birthday experience, they had learned the power of direct mail.

I was hawking Add-Mate adding machines along University Avenue and ran into the pair. They told me that they had a shipment of distrained Christmas trees in Iowa that they had bought in Italy.

The Boy Scouts of America were going to sell the trees and make some good money for them. Unfortunately, they needed a little more than $600 to free up the trees so they could get them to the scouts. They told me that if I would give them the money, they would make me a one-third partner in their business. I thought it was a good idea and told them I would get back to them.

Celeste knew Millard and Morris, as well as their wives. When I ran the idea by her, she almost had a fit.

"We have $1,400 in the bank, and you want to give half of it to those two birthday boys? Absolutely not!"

So much for that. Celeste was always very conservative.

End of story: Millard and Morris graduated from law school and moved to Montgomery, "where the action is," and opened a law office.

Due to solicitation and advertising by lawyers being illegal at the time, it was not six months before they were being threatened with disbarment. They mended their ways and seemed to be doing very well.

According to what I was told, one day Millard walked into the office and announced to Morris that he was leaving. The night before, an Angel of the Lord had appeared at the foot of his bed and told him to leave Montgomery and go to South Florida and be a missionary to the Seminole Indians. He told Morris to buy him out, as he was leaving.

Morris began the practice of law without his long-time partner. He was the president of the Montgomery Jaycees and asked me to come down and speak to them. I spoke to them. And after the speech

Morris said that he was impressed. In fact, he was so impressed, he was going to nominate me as One of the Outstanding Young Men of America.

A few weeks later, I was notified that I had been named as One of the Outstanding Young Men of America. I acquired a certificate and a pewter key indicating my elevation to such an auspicious honor.

Although I was very honored to be included with many famous young men, I always suspected Morris was the idea behind the honor, and may have made a little money off the keys and certificates. Anyway, the key looks good on a nice tie.

Millard went on to organize Habitat for Humanity and served as president of that organization for many years. He did a lot of good for a lot of deserving people.

Morris became the unofficial chairman of the Jimmy Carter Presidential Campaign. Using his contacts there, and his experience with direct mail solicitations, he organized the Southern Poverty Law Center. This group did some good work while Morris was in charge. He told me once that he had raised enough money for the organization to continue practically unabated in perpetuity. Unfortunately, it seems to have now descended into nothing more than an ultra-liberal name-calling organization, fat off donations, that finds racists under ever mattress. Seems the SPLC has outlived its usefulness.

Regardless, knowing Millard and Morris was fun while it lasted.

SCHOOL PRAYER CASE

I have tried a lot of cases. A few stand out in my mind. The school prayer case was one because it had nationwide implications. I suppose it is worth mentioning here.

I was hired as the local school board attorney. Little did I know when I accepted the position that a teacher had sued the system for sanctioning prayer in our public schools. He was from Valley Head and was represented by the American Civil Liberties Union.

At the time I was employed, the case was pending in the U.S. District Court for the Middle District of Alabama in Montgomery. Ira Dement was the U.S. District Judge trying the case. I had grown up with him in West Town in Decatur. We lived on 6th Avenue West and his family lived on 5th Avenue West. I did not know him too well growing up as he was 3 or 4 years older than I was. However, his younger brother Louis, was in my class at Decatur High School.

I stepped right into the middle of the trial. My first appearance was within a couple of weeks of when I was hired. We went to Montgomery and defended the school board the best we could, citing all the law supporting that students had the right to pray in school.

Long story short -- you know the outcome. Judge Dement ruled that prayer in public schools violated the constitution and was therefore illegal. I gave notice of appeal to the 11th Circuit Court of Appeals in Atlanta.

While the case was pending, Bill Pryor, a protégé of Jeff Sessions, wanted to follow Sessions as Alabama Attorney General. Sessions had been elected U.S. Senator. Prior called me and asked if he could take over as counsel for the school board during the appeal. First, it would be good for him politically. Second, he believed he could win the case.

He was a good lawyer and I knew that he would do a good job. Plus, he could lose the case just as well as I could because it was a loser.

Being a good Republican, I told him that I was perfectly willing for him to take over as General Counsel. I hoped it would be beneficial for its publicity value. I wanted him elected as well.

I told the Superintendent, Richard Lands, that Prior would lose the case. I told Prior that the most he could do was change 14 words in the Dement Opinion.

He argued the case, along with attorneys from Judicial Watch in Washington, and successfully changed the opinion – 14 words that allowed students to pray in school on their own time so long as religion was not sanctioned by the school. Or, something like that.

Anyway, that's how you got prayer taken out of the public schools. In my opinion, although it might be a correct decision constitutionally, it has wrecked havoc on our society.

The anti-religious bent in America has resulted in school shootings, bullying, and any number of horrible interactions. Taking the bible at its word, we have sewed to the wind and we are reaping the whirlwind. No left leaning liberal would ever agree with that statement.

My board wound up paying the legal expenses of the ACLU. Pryor went on to become a judge on the 11th Circuit Court of Appeals, and is a candidate for a U.S. Supreme Court appointment. Jeff Sessions became U.S. Attorney General while I did my usual, piddling around fat, dumb, and happy.

MIDNIGHT IN THE GARDEN OF GOOD AND EVIL

While I was sitting in my usual, Dr. Charles Hillis walked into my office and employed me to represent him in a domestic matter in Savannah, Georgia.

It seems that his family had been one of wealth and owned one of those famous mansions in Savannah. It was called the Hamilton-Turner Mansion. I think there are 36 mansions in down town Savannah. Don't hold me to that number.

It was in April, 1996, Dr. Charles and Nancy decided to sell the mansion for something around $500,000, if my memory serves me correctly. The fight was over how to divide the money.

Nancy got around $325,000 from Dr. Charles as alimony and child support for their son.

When the doctor walked in with his strange story, I knew that I would soon be visiting Savannah. The trial went on until late 1997. Dr. Hillis ran low on finances due to the litigation. He didn't have to pay any more money and the son came to live with him for a while.

There were several interesting aspects to the case. According to Dr. Hillis, his family mansion was next door to the mansion where the book *Midnight In The Garden of Good and Evil* was set.

After my initial interview, I immediately bought the book and read it cover to cover as quickly as possible. Great book, quick read.

Seems Dr. Hillis inherited the mansion and was practicing medicine in Savannah.

He was quite successful until he married Nancy, a gorgeous woman, who claimed to have been Miss. Tennessee in the Miss America Pageant. We never could confirm whether that was true or not. In court, she maintained that she had held the crown. Now, she was one of the leading characters in the book.

Nancy Hillis was Mandy, the woman who drove car with her knees while putting on makeup going down the highway.

In representing Dr. Hillis and traveling back and forth to Savannah, I concluded that Savannah is a city of interesting characters.

I was fortunate to meet John, whose last name I can't remember. He was the guy who would tie a thread to a fly's leg and walk around the courthouse area with the thread up in the air tied to the fly. I met him at the famous restaurant near the courthouse, but I can't remember the name of the café either.

Sonny Seiler came into the courthouse one day and I shook hands with him. I knew he was a lawyer, but he quickly informed me that he owned Uga, the Georgia English Bulldog. His family had owned the Georgia mascot through some seven generations. He showed me a picture, and said, "Damned good Dog."

I then went into the courtroom where I tried the case before a female judge who was barefooted.

At recess, I asked one of the security guards if everyone in Savannah was a character. He said that if they weren't a character from Savannah, when they crossed that bridge coming into the city, they would become a character.

I drove out across the bridge and no wonder. It was named after Herman Talmadge the notorious senator from Georgia!

After considerable litigation and very expensive lawyering, Charles and Nancy tired of fighting and Nancy declined to go forward with the case. It was dismissed for want of prosecution in late 1998.

In the meantime I bought a Bird Girl replica of the famous tombstone for Celeste.

CIRCLE UP FOUR

Very few of my friends ever knew I was a square dance caller.

Celeste and I began square dancing in Tuscaloosa with the B.F. Goodrich Square Dance Club.

We loved it. When we arrived in Fort Payne, we looked for a square dance club and found the DeSoto Squares.

We had the whole deal -- the boots, shirts, ties, crinoline skirts, the works. we took the children with us to the square dances. One or two times a guest caller failed to show up. Everyone was disappointed. Celeste said, "Bob, you need to learn to call so that when the caller doesn't show up, you can take over."

She always had more faith in me than I had in myself.

She and I went to a callers school in North Carolina. When we came back:

"Well, grab your partner and circle up four. Now bow to your partner, corners all, join hands, circle to the left, go around the hall. Walk around your left hand lady, see-saw your pretty little baby, and back to your corner, left allemande, here we go, right and left grand, every other girl, with every other hand. Meet your mate and promenade. And so on.

Square dancers collected plastic badges. I had a badge made that were wings that said I flew with Bob. We awarded the badge to everyone who flew with Celeste and me to a far away place to square dance.

We flew into Knoxville with Ronald and Peggy Cagle. We went to a great square dance. When we started to fly home, the little Mooney sputtered and almost didn't make it off the runway. I pushed it as hard as I could to get to altitude – barely made it. We sputtered on to Fort Payne in the dark. It was one of those experiences in flying when you reach the PMP, Point of Maximum Pucker.

We hobbled home with the roughest engine you have ever heard that kept flying. The following morning I checked the fuel tanks. The fuel was red! Someone trying to help me had filled my tanks with automobile fuel. Unbelievable.

CELESTE AND THE HOT TUB

It was about this time Celeste said that we needed a swimming pool. Tommy and Tammy were growing up and they needed a pool.

"Celeste, we live on the brow of Lookout mountain. How can we possibly have a swimming pool?"

"When we were going to build up here, you had the coal miners bring the spoil over here and build a shelf where we could build our house below the bluff line. We can fill in for a pool. After all, the Martins have one."

Hard to argue her points. "Okay. Sunday, we will drive over to Rome and look at some of those pre-fab pools."

We drove over and found the perfect pool. All we had to do was get a wide load hauler to haul one over to our house and deliver it down behind our house. I had to think quickly.

On our way home I said, "How about a hot tub? We can put it down behind the house without the expense of cutting trees, hauling in fill dirt, and worrying about kids falling over the edge down the mountain?"

I could see the light bulb above my darling wife's head. "That is not a bad idea. Plus, it might be good therapy if any body is sore."

Fortunately, the graduate nurse came out in Celeste. The therapy idea worked. I arranged for us to go to Gadsden, to Lowes, and buy a hot tub.

At the store, we found the perfect tub. It was 500 gallons, four seats, and came with a Bogotá of red wood. Celeste loved it as did Tammy and Tommy.

$2,400 and they would deliver it. I gave them a check for $1,000 to hold it for us while we prepared a place for it.

I hired Tommy's future father-in-law, Gene Guffey, a good carpenter, to come to the house and build a deck for the tub.

Gene picked out a place behind the house where there was a huge rock he could anchor the deck. Celeste liked the place. Gene built a beautiful deck with a bench all the way around while the 30-mile view off the mountain was perfect.

I went to Gadsden, paid the balance and the family anxiously awaited the hot tub and Bogotá.

Lowes made a mistake. They delivered a 750 gallon 7 place hot tub that was too large for the Bogota'. After Gene made some measurements, he said he could enlarge the Bogota' by 5 ½ inches on all four sides and the tub would fit.

While we were having the electricity wired in, Gene enlarged the Bogota' around the tub. Perfect fit!

I told Celeste, "Look, we bought a tub for $2,400. The one they delivered was the one that cost $3,200. The guy gave us a $50 discount. So, we owe Lowes $750."

She agreed. I went to my private stash and got $750 and gave it to her.

"Take the twins and go back to Gadsden and tell the folks at Lowes that they made a mistake, and we would like to pay for what we received as a result of their mistake."

I gave her the $750 and she and the twins left for Gadsden.

When they returned I noticed that the Volvo station wagon was packed full of packages and sacks in the back.

The three of them were joyous as they came into the house.

"Was Lowes happy that we corrected their mistake?"

"Oh, yes, everyone was happy. Get the stuff out of the car, kids."

"You've got an awful lot of stuff there. What did you do, go school clothes shopping?"

"Sure did."

"Credit card?"

"No cash."

"Did you use the money I gave you to pay Lowes to buy all that stuff?"

"Of course. You didn't really expect me to give all that money to Lowes, did you?"

"Celeste, you are a crook. You cheated Lowes while I tried to make it right."

"Bob, do you know how many times I have been cheated by retailers? You don't shop. They treat men different from women. I have been cheated so many times, I can't count. For once, I got even with them. Yahooo!"

"But it was my money that I gave you to be honest."

"Tough stuff, big boy. Help me unload the car. Yea! For once I scored!"

I tried to feel bad about it, but she was probably right. Retailers probably do work lady shoppers, and she did hit a score. Somehow, I felt I was involved in it, but my conscious was clear. I tried to do the right thing.

After all these years, I do enjoy the hot tub, particularly at sunset.

GOLFING HERO

I don't remember how it happened, but there was a time that Roland and I teamed up in golf against two good friends - Jimmy Wiley and Bobby Ray Smith. We played golf matches across the country.

Wiley had grown up with Roland and me playing golf early at the Decatur Country Club. He was not a caddy; he was the son of a local doctor. However, he played with the caddies and other teens his age. He and Roland became the best golfers in Decatur. They fought for club championships on an annual basis. Roland was champion three times, and I do not know how many times Jimmy claimed the cup.

Bobby Ray Smith was a natural athlete. He had been the quarterback of the football team and was a natural golfer. He and I were good golfers, but neither of us was as good as Roland or Jimmy. So we made good competitors. But, how it began, I do not know.

When I was a successful trial lawyer, Roland was a successful manufacturer's representative in the metal fastener industry. Jimmy had become a doctor, and Bobby Ray was a successful contractor. We could afford it, so we loaded up in Roland's airplane and flew to such places as Doral, Sawgrass, and other exquisite venues. As with almost all golfers, we put a wager on each round.

We played pretty even. Rarely did either team take home the other's money. Usually a final press on the 18th hole resulted in no blood for either team.

There were a couple of times that stand out in my memory because I became a hero. The first time was at Decatur. We had played 18, and had broken even. We had time, and decided to play an additional three holes that brought us back to the clubhouse for $100 a hole. Wiley and Smith won the first hole. We were one down. They won the second hole, and we were two down-- $200 – one hole to go. We pressed. The final hole could cost us $400.

Roland said, "Herman, we've got to win this one, or we will never live it down. This is my home club. We have got to win!"

Smith and Wiley drove straight down the fairway. Roland kept up with them. I pushed my drive into the right rough about 200 yards from the hole.

On the cart, Roland said, "We can't half this hole, we still lose. We have to win, and it looks like you may be out of it."

I was away and knew I had to make a perfect shot. The hole was designed to tempt the golfer to try to clear a line of pine trees as the direct line to the hole or go around the trees to the right and stay in the fairway. The line of pines was at least 30-feet-high. They were directly between me and the hole. They were about 50 yards back from the green. I had to clear the trees and carry the green.

We had to have a birdie, as a par was a loss. I hit a three wood and cleared the trees. None of us could see where my ball came down. We rode up to Roland's ball. He, along with Smith and Wiley, cleared the trees. Roland and I thought the three of them were on the green. We had no idea where my ball was.

When we came through the trees, we saw four balls on the green. One was only 6 inches from the cup. Roland and I agreed that we had had the lick. The one at the hole was a tap in. The others had 8-to-15-foot putts.

Arriving at the green, will wonders ever cease? My ball was the tap-in. I tapped in for a birdie. Roland, Wiley, and Smith missed for pars. Moments you want to live forever! We broke even! Roland talked about my second shot for months. I felt pretty good about it. But there was more to come.

The mineral business and world travels began to take all my time. As a result, my golf game had faded a bit. Roland invited the three of us to go with him to Jacksonville and play one of his very favorite courses, Hidden Hills. I was willing to go, but I was not playing every week like they were.

Before we left, I said that I would only bet if they would stroke my ball. I wanted two strokes to the side. Smith and Wiley said absolutely not. They would give me one stroke to the side. I countered by saying, I would take only one stroke on the 18 if I could call the time and place to use my stroke. They agreed, thinking they had put one over on me. I planned for Roland to carry me most of the way, and I would use my stroke when it was most advantageous for us.

It was a hot Florida day, approaching 100 degrees. We took plenty of water and were off. We had a great adventure on Number 4. I sliced my ball into a row of saw palmetto bushes to the right of the fairway. I knew I was out of play, but I was not giving up a brand-new Titleist. Being an old caddy, I dove into the saw palmettos that were so large they were over my head. It was dark. I saw the ball and went for it. Just then, everything around me went cold and the saw palmettos began to tremble, rattle, and shake. I grabbed the ball and told my playing partners, "There's something in those saw palmettos. Come and see."

Bobby Ray said, "There's nothing in there," and dove into the area where I had been. He came out in a hurry! "Herman's right! There's a demon in there! I felt it! When I got in there, it went stone cold, almost freezing, and the saw palmettos began to rattle like they were being shook by a giant. It's a demon. Let's get outta here!"

I asked Roland to go in there and see what he thought. He refused. "I'll take your word for it."

"What about you, Jimmy? Will you take a look?" I asked.

"I haven't lost anything in there. Let's go."

As we were going up the fairway, Roland asked, "Do you really think there was a demon in there?"

"I'm not much on demons, but there was something paranormal in there. I know that. It was like some places where I have been that a murder had occurred. The cold was clammy and seemed to drop on me as the saw palmettos began to rattle and shake. I don't know what it was, but I'm not going back."

Our golf games sort of fell apart for the rest of the front nine. On the back, Roland and I were beginning to lose big time. He couldn't hold us in, and all I could do was half a few holes.

We began to press the bets, and by the time we reached 17, we were $700 down. Roland asked me if we should press 18.

I didn't see that we had a choice. This was the most money I had lost in golf in all my life. We pressed the $700 to win. Now if we didn't win, we had $1,400 riding on the final hole. If there was a half or a tie, we lost the $700.

The hole was a par 5. From the tee box, the fairway fell off into a deep valley; and then on the second shot, the golfer had to reach the top of the opposing hill. The fairway then took a 90-degree right angle, continuing steeper up the hill to the hole. It was one of the toughest holes I have ever played.

All of us drove into the bottom of the valley. On their second shots, Roland, Wiley, and Smith cut as close as they could to the trees lining the right of the fairway. They were attempting to make the climb to the green easier. I hit my shot to the middle of the fairway just past the 90-degree turn.

Roland said, "Looks like you are out of it unless you can pull a three wood like you did that time."

I didn't have much hope of that, but I was sure going to try. I was away and hit a three wood up the hill to the green. Wiley, Smith, and Roland all went to the green. I suppose I got a very lucky bounce because all of us were on in three.

Unbelievably, all of us made our putts for four birdies.

Smith said, "Boys, that was fun. Too bad you lost so much money, but it's bad luck not to collect your golf winnings. Looks like you guys owe us $1,400. We will take cash or a check."

I said, "Yeah. You'd be right except for the fact I made an eagle."

"You didn't make an eagle. You made a birdie just like us."

"Really, I claim my stroke!"

With all the excitement of the demon, the others had forgotten my stroke on my call. I called it when it meant the most. We broke even.

Smith and Wiley said they could never forgive me for that. I didn't care; they didn't get my money, even when I was not playing good golf. Sometimes you just have to out think 'em and keep your eye on the prize.

KAREN PETTY HOLCOMB

Consistent with what the fortune teller told me so long ago, a second woman would figure prominently in my life.

In 1986, Karen Petty Holcomb, of Harrison, just outside Chattanooga, on Chickamauga Lake appeared in my office. She had been sent to me by an old friend, Conrad Finnell, a lawyer in Cleveland, Tennessee. She wanted me to represent her in a divorce action against her husband, Judge Richard Holcomb.

I didn't want to take a case against a judge, but I always lived by the rule that there are my clients and people who aren't my clients. It's open season on those that aren't. So I agreed to help her.

Long story short, I helped rejuvenate and reconcile the marriage. The Holcombs continued to enjoy a happy marriage until he passed away. At that time, she believed that the hospital had killed her husband by administering an incorrect drug when he came to the emergency room.

The staff practically admitted their error. Karen contacted a local lawyer who investigated the case and said that she had an open-and-shut medicial malpractice case. However, according to the judge's history and medical records, he would have passed away in a few months. Therefore, the damages in the case were not sufficient to continue on.

Karen remembered me and showed up in my office. I handle medical malpractice cases and agreed to investigate the facts of the case. Sure enough, the hospital administered the death-inducing drug by accident. The medical history of Judge Holcomb was terrible. He was suffering from cancer, congestive heart failure, and numerous other maladies that could have killed him at any time. He was a person in very poor health. We spent a great deal of time investigating the medical records trying to find something to assuage the hurt being experienced by Karen. Like Tennessee Counsel, the evidence was overwhelming that the good Judge would not have lived more than one or two months, no matter what the hospital did.

During the time that I was working the case, I had occasion to have dinner with Karen, and we slowly began to see each other as old friends. I visited her on the lake, and she visited me on the mountain. Seeing each other regularly, we became a bit more than friends. I helped her in her grief, and she helped me in mine.

Eventually, we began to hang out together, travel together, go to football games, stay in her condominium in Florida, attend family functions, and generally behave like old married folks.

Karen, influenced me to write the Neelley Book, BB&D, while we were attending the Alabama Writer's Symposium in Monroeville a few years ago. She has been very supportive in everything I try to do.

I always say, "growing old is the greatest adventure of life." It is quite unbelievable. Karen has been a blessing provided by the Lord to help me through old age. For a couple of old geezers, we do have a good time.

DOG ISLAND

No book about my life can be written without Dog Island.

I think it was 1971. Recently divorced John Tcherneshoff had flown his Cherokee with his children down to Disney World. I had flown our Mooney with Celeste and Michelle. We landed at Kissimmee, Florida, near the park.

After a wonderful time we were flying home, cutting across the Gulf to the Florida Panhandle.

I looked down and saw an island with a dirt runway.

"What is that island down there, John?"

"Says here it is a private airport. Let's land and see what is going on."

He landed and I followed him in. A man met us in an old station wagon and offered to carry us to "the hut." We accepted and climbed in.

The hut turned out to be a Quonset hut left by the U.S. Navy in WWII. It was occupied by Dewey and Doris who sold some snacks, drinks and sandwiches now and then.

The only commercial business on the island was The Pelican Inn, a ten unit efficiency motel.

The island was 9 miles long and almost a mile wide at its widest place. A ferry from Carrabelle, Florida two miles away, came over twice a day.

We walked down to the beach, inspected the inn, visited with Mr. Lewis, whose family had developed the island after the war, and flew home.

Within a few weeks we flew back to the Island and stayed in the Inn for four days. During that time we explored the island, swam, fished, and cooked out. We loved it.

The next time we visited, we drove down in John's car. We took it across to the island on the ferry. We had rented a circular house built up on stilts. John Parked up under the balcony that went around the house.

The kids had a ball gathering shells, swimming and exploring. John and I cooked out while Celeste took care of things in the kitchen. Later, we took the kids snipe hunting. Fun – they still remember it.

After we went to bed, we heard these banging noises all night. It seems the children had gathered beautiful shells all day and the animals were crawling off the balcony and hitting John's car.

A few weeks later, Celeste, Michelle and I flew in. This time, we explored the island by beginning shortly after dawn and walking completely around the island by dark. Michelle collected some fantastic shells on this trip. They are still spread around the house.

When Tammy and Tommy came along, we introduced them to Dog Island and continued to "raise" our children down there.

Earlier, we had bought a lot with intention to build, but we could never find time to do it. I did get to introduce my nieces and nephews from New York to the island. They didn't like it then, but they now look back on it with fond memories.

After Celeste past away, I took Roland to the island. We were to stay several days. After one night, he was ready to go home. I asked why.

"I'm not staying anywhere I can't get breakfast by room service. Let's go home."

Soon, a hurricane destroyed the hut and many of the homes on the island. I was glad he had not built at that time.

A couple of years ago I visited the island taking Karen Holcomb and Poodle Dog Red with me. Other than toilet paper, dishes, and linens, if you don't take it with you, you will not have it on Dog Island.

We always visited the IGA in Carrabelle the night before the ferry if we drove down. Otherwise, we hauled it on the plane from home.

Karen, Red and I drove down. When we visited the IGA, Karen filled one ice box with water. I told her that the island water. That didn't register. We hauled enough water for a scout troop.

Our visit was preceded by the most severe rain storm ever to visit the Panhandle the week before. When we arrived at the Pelican Inn we noticed that we were the only occupants. Then we saw the sign on the door, "Do Not Drink The Water."

Karen didn't say anything and I appreciated that. Because of her, we had water—except for Red. He immediately took a drink out of the toilet. Bad mistake. Talk about "sick as a dog." We witnessed it. It took two days for him to recover enough to take a walk on the beach with us.

I always enjoy walking the beaches of this isolated paradise. One never knows what gifts the ocean may give as there were many ship wrecks near the island in antiquity.

Red was having a great time running and playing the surf. I noticed something in the shallow water.

"What's that?" I asked pointing to the item.

Karen waded in and fished it out of the sand. "It's a sword," she said picking it up.

Sure enough, it was a barnacled encrusted short Spanish officer's sword in the scabbard.

We debated giving it to Florida State University in Tallahassee and decided to keep it. I was not sure whether that was legal nor not.

Karen decided to keep it and still has it as it falls apart due to age and rust. I anticipated it was at least 700 years old.

Oh, we still own the lot and I am sure not a one of my children will ever agree to sell it.

WHY I HATE AUBURN

I think it is nice for a personal letter to have a post script. This is my post script to you.

Jerry Barksdale and I decided to hike the length of Little River Canyon on Lookout Mountain.

We learned very quickly that it was some of the most inhospitable country in the world. The rocks that looked interesting from the rim were larger than automobiles. The river that looked like a trickle from the rim, was a torrent. Still, we pressed on.

At one point the river filled the entire canyon backed up slightly by a 5 foot waterfall. We had to climb up the Eastern side of the canyon to portage around the waterfall.

On the climb, Jerry lost his back pack, and we watched it tumble down the canyon wall go over the falls, and lodge in some rocks. We were able to rescue it when we climbed back down.

With the rushing water coming over the falls echoing in our ears, we found the back pack. Looking around, we knew that we were in some wild country.

Jerry said, "Bob, you know, we may be one of a very few white men to ever stand in this place and see this beautiful falls."

I agreed and turned to drink in the astounding scenery.

Then I saw it!

Some rotten no good SOB had taken a spray can of red paint and painted on the rock ledge creating the falls, "War Eagle."

Then Jerry saw it. "I can't believe this. We are in one of the most isolated spots on earth and some Auburn Fan has defaced it by writing that horrible war cry."

"Well, at least we know we aren't the only white men to visit this spot," I responded.

We hiked on.

Two years later, Roland and I decided to do some spring skiing. It was early April. We took my Baron and flew into Salt Lake City to ski some of the Wasatch Mountain slopes.

We rented a car and drove to Cottonwood Canyon. We had decided to sky one of the most difficult slopes in the area – Snowbird. It was not for the novice nor the faint of heart.

Roland and I boarded a gondola and rode to the summit. Everyone didn't go all the way to the top, but with three other hearty skiers, we pressed on.

The summit was pretty high up and the slopes down were expert, but we were good skiers, and down we went.

The 20 minute trip was adventurous and exhilarating.

"Let's go again," I said heading toward the gondola port.

"Let's not go to the summit this time," Roland responded. "That first drop up there is pretty steep.

You've gotten me into ski messes before. Remember that Palma lift at the top of Steam Boat Springs?"

I remembered. He, Michelle and I went to the top. The last 100 yards required the skier to straddle a little seat attached to a cable, while the skis were in the snow, and the lift was pulling the brave ones to the summit.

Of course, Roland missed the seat. However, his coat didn't, and the result was he was dragged to the top of Steam Boat Springs by his coat caught on the lift.

When the cable went around the huge pulley, he was released. To say that he was angry is putting it mildly.

Now, I was encouraging him to return to the summit at Snowbird. Reluctantly, he agreed, and up we went.

The top was pretty high. You could almost see Park City. We caught our breath and rested a minute in the gondola shack.

While we were resting, I noticed that we were not exactly at the top of the mountain. There was still 100 feet, or more, that could be climbed for a greater adventure. I suggested we side step up to the top and ski down from there.

Roland didn't like it, but, like he said, "A faint heart never banged a cook." And we were on our way.

We side stepped up the mountain for at least 45 minutes. When we reached the pinnacle, it was a very small area on a rock bluff. We were ringing wet with sweat and had to rest for a while.

Looking out over the vast panorama from our lofty perch, Roland said, "I can't believe I let you talk me into this. All my life you have been getting me into shit I didn't need to be in. Now, look at us. How are we going to get down from here?"

On top of the mountain the mid-morning spring weather was beginning to moisten the snow. I figured we had better get down while the getting was good.

Otherwise, we were going to have trouble around noon or thereafter. It's hard to ski in slush.

"Well, we need to get ourselves on down the mountain. We can't wait for the snow to melt," I encouraged Roland.

"I can't believe this! We've got a 60 foot drop to get off this peak. One mistake and we will be taken off the mountain by the Ski Patrol. I'll bet you there haven't been 10 fools ski off this place. This is insane."

Admittedly, we were up in the air. I could now make out the outskirts of Park City some 20 miles away. It was high and I was trying to get up enough nerve to go over the edge down slope.

As I was contemplating, I rubbed the wet snow off a large rock nearby. I couldn't believe it! There, for the world to see, some rotten SOB had scratched, "War Eagle" on the stone!

I turned to Roland. "See that? Some rotten Aubur nite has been up here and defaced the place. That's it! I'm going over the edge."

"I've got to figure another way," Roland responded. "I don't want to make that first drop."

"Try to go back down the way we came up. Otherwise, wait for the spring thaws. That "War Eagle" has pushed me over the bluff."

I stood up, pointed my tips in the mountain air, leaned forward, and dropped about 60 feet to a slope that carried me another 200 yards down the hill. It felt good. I turned and looked for Roland. Within seconds, he was standing beside me.

We relaxed going on down, and finished our trip without incident. Roland talked about the great adventure for several years.

Me? About all I remember was "War Eagle" scratched in the rock at the top of Snowbird.

And that, ladies and gentlemen, other than the 40-0 game in Birmingham, in 1958, is the reason I hate Auburn.

CONCLUSION

My first book, *An Adventure with John*, was my life's work. It is an interpretation of the Book of John in the Bible. My second book, *THE LAWyer*, was about humorous and exciting things that have happened to me while practicing law. My third book, *Beaten, Battered and Damned*, described our defense in the Neelley trial and the things I went through during the Drano murder defense. In the end, looking back, that book is really about Alabama politics.

As Karen said, "You are the real-life Atticus Finch."

Now this book is the story of my life involving some of the wild and crazy things I have done and the unbelievable people I have met.

She says, "In this book, you sound like Forest Gump."

I guess that about sums it up. On the one hand, I am the fictional character, Atticus Finch. On the other, I am the fictional character, Forrest Gump.

In reality, I'm the notorious Robert B. French, Jr., tromping through life yelling, "Give me a chance," and "Roll Tide!"

In the end, just call me Herman.

AFTERWARD

I do not believe there is a way to write a biography without leaving out some things that you wished you had put in. So, without further ado, I am going to put down here some of the things I wished I had put in their proper order in the book.

ANOTHER CLOSE CALL

I have always thought the Lord has something for me to do before I join that innumerable band in that moves to the eternal resting place. It seems so because I have escaped death and destruction so many times. Some of those experiences have been articulated in this book. Many of them simply repose in the dark gray matter of my brain and only come up now and then.

There's no need to discuss little things like having a stiletto stuck up under my throat and learning that I could stand on my toe nails.

No need to talk about the captain of the guard running over to us and saying, "Get out of here! When that boat comes ashore, they are going to kill you to find out what's in your brief cases."

Nah, things like that were fairly common place. Here's one that wasn't:

A client came in and hired me to get his pickup truck that would not be released from the custody of the State of Alabama. It seems his vehicle had been stolen, caught within hours, and taken to a state yard at Taco-Bet. Taco-Bet was famous as an Indian trading place and remained a huge flea market and trading post open every Saturday. It was located in the Dutton community at the top of Sand Mountain above Scottsboro, Alabama, east of the Tennessee River.

The client had been trying to have his truck released from the Alabama Bureau of Investigation for three months. They would not release the vehicle pending the conclusion of their investigation to prosecute the thief. Seems the perpetrator had stolen several vehicles and this was the only one the State had been able to catch.

It was the middle of July – hot as torment – had not rained in weeks – and it was miserable outside. I told the client that he and I would have to go over to Taco-Bet and see the vehicle. Then, I would file appropriate papers to get it back.

When we got to Taco-Bet, the owner of the local store, who also owned the state yard, let us in to investigate the pickup, after we had produced the title to the vehicle.

There were several vehicles in the yard, including some heavy equipment. My client's pickup was wedged up against the back of the store too close to open the door. To see what was going on with the truck, I opened the driver's door and slid across the seat. The client got in, closed the door and sat under the steering wheel.

We sat there and talked a few minutes in the sweltering heat while I made notes. All the while, I heard this buzzing noise. I asked the client, "What's that racket?"

He replied, "I donno."

It was then I saw it – a wasp nest as large as a soccer ball between under the dash board and right wall. Those horrible insects were feverishly working their enormous nest. I froze.

Under my breath I said, "Open that door easy, and slide out slowly. We are very close to being stung to death."

The client saw the nest and did as I instructed. I then took about 3 minutes to slide across the seat and exit the door. I was wringing wet with sweat when I finally made it out of the truck.   We slammed the door and I thanked the Lord for my life once more.

Had we disturbed the nest, we would have been swarmed, and stung to the point we would have been dead before the ambulance could arrive.

That was a very close call.

BLACK JACK PAYNE

No story of my life would be complete without mentioning a life changing event. I don't know how I missed this one recounting my years at the University, particularly law school.

Please remember, Celeste and I arrived in Tuscaloosa with $40, some rent paid, a car payment, and a dog.

Within two weeks I was working at Snipes Business Machines and she was an obstetrics nurse on the OB Ward at Druid City Hospital.   I worked every day through Commerce and Business Administration. When I got my degree, I was fortunate enough to land the best job of my graduating class at B.F. Goodrich in Tuscaloosa.

After I declined the finest promotion a young man could be offered, I went to law school. During those years, I worked 40 hours a week at the plant and went to school 4 hours a day. It was not an easy life.

As I guess I said in the earlier part of this book, I was the only Republican in law school. Some of the professors held it against me that I was a Republican, going to law school, and making as much money as a full professor. Plus, I drove a little red Austin-Healy sports car every day. In addition, having a photographic memory helped immensely with my class work. I was a straight A student. I may have had one B entering the last semester of my junior year. Regardless, I had more than enough quality points to graduate.

Enter my well-structured life – Professor John

C. Payne.

Among other things, Professor Payne taught property. Real estate is real estate, but wills and trusts are a different animal altogether. I don't remember who taught real property the semester I took it, but no problem, another A. Now it was time for Property IV, taught by Professor Payne, who took a particular delight in giving low grades in Wills and Trusts.

Because of his proclivity for low grades and his general demeanor, the students nicknamed him Black Jack Payne behind his back. He lived up to the name. He was constantly doing research in the library wearing a green celluloid visor and green bands on his white shirt arms. He was gray headed and wore small spectacles. In short, he appeared to have just stepped out of a Charles Dickens novel. And, he would have done just fine penalizing Oliver Twist.

I thought he was a very good instructor, and believed I had Property IV knocked. If I got a B in that course, I would probably graduate with honors, Order of the Coif, and Law Review. It was simply no hill for a climber.

Never absent nor tardy, I turned in all work required and thought I had aced the final. Wrong.

I went to Professor Payne's office door to look at the posted grades on the door facing. I found my name and almost passed out. I had made a D! This was the lowest grade I had ever made at the University. Hurrying home, I discussed it with Celeste.

"Go see Professor Payne. Maybe there is a mistake. He'll make it right."

I did as Celeste suggested. When he invited me to open his isinglass door, I found him studying in his green visor.

"Professor Payne. You have given me a D in Property IV. I strongly disagree with that grade. I scored high on all assignments, and I think I did well on the final. There must be some mistake."

"I didn't give you a D, Mr. French. You earned it. Your essays on the final were terrible. It was you who do not have a firm grasp of wills and trusts."

Thinking I now knew why the students called him "Black Jack," I persisted. "Professor Payne, this D knocks me out of Order of the Coif, Law Review and graduating with honors. This can't be."

"Mr. French, I have examined your record and you have outstanding scholastic aplomb. So, I will make you a deal. Take the course over, and I'll erase the D, and give you whatever you make next time."

"Well, that's an awful lot of trouble, but if I did it as badly as you say, it seems fair. I'll do it."

Celeste thought that the proposal of Professor Payne was fair. Maybe I did really fail Property IV. I would never agree to that. I knew that I did better than a D. However, I would really apply myself next time.

I studied Wills and Trusts like a maniac. I turned in a perfect very complicated trust agreement. I drew a will that any executor would have been proud to probate. I wrote final essays that were capable of being published. Obviously, I had aced the course.

After sweating out the classes and assignments and final in a basement classroom of Farrah Hall, it was finally over. I went to Black Jack Payne's door. I truly expected an A or a B at the very least. Confidently, I looked at the grade posting on his office door facing.
Black Jack Payne gave me an F!

I never spoke to him again and concentrated on simply getting a law degree. All honors were gone, so forget it. I had more than enough quality points to graduate, so I just sailed on through with as little effort as possible.

The law students didn't call him "Black Jack" for nothing.

THE JOHN WAYNE BELT BUCKLE

When I was completing my representation of John Wayne, everyone was celebrating that the transaction had been completed, the documents signed, the advance royalties had been paid, and it was time to leave. It had been a very successful trip. My pilot was ready to fly me home.

The president of the new mining corporation, that had signed the lease to mine the minerals on Mr. Wayne's Nevada ranch said, "Gentlemen, we thought this might be a successful negotiation. In celebration of this event, we had Cartier, of New York, strike even solid silver belt buckles. I want to give on to Mr. Wayne, I'll have one, and our officers will have one."

John Wayne interrupted, "Give Alabama Bob one of those buckles."

I couldn't believe it. The buckle was an original silver eagle, struck especially for the occasion, never to be repeated. It was a very large piece of silver, perhaps 7 ounces, with a unique eagle head displayed, and "Cartier" stamped on the back.

The president of the new corporation looked over at me and pitched the light blue flannel Cartier sack containing the silver buckle to me.

I had an idea of the value of the buckle, and I knew the importance of the lease we had just signed, to I thanked him profusely. I thanked Mr. Wayne for considering me, and I looked at the magnificent buckle.

The buckle became my most prized possession because John Wayne had thought enough of me to get one of the very expensive buckles for me. I prized it so much that I very rarely wore it because I was afraid something might happen to it.

Several years passed by. My dear friend Jerry Barksdale came over to see me. At that time, we were pilgrims on the spiritual path, and very seriously pursing the spiritual life. Somehow, we found ourselves in Eddy Brown's bedroom, on Sand Mountain, above Trenton, Georgia. We began discussing the aspects of the spiritual life. I was deep into writing my book explaining the Gospel of John at the time. I would later publish it as *An Adventure with John.*

I pointed out that quality is how slowly a thing wears out. Everything a person owns is wearing out- some more slowly than others. Yet, all possessions demand attention constituting an impediment on the spiritual path.

Jerry agreed with me. "If that is the case, and I truly believe that it is, then one might make great strides on our journey, if one could divest himself of the thing he treasured most. Because, as you say, that possession is draining our attention every time it crosses the mind, or must be attended to. What's your most prized possession, Bob?"

Thought long and hard. I had many treasures, a Porsche, an airplane, property on an island in the Gulf, a great law office among others. I could do without all those things, but my most prized possession was something very few people knew about- my John Wayne belt buckle.

"My most prized possession is the 7-struck Cartier belt buckle given to me at John Wayne's house in Newport Beach, California."

"Could you part with it if it was hindering your progress on the spiritual path?"

"I believed I can do it. It will be very difficult, but I'll give it to Eddie."

"That's mighty strong, Bob. I don't know that I could do it, Jerry responded.

Brown interjected. "In that case, I will give Jerry my most cherished possession."

He went to his gun cabinet and brought out a Browning .44 magnum 9" pistol. "This has never been fired," he said handing the pistol to Barksdale.

Jerry admired the pistol. "Are you sure you want to do this, Eddie?"

"If French can give up his buckle, which I have never seen, the least I can do is get rid of this jewel, because I love it, and have seen one like it."

Jerry said, "I'm sorry, I do not know what my most prized possession is. Right now, I don't have one. Perhaps this pistol Eddie gave me will become mine."

We left, and I was feeling released from the selfishness that caused me to look at that buckle now and then, and admire it, and be happy to own it. I was determined to deliver it to Eddie Brown.

A couple of days later, I was going to see Eddie. I decided to give him the buckle then. I took the buckle from my jewelry box and admired it. I couldn't give it up. I looked through my buckles and found a very nice eagle buckle. I put it in my pocket.

When I saw Brown, I said, "Hey Eddie, here's my most prized possession." I handed him the buckle.

"That's a beautiful buckle Bob. I really appreciate receiving your John Wayne buckle."

He took off his buckle, put it in his pocket, and put the new eagle buckle I gave him on his belt, and cinched it up.

We went about whatever we were going to do. However, I knew that he knew that was not the John Wayne buckle I had given to him. That bothered me. I was a fraud and a failure on the spiritual path. I was not only too attached to a physical item, I had lied about it. Horrible.

A few days later, I was with Eddie again. "Here, this is the real John Wayne buckle. I'm giving it to you. Give me my old buckle back."

Brown laughed and admired the silver eagle he was holding in his hand. "I knew you did not give me the John Wayne buckle. Now I have the real thing. It's beautiful.

Thanks. I'm not going to put it on. It's too nice to wear with jeans."

Time went by. I felt better about the entire situation. I saw Brown again. He was wearing the old buckle.

"Hey. I want the old eagle back. You have the John Wayne buckle."

"No. You gave me this phony buckle, and every time you see it, I want you to remember your weakness when it came to parting with a prized physical possession."

Lesson well learned. It has now been 25 years. Brown still has both buckles, and still wears what he calls, "Bob's weakness buckle." I doubt he has ever worn the John Wayne Buckle. However, I did notice, the last time he showed it to me, that the light blue flannel Cartier sack it was carried in was worn threadbare. He must look at it and show it a lot.

Barksdale gave the Browning pistol to his best friend, Glenn Duncan of Laramie, Wyoming.

Me – I have survived the lesson of the buckle. However, is it failure to hope Brown will give it to my grandson after I'm gone? Maybe.

ROLAND'S WISE SAYINGS

There were words or phrases that Roland said over and over all our lives. I do not know whether all, or any of them, were original with him. He just embedded them into my brain over our 68-year relationship. Now that he's gone, I catch myself repeating some of his phrases when the occasion requires it. I was told I should write them down, and share them with the readers of this book. I've been making notes the past few months when I slip and say something and say, "Roland used to say that." So, here are some Rolandisms that come back to me from time to time:

1. "Here I sit, fat, dumb and happy."
2. "Let's don't and say we did."
3. "You're not tall, dark and handsome. You're short, light and ugly."
4. "Drink your whiskey and shut up.
5. "My car is so old the wheels will barely hold it up."
6. "Fly low and slow."
7. "This plane is so slow, we've got to flap harder."
8. "You go ahead, I'll watch."
9. "He is so dumb he thinks ping pong balls is a Chinese venereal disease."
10. "That guy is so horny, he would bang a bush if it had a bird in it."
11. "Make the best of things because they can always get worse. And they usually do."
12. "If you say I said it, I'll deny it. If they believe you, I'll say you said it."
13. "Some say don't. Some say do. If you think don't, don't do."
14. "Come hell or high water, that's my story and I'm sticking to it."

15. "To me, somewhere over the rainbow is somewhere under the hill."
16. "I think I have a bladder the size of a pinto bean."
17. "The preacher preached hell fire, he should have burned up."
18. "That guy thinks he is going to steal my girl, I wish he would."
19. "I feel just like Jesus, crucified between two thieves."
20. "I might not be a millionaire, but with good credit, I can live like one."
21. "If I live to be 30 years old, I'll never forget old what's-her-name."
22. "He's about as funny as gonorrhea, and that's not funny unless someone else has it."
23. "My mother told me not to do that. I should have listened."
24. "You want what? How about I hit you in the back and start you to breathing?"
25. "That was as fast as Epson Salts through a widow woman."
26. "That ain't no hill for a climber."
27. "He sweats less than any white boy I've ever seen."
28. "He's feeding an alligator hoping it will eat him last."
29. "If I had a dog that looked as bad as her, I'd shave his butt and teach him to walk backward."
30. "Look at your date's mother. If she's ugly, don't ask her out again."
31. "That girl is as ugly as ugly on a mule."
32. "That girl was so cultured, she wouldn't say fart. She would only say poot."
33. "She said that she was a coal miner's daughter. She should have stayed in the mine.
24. "It's such a mess. I'm a fucked turkey."

25. "That ball went into the woods so far Lassie couldn't find it if it was wrapped in bacon.

26. "Animals are a lot of fun when they belong to somebody else."

27. "It was so hot out there my sweat had sweat."

28. Interestingly, Roland never said, relax. He always said unlax.

29. He never said however. He always said, howsomever.

30. He never said perhaps. He always said, mayhaps.

31. Roland never said "Hello, Hi, nor Hey." He always said "How."

32. Roland never said restroom. He always referred to the facility as the pissery.

33. If something was particularly good, he would say. "That's as smooth as the groove on a polar bear's tool."

34. Roland swung his old 3-wood and hit Allen Humphrey in the head. He apologized. Later he said, "That the swing just wasn't that good anyway." For the rest of our lives, if he hit a bad shot, he would say, "That swing just wasn't that good anyway."

35. Roland never said water, it was always la-la. "Give me a swig of that la-la. Aw bad, my ball went into the la-la."

36. "We might get what we need at Serious and Roebucks."

37. Coca-Cola came out with an advertising campaign showing a man drinking a coke and saying, "Ah, the pause that refreshes." Roland would say that every time he came out of the toilet.

38. He said that if he ever opened a barber shop, he would name it after a tree, "Eucalyptus."

39. Whatever he was reading, he would say, "It says here in fine print...."

40.   If Roland was asked to go somewhere he did not want to go, he would say, "Can't go there, too far and snaky.

41.   If he did something wrong, he would throw up both hands and say, "Don't shoot, I'll marry your daughter."

Photo Album

My Mother in High School

Above: Uncle Arnold and my grandmother Hester A. Sibley the grandchildren called her Wava.

Right side: My grandmother Anna Loper French.

Mr. French -My Dad and Receipt of
Bob's delivery expanse.

Dot and me in the pasture on the dairy

Hester, Daina, Me, Kitty (kitten) Dot and Bingo (dog)
Summer 1941

SCHOOL YEARS

First Grade

Second Grade

Fifth Grade

Senior Class Picture

Sgt. French and Roland

Engaged to Patricia Sparhawk

Nancy Carolyn Long and Me

End of Civilization as we knew it.

Courting Celeste
Newburgh, NY

Wedding Day Picture

Lenny Vandewal and Me at the Radio Station
We Built

Hester, Me, Daina, Dot and Daddy
While I was at the University

Young Management at
Goodrich

In charge of Housekeeping at
BF Goodrich (BFG)

French Family

Dot, Bob, Mom, Daina, Rebecca, Hester and Dad
At the University of Alabama when I was in under graduate school 1957.

Proud Father of Michelle

Young Republicans returning from 1964 Goldwater Convention in San Francisco. Jimmy Holliman Celeste with the patch over her eye where Carol Ann hit her with a Goldwater sign, Ed Nelson, Carol Ann Barksdale, Jimmy Sizemore, Jerry Barksdale and me. Note our Goldwater hats.

A Message from

BOB FRENCH
Candidate for the U.S. House of Representatives

"For many years I have been worried about the gradual centralization of power and control in Washington. My concern changed my party affiliation from Democrat to Republican in 1959. I have seen the Democrat Party repudiate Alabama while we have blindly supported it. As a "State's Rights" Alabamian, I have had enough.

I have not been satisfied with the way my vote has been cast by life-long politicians representing me in Washington. Alabama politicians in Washington have merely echoed the policies laid down by the National Democrat Party. Their records prove this. They have voted to give foreign aid to the Communists, they have voted to disarm America without disarming the Russians, and they have supported many other issues which I believe Alabama People are opposed to. I think it is time we had *a voice* in Washington, *and not an echo!*

I believe that America should return to the principles of God, Country, and Self, and in that order. I find it strange that the courts can ban the Bible in our schools, but can find no way to ban filthy and obscene literature on our newsstands.

We are losing the Cold War. We are not conducting our foreign affairs with the confidence and dignity befitting the greatest nation on earth. Until our foreign policy is defined we are going to continue having decisions damaging American prestige and costing American lives. I will support a firm aggressive foreign policy.

All incumbent Alabama Congressmen voted for Emanuel Celler, author of the Johnson Civil Rights Bill, to be chairman of the powerful House Judiciary Committee. They also voted for Adam Clayton Powell, the Negro Harlem Democrat, to be Chairman of the Education and Labor Committee in the U.S. Congress. Some Alabama Representatives voted for the junkets Powell has taken overseas with white women. I promise that I will use your vote in Washington to oppose Powell or Celler ever holding positions of influence in the U.S. Congress.

1964 is a year of decision. Will Alabama continue to be beaten to her knees by the National Democrat Party? OR WILL WE CHANGE HISTORY?

The decision is yours!"

Vote For

Bob FRENCH

REPUBLICAN FOR

U.S. CONGRES

French brochure
Running for Congress

| VOL XII | SEPTEMBER-OCTOBER, 1968 | NO. 5 |

President Roy Nixon presents awards to the FOYM of Alabama. (L to R) are Clayton Pruett, Jr., Livingston; Forrest David Matthews, Tuscaloosa; Robert B. French, Jr., Ft. Payne; James M. Grant, Jr., Bellion, and Nixon. The FOYM program is sponsored jointly by the Jaycees and Liberty National Life Insurance Company.

ALABAMA'S FOUR OUTSTANDING YOUNG MEN

BOB ★ MICHELLE ★ CELESTE

BOB FRENCH

IS THE KIND OF MAN ALABAMA NEEDS IN THE U. S. CONGRESS!

★ Graduate of Decatur High School.
★ Veteran—Korean Conflict.
★ B.S. and LL.B. Degrees from the University of Alabama.
★ Married 9 years, father of 5 year old daughter.
★ Lifelong worker in the Baptist Church.
★ Member of Alabama Bar Association and Tuscaloosa Bar Association.
★ Worked his way through school.
★ Served on Workmen's Compensation Committee of Associated Industries of Alabama.
★ Selected as one of the Outstanding Young Men of America by National Junior Chamber of Commerce.
★ Past Secretary-Treasurer of Tuscaloosa Personnel Association.
★ Worked closely with National Safety Council to promote industrial safety.
★ Knows problems of being an underprivileged youth; has worked to promote organizations dealing with Alabama Youth.
★ Bob French knows hard work. He has worked on a farm, chopped and picked his share of cotton. Beginning work at age 11, Bob has worked as: a grocery clerk, newsboy, service station attendant, stock clerk, movie usher, caddy, soda jerk, delivery boy, salesman, personnel man, and attorney. Bob French has truly pulled himself up by his own bootstraps. His next job will be working for you as a United States Congressman.

293

Turkish Belly Dancer- came to our table in Istanbul.
That's Edgar, on my right and a businessman we met there

Barry Goldwater and Me

Vice President Sprio Agnew, Me & Mayor
George Siebels (Mayor of Birmingham)

294

Bob and Barry Goldwater

President Nixon and Bob

Mom and Dad's 50th Anniversary

Roll Tide Porsche

Enjoying "Dog Island" 1971

My Dear Moth

Celeste & I at our
40th Wedding
Anniversary 1997

The day we adopted "TNT" Tommy and Tammy

The French Family
Tommy, Celeste, Michelle, Bob and Tammy

Hester, Dot, Bob, Rebecca and Daina
Thanksgiving